MEASURING TRANSACTIONS
BETWEEN WORLD AREAS

NATIONAL BUREAU OF ECONOMIC RESEARCH

Studies in International Economic Relations

1. PROBLEMS OF THE UNITED STATES AS WORLD
   TRADER AND BANKER   *Hal B. Lary*

2. PRICE AND QUANTITY TRENDS IN THE FOREIGN
   TRADE OF THE UNITED STATES   *Robert E. Lipsey*

3. MEASURING TRANSACTIONS BETWEEN WORLD
   AREAS   *Herbert B. Woolley*

MEASURING TRANSACTIONS BETWEEN WORLD AREAS

BY HERBERT B. WOOLLEY

PUBLISHED 1966 BY

NATIONAL BUREAU OF ECONOMIC RESEARCH, *New York*

DISTRIBUTED BY

COLUMBIA UNIVERSITY PRESS, *New York and London*

Printed in the United States of America

RELATION OF THE DIRECTORS TO THE WORK AND PUBLICATIONS OF THE NATIONAL BUREAU OF ECONOMIC RESEARCH

1. The object of the National Bureau of Economic Research is to ascertain and to present to the public important economic facts and their interpretation in a scientific and impartial manner. The Board of Directors is charged with the responsibility of ensuring that the work of the National Bureau is carried on in strict conformity with this object.

2. To this end the Board of Directors shall appoint one or more Directors of Research.

3. The Director or Directors of Research shall submit to the members of the Board, or to its Executive Committee, for their formal adoption, all specific proposals concerning researches to be instituted.

4. No report shall be published until the Director or Directors of Research shall have submitted to the Board a summary drawing attention to the character of the data and their utilization in the report, the nature and treatment of the problems involved, the main conclusions, and such other information as in their opinion would serve to determine the suitability of the report for publication in accordance with the principles of the National Bureau.

5. A copy of any manuscript proposed for publication shall also be submitted to each member of the Board. For each manuscript to be so submitted a special committee shall be appointed by the President, or at his designation by the Executive Director, consisting of three Directors selected as nearly as may be one from each general division of the Board. The names of the special manuscript committee shall be stated to each Director when the summary and report described in paragraph (4) are sent to him. It shall be the duty of each member of the committee to read the manuscript. If each member of the special committee signifies his approval within thirty days, the manuscript may be published. If each member of the special committee has not signified his approval within thirty days of the transmittal of the report and manuscript, the Director of Research shall then notify each member of the Board, requesting approval or disapproval of publication, and thirty additional days shall be granted for this purpose. The manuscript shall then not be published unless at least a majority of the entire Board and a two-thirds majority of those members of the Board who shall have voted on the proposal within the time fixed for the receipt of votes on the publication proposed shall have approved.

6. No manuscript may be published, though approved by each member of the special committee, until forty-five days have elapsed from the transmittal of the summary and report. The interval is allowed for the receipt of any memorandum of dissent or reservation, together with a brief statement of his reasons, that any member may wish to express; and such memorandum of dissent or reservation shall be published with the manuscript if he so desires. Publication does not, however, imply that each member of the Board has read the manuscript, or that either members of the Board in general, or of the special committee, have passed upon its validity in every detail.

7. A copy of this resolution shall, unless otherwise determined by the Board, be printed in each copy of every National Bureau book.

(Resolution adopted October 25, 1926, as revised February 6, 1933, and February 24, 1941)

To Peggy for patience

This study was made possible by funds granted by the Ford Foundation to the National Bureau. The Ford Foundation is, however, not to be understood as approving or disapproving by virtue of its grant any of the statements made or views expressed herein.

CONTENTS

PREFACE   xv

FOREWORD, by Solomon Fabricant   xvii

1. INTRODUCTION   1
   A. Objectives of the Study   1
   B. Nature of the Record and
      Plan of the Book   3

2. CONSTRUCTING THE RECORD   6
   A. Design of the Record   6
      1. The Geographic Dimension   6
      2. The Item Dimension   14
      3. The Time Dimension   16
      4. The Currency Dimension   17
   B. Preparing the Record   17
      1. Special Studies   18
      2. Some Deficiencies in the Record   18

3. WORLD TOTALS   20
   A. The Course and Composition of
      World Trade in 1950–54   20
   B. Discrepancy in Total Credits and
      Debits for Goods and Services   24
   C. Over-All Errors in the Financial
      Accounts   26
   D. Distribution of Net Error by Country   32
   E. Concluding Observations   34

4. GOODS AND SERVICES TRADE   35
   A. The Geographic Structure of Trading
      over the Five Years   35
      1. Gross Transactions in the
         Two-Valued Matrix   35
      2. The Effect of Redirecting Petroleum
         Trade and the Influence of Middlemen
         on the Trading Pattern   37
      3. Net Transactions in the
         Two-Valued Matrix   38
   B. The Annual Matrixes   41

   C. The Nature of Specialization in Trade:
      The Services Matrixes   42
      1. The Nature of Trade in Services   42
      2. Further Comment on the
         Services Matrixes   43
      3. The Contrasting Patterns for
         Merchandise and Services   46
   D. Concluding Observations   48

*5. FINANCIAL FLOWS AND
   MULTILATERAL SETTLEMENTS*   49
   A. The Pattern of Financial Flows, 1950–54   49
      1. Unilateral Transfers, Capital,
         and Gold   49
      2. Multilateral Settlements and Error   52
   B. Bilateral Balances, Liquid Assets, and
      Multilateral Settlements   54
      1. Problem of Measuring Surpluses
         and Deficits   54
      2. Over-All Deficits of the U.S.
         and the U.K.   55
      3. Continental European Surpluses   57
      4. Main Multilateral Links   57
   C. Multilateralism and the Measurement
      of Multilateral Settlements   59
      1. The Concept of Multilateralism   59
      2. Components of the Final Matrix
         of Multilateral Settlements   61
      3. Amount of Multilateral Settlements   62
      4. Significance of the Multilateral
         Settlements Network   64
      5. Statistical Limitations to the
         Multilateral Settlements Matrix   67
      6. Three-Area, Four-Area, and
         Five-Area Consolidations of the
         Two-Valued Matrix   70
   D. Structure and Movement of Financial
      Flows: The Annual Record   70
      1. Stability of Direction in Trade
         Balances and in Financial Flows
         Between Areas   71

2. Consistency of the Two-Valued
   Matrixes of Financial Flows   74
3. Systematic Variation in
   Multilateral Settlements   75

6. *CONCLUSION*   77
   A. Summary   77
   B. The U.S. Deficit and
      Multilateral Payments   79

APPENDIXES
   A. Two-Valued Matrixes for the
      Whole Five Years 1950–54   87

B. Two-Valued Matrixes,
   Annually, 1950–54   95
C. Effects on the Record of
   Redirecting Petroleum Trade   124
D. Divergence in the Two-Valued Record
   of Goods and Services Transactions 130
E. Valuing Imports F.O.B.   139
F. Estimating Bunker Sales   148

Glossary   151

Index   153

TABLES

1. Transactions Between Four World Areas, 1954   4

2. Comparison of Total Merchandise Credits in International Payments Statistics with *IFS* Export Totals, 1950–54   8

3. The Course and Composition of World Trade in 1950–54   23

4. Balances of All Areas with All Areas from the Two-Valued Matrixes and of Sixty-Eight Countries with All Areas, 1950–54   27

5. Balances of All Areas with All Areas Compared with Total Net Credits and Debits of Countries with All Areas, by Type of Transaction, over the Five Years 1950–54   29

6. Net Error in Country Accounts, 1950–54   30

7. Summary of Error Term in Country Accounts over the Five-Years 1950–54   33

8. Balance of Payments of the United States and the United Kingdom, by Partner Area, over the Five Years 1950–54   56

9. Offsetting of Credit and Debit Balances in Interarea Settlements over the Five Years 1950–54   63

10. Distribution of Nonsterling EPU Countries by Pattern of Balances to Be Settled with Nonsterling EPU Area, U.S., and Sterling Area, over the Five Years 1950–54   64

11. Balances to Be Settled Multilaterally by Nonsterling EPU Subgroups with the Sterling Area and Nonsterling EPU Area, over the Five Years 1950–54   65

12. Balances of Sterling Area Subgroups to Be Settled Multilaterally with Nonsterling EPU Area Subgroups, over the Five Years 1950–54   66

13. Balances of U.S., Canada, and International Organizations to Be Settled Multilaterally with the Sterling Area and Nonsterling EPU Area, over the Five Years 1950–54   67

14. Three-Area, Four-Area, and Five-Area Consolidations of Two-Valued Matrixes over the Five Years 1950–54   69

15. Stability of Direction of Trade and Financial Balances in Annual Matrixes, over the Five Years 1950–54   71

16. Bilateral Balances and Multilateral Settlements in the U.S. Balance of Payments, 1950–62   82

A-1. Two-Valued Matrix of Gross Goods and Services Transactions Between World Areas, 1950–54   88

A-2. Two-Valued Matrix of Net Goods and Services Transactions Between World Areas, 1950–54   89

A-3. Percentage Distribution of Gross Goods and Services Transactions Between World Areas, 1950–54   90

A-4. Net Transactions Between World Areas, 1950–54, by Type   92

B-1. Gross Goods and Services Transactions Between World Areas, Annually, 1950–54, as Reported by Area Credited   96

B-2. Gross Goods and Services Transactions Between World Areas, Annually, 1950–54, as Reported by Area Debited   97

B-3. Net Goods and Services Transactions Between World Areas, Annually, 1950–54   98

B-4. Gross Merchandise Transactions Between World Areas, Annually, 1950–54, as Reported by Area Credited   99

B-5. Gross Merchandise Transactions Between World Areas, Annually, 1950–54, as Reported by Area Debited   100

B-6. Net Merchandise Transactions Between World Areas, Annually, 1950–54   101

B-7. Gross Services Transactions Between World Areas, Annually, 1950–54, as Reported by Area Credited   102

B-8. Gross Services Transactions Between World Areas, Annually, 1950–54, as Reported by Area Debited   103

B-9. Net Services Transactions Between World Areas, Annually, 1950–54   104

B-10. Gross Transportation Transactions Between World Areas, Annually, 1950–54, as Reported by Area Credited   105

B-11. Gross Transportation Transactions Between World Areas, Annually, 1950–54, as Reported by Area Debited   106

B-12. Net Transportation Transactions Between World Areas, Annually, 1950–54   107

B-13. Gross Travel Transactions Between World Areas, Annually, 1950–54, as Reported by Area Credited   108

B-14. Gross Travel Transactions Between World Areas, Annually, 1950–54, as Reported by Area Debited   109

B-15. Net Travel Transactions Between World Areas, Annually, 1950–54   110

B-16. Gross Investment Income Transactions Between World Areas, Annually, 1950–54, as Reported by Area Credited   111

B-17. Gross Investment Income Transactions Between World Areas, Annually, 1950–54, as Reported by Area Debited   112

B-18. Net Investment Income Transactions Between World Areas, Annually, 1950–54   113

B-19. Gross Government Transactions Between World Areas, Annually, 1950–54, as Reported by Area Credited   114

B-20. Gross Government Transactions Between World Areas, Annually, 1950–54, as Reported by Area Debited   115

B-21. Net Government Transactions Between World Areas, Annually, 1950–54   116

B-22. Gross Miscellaneous Services Transactions Between World Areas, Annually, 1950–54, as Reported by Area Credited   117

B-23. Gross Miscellaneous Services Transactions Between World Areas, Annually, 1950–54, as Reported by Area Debited   118

B-24. Net Miscellaneous Services Transactions Between World Areas, Annually, 1950–54   119

B-25. Net Transfer Transactions Between World Areas, Annually, 1950–54   120

B-26. Net Capital Transactions Between World Areas, Annually, 1950–54   121

B-27. Net Gold Transactions Between World Areas, Annually, 1950–54   122

B-28. Net Settlements Transactions Between World Areas, Annually, 1950–54   123

C-1. Adjustments of Merchandise Matrix (Tables B-4 and B-5) to Channel Oil Purchases from Free World Sources Outside the United States, United Kingdom, and Continent Through the United States and United Kingdom, 1950–54   125

C-2. Two-Valued Matrix of Gross Goods and Services Transactions Between World Areas, Adjusted to Redirect Petroleum Transactions, 1950–54   126

C-3. Percentage Distribution of Unadjusted and Adjusted Goods and Services Transactions Between World Areas, 1950–54   127

D-1. Analysis of Divergence in Annual Gross Trade Flows Between Areas   131

D-2. Analysis of Divergence in Year-to-Year Changes in Gross Trade Flows Between Areas   132

D-3. Analysis of Divergence in Changes in Gross Trade Flows Between Areas from 1950 to 1954   134

D-4. Analysis of Divergence in Annual Trade Balances Between Areas   134

D-5. Analysis of Divergence in Year-to-Year Changes in Trade Balances Between Areas   136

D-6. Analysis of Divergence in Changes in
Trade Balances Between Areas from
1950 to 1954   137

E-1. Share of Freight and Insurance in
C.I.F. Value of Merchandise Imports

for Twenty-Seven Countries, by
Partner Area, Annually, 1950–54   143

F-1. Estimated Value of Sales to Ships'
Bunkers, 1950–54   149

CHARTS

1. The Course of World Trade: Goods and Services Credits and Debits by Type of Transaction, Annually, 1950–54   21
2. Over-All Discrepancies in Trade and Financial Accounts, Annually, 1950–54   28
3. Combined Goods and Services Balances Between World Areas over the Five Years 1950–54: Six-Area Consolidation of the Two-Valued Matrix   39
4. A Comparison of Merchandise and Services Balances Between World Areas over the Five Years 1950–54: Six-Area Consolidation of the Two-Valued Matrix   47
5. Financial Balances Between World Areas over the Five Years 1950–54: Six-Area Consolidation of the Two-Valued Matrix   50
6. The Circular Flow of Multilateral Settlements over the Five Years 1950–54   53
7. Annual Financial Balances Between World Areas, 1950–54: Six-Area Consolidation of the Two-Valued Matrix   72
8. Multilateral Settlements of the U.S. with Partner Areas, 1950–62   81

PREFACE

The origins of this study go back to Walrasian general equilibrium theory, the *Tableau Economique* of Quesnay, and the circular flow of Say. Like analyses of money flows and input-output studies, it explores the interrelations between parts of a whole—in this case, the whole world economy. It is best described as a kind of input-output analysis, but between countries instead of industries and for all types of transactions not simply current production; for an earlier generation it was the other way round. Leontief himself, in presenting his input-output analysis, described it as like an international trade table, but between industries within a country rather than between countries.[1]

Analyses of trade between countries have long been made, and when the ideas for the present study were forming, *The Network of World Trade* study of the League of Nations and a trade matrix analysis by Frisch were the subject of current interest. My interest in working on trade and payments relations between world areas crystallized in the early postwar years in the course of my work at the Department of State on the international trade and payments aspects of the U.S. foreign aid program. After making a series of efforts to relate the international payments prospects of the European countries to the prospects for world trade and payments generally, I came to the conclusion that a methodological study covering a period of years was needed.

Many officials of the U.S. government, foreign governments, and international agencies aided in preparing the records, but a prime debt is owed to the Balance of Payments Division of the International Monetary Fund, which made space and files available and spent much time discussing methodology and details of particular accounts. A conference of more than a dozen specialists in trade and payments advised on the project; and particularly helpful comments were received from Walther Lederer of the Commerce Department and Poul Høst-Madsen of the International Monetary Fund on a preliminary progress report given to a Universities-National Bureau Conference on International Economics.

The National Bureau's Director of Research, Solomon Fabricant, provided the continuing support, interest, general guidance, and stimulation so necessary for a prolonged project. The Associate Director of Research, Hal B. Lary, brought to bear the fresh perspective of an informed outsider. I wish to thank the Directors' reading committee: Lester V. Chandler, Gottfried Haberler, and Willard L. Thorp. I also benefited from the useful comments of Ilse Mintz, Robert Lipsey, and Zvi Griliches, who served on the Bureau's staff reading committee.

Besides the collaborators on the project—Cornelius Dwyer, Herman Karreman, Robert Lichtenberg, and Walther Michael—the work depended heavily upon the often tedious labors of many research assistants; Deborah Schoen Becker, Dianne Silverman, and the late Carmellah Moneta made particularly noteworthy contributions. Virginia Crowley, Bureau librarian, helped greatly in securing specialized materials from all over the world. Louise Smith was for a number of years secretary for the project. I am grateful to Rosa Lechner for work on the preliminary charts and to H. I. Forman for drawing the final charts. The book has gained greatly in readability and brevity from editing by Marie-Christine Culbert.

Finally, I wish to express my appreciation for the freedom which the Bureau has provided me to develop a set of ideas and a program of research circumscribed only by the available resources.

May 1965   *H. B. W.*

---

[1] Wassily W. Leontief, *The Structure of American Economy, 1919–1929*, Cambridge, Mass., 1941, pp. 4 and 12.

FOREWORD

During the years following the Second World War widespread concern with foreign exchange problems and currency inconvertibility prompted many countries to develop their international payments accounts with some regional elaboration, and the International Monetary Fund sought in its *Balance of Payments Manual* to set guidelines for reporting transactions regionally. The opportunity therefore existed for someone to try to bring together the payments accounts of all countries and to fit them into a comprehensive, interlocking scheme showing trade and payments flows between world areas.

This was the task Herbert B. Woolley set for himself in a study begun at the National Bureau in 1953 with the financial support of the Ford Foundation. The results of Woolley's investigation are given here. (As mentioned elsewhere in this book, preliminary reports on parts of the study appeared in 1957, 1958, 1959, and 1961.) This book presents the first detailed matrixes ever made of transactions (other than merchandise trade) between major world areas and provides essential background on the problems encountered in moving from the balance of payments estimates of individual countries to a world system of regionally integrated accounts. This experimental work has been performed for each of the years 1950 to 1954 and covers the following main types of transactions—merchandise, services, unilateral transfers, capital and gold movements, and multilateral settlements. The study describes the statistical methods used to construct the record, evaluates the limitations of the data for descriptive and analytic uses, and considers the implications of the results for the concept and measurement of multilateral settlements.

The significance of this investigation is perhaps even greater now than when it was started, as indicated most recently by the Review Committee for Balance of Payments Statistics in its report to the Bureau of the Budget. "The importance of viewing balance of payments problems in a world context," the report states, "is becoming more widely recognized." Two reasons may be distinguished for this growing interest in the regional dimensions of international payments, one concerning policy formation and the other the underlying statistical basis. On the first, the Review Committee's report observes, among other things, that:

The initial impact of any measures taken by the United States to strengthen its balance of payments will not necessarily fall entirely on the surplus countries, but will be felt most quickly in countries with which the United States has the closest relations in trade and investment. Some of these may be countries whose own payments positions may be precarious. Similarly, measures taken in other countries to strengthen their balances of payments may have an adverse effect on the U.S. balance of payments.

With respect to the compilation of the statistics, the Review Committee stresses the advantages of cooperation between national statistical authorities and adds:

It might be supposed that some balance of payments transactions of a given country could be measured more reliably on the basis of the statistical information on those same transactions as compiled in other countries. . . .

It is [however] extraordinarily difficult to judge the comparative reliability of estimates for purportedly the same items which are prepared in different countries according to different statistical approaches and methods. . . .

International reconciliation and mutual use of the data collected by different countries are difficult, time consuming, and often frustrating. . . .

Woolley's project was a pioneering effort to face up to these problems, and his report will help in evaluating both the cost and the usefulness of devising solutions. One basic and simple point that emerges is that successful international collaboration in this area requires that the various national statistical offices be willing to prepare their estimates in appropriate detail by regions and by major countries.

Even if this elementary condition is, in time, more adequately met than at present, the experience gained in executing this project suggests that the preparation of regionally integrated accounts on a regular and systematic basis is likely to prove costly in terms of the skilled manpower required and likely also to yield current statistics only with a delay determined by the most laggard among the reporting countries.

Another difficulty highlighted by this study is that the consolidated payments network will, at best, still be subject to the well-known "errors and omissions" which beset national balance of payments statisticians. For this reason, and perhaps also on conceptual grounds, there may be questions concerning the meaning of Woolley's residual calculation of net multilateral settlements. Without diminishing the importance of multilateralism as an objective of policy, one may conclude that the statistical expression of

this concept in the form of data on multilateral settlements encounters greater difficulties and presents more ambiguous results than seems to have been generally supposed.

Woolley's study explores these and related questions more systematically, I believe, than anything hitherto available and provides comprehensive statistics on the network of international payments where previously scholars have had to work only with very partial data and abstract models. It is hoped that, in addition, this report will contribute to an understanding of the possibilities and the problems of developing better information on the pattern of international economic and financial relations and thereby ultimately help also to strengthen the basis for policy formation in this area.

SOLOMON FABRICANT
Director of Research

May 1965

1

INTRODUCTION

A. OBJECTIVES OF THE STUDY

As the handmaiden of politics, economics has concentrated upon the activities bounded by the control of the sovereign and the resources under its jurisdiction. The main schools of economic doctrine from the mercantilism of the eighteenth century to the neoclassicism of the twentieth, accepting the existence of a social structure and a market economy established under the protection of a political power, have been largely concerned with the consequences of different courses of public policy for the income and wealth of a country's citizenry.

Therefore, the social accounts of the economist are "national" accounts. The national product and income accounts deal with the composition and disposition of domestic (or national) production; money flows and input-output accounts deal with interrelations among sectors of the economy. Economic relations with other states enter these social accounts in lines or sectors for exports of domestically (or nationally) produced goods and services and for imports from other countries received in trade, and the elaboration of foreign trade is made appropriate to the sectoral development of the account. The social account focusing upon the relations between residents (or nationals) of a given country and those of other countries—i.e., the balance-of-payments account—was until recently rarely elaborated by partner area and was usually employed analytically without regard to regional dimensions. With each state concentrating on its own problems, the operation of the economic system of the world as a whole has received insufficient attention, and the social accounting framework has not been developed to illuminate it.

In the post-Napoleonic era, when Britain was the financial and trading center of the modern world,[1] it

[1] Albert H. Imlah, *Economic Elements in the Pax Britannica*, Cambridge, Mass., 1958.

was natural for British writers to deal with external economic relations as though the rest of the world were a unit. The *Pure Theory of Foreign Trade* of Alfred Marshall, for example, treats of the relations between a country and the outside world—a two-country model—as though nothing new would be involved in the trading relations among three or more countries. The world then consisted of Britain, a handful of lesser national states on the Continent, and a scattering of small powers outside Europe; large areas of the Middle East, Asia, and Africa were integrated into the exchange economy of the West only through the European empires. In such circumstances the effect of actions by the big economic power, Britain, spread widely over the whole world, and smaller powers could disregard the effects of their economic actions on the rest of the world. It was, perhaps, sufficient for Britain to be concerned with the impact of her actions on the world as a whole. In such a setting, principles drawn from an analysis of the two-country model may have served, but the conditions of the mid-twentieth century require more elaborate models.[2]

Today's world is not such a unimodal system of national economies dominated by a single financial and trading center. The largest trading country, the

[2] There is some question whether the two-area model was adequate even for the era of *Pax Britannica*. R. A. Mundell, in restating "The Pure Theory of International Trade" (*American Economic Review*, March 1960, pp. 67 ff.), finds the results of the two-country model applicable to the multiple-country case only when all foreign exports are *perfect* substitutes for each other. In that special case, foreign countries can be treated as one country—the "rest of the world." When gross complementarity exists among the exports of various countries, the consequences for one country of such events as productivity changes, tariff changes, price changes, and unilateral transfers may differ from those in the two-country cases. From available data it can be seen that exports of different countries are far from perfect substitutes and that complementarity is widespread.

United States, provided a market for 18 per cent of the merchandise exported by other countries in 1959 (and supplied 21 per cent of that imported by other countries). In contrast, Britain in 1860 provided a market for an estimated 31 per cent of all non-British exports.[3] The rise of the United States and more recently of a rapidly growing Continental grouping has produced a world in which the unilateral actions of either the United States or the United Kingdom and the concerted actions of the Continental complex impinge importantly upon each other and on different groups of countries outside Europe. Moreover, new constellations of countries are being born, large enough to have a noticeable influence. The Soviet countries—trading largely among themselves, following essentially autarchic trading policies toward non-Soviet countries, and consciously employing trade as a political instrument—came in the years after World War II to form a bloc. Looking ahead we must anticipate that the increased political consciousness and assertiveness of the developing countries may lead to concerted action with a world-wide impact.

In such a world, enlightened national self-interest requires the explicit recognition of interdependence. The health of the economic system of the world is the necessary concern not only of all countries acting in concert in the United Nations but also of regional groupings of countries acting together and of the major economic powers acting individually. A small country can still behave without regard to the effects of its actions on the rest of the world, but the larger countries have, by their very size, lost the possibility of doing so. Just as the United States, in arriving at a position of leadership on the world scene, has been compelled to recognize the direct and indirect effects of its actions on the different parts of the world, so other leading countries or groups of countries must be sensitive to the effect of their behavior on world economic relations.

To find solutions to the problems of one area of the world without intensifying or creating new problems for other areas requires a framework of analysis and a body of data encompassing all the economic activities of the world and expressing the interrelations of national economies. Problems of economic interdependence cannot be assessed without an or-

ganized and consistent record which can be used as the basis for weighing the consequences of alternative policies and programs or of economic changes originating anywhere in the world for different parts of the world's economy. It was to make a contribution toward developing a technique of description and analysis encompassing the world economy and relating all important phases of international economic life to one another that the present study was undertaken at the National Bureau at the beginning of 1953.

The ideal record would approximate a Walrasian general equilibrium system covering the internal activities of all countries and linking them up, product by product, sector by sector, and encompassing not only current production and exchange but also savings, investment, international capital flows, unilateral transfers, and monetary phenomena.[4] Preparing such a comprehensive record would have been far beyond the resources available. Hence we set a more limited objective, one which, nonetheless, was comprehensive in focusing on payments relations among all countries. National boundaries (important hindrances to the free play of economic forces around the world) provide a convenient means of delimiting research and analysis. Moreover, there is particular advantage in dealing first with the international economic relations of countries since governmental policies must work toward maintaining a balance in external payments. For most countries,

[3] Imlah, *Economic Elements*, p. 191. Percentages for 1959 were calculated from the trade table in *International Financial Statistics* (May 1960), allowing 6 per cent of world imports c.i.f. for freight and insurance. U. S. exports include military aid goods.

[4] Jacob Mozak, in his Cowles Commission Monograph (No. 7) *General Equilibrium Theory in International Trade* (Bloomington, Ind., 1944), outlined such a system in theoretical terms. Hans Neisser and Franco Modigliani, in their quantitative analysis *National Income and International Trade* (Urbana, Ill., 1953), explored an international model in which the merchandise trade of all countries was linked up with their national incomes; J. J. Polak made a similar study, *An International Economic System* (Chicago, 1953). Both of these studies dealt with merchandise trade only and, like the League of Nations study *Network of World Trade* (Geneva, 1942), disregarded other international transactions. Moreover, their empirical data referred to the interwar period. Polak, working with Rudolph R. Rhomberg, has reported some progress in removing these deficiencies. In their article, "Economic Stability in an International Setting" (*American Economic Review*, May 1962, p. 110), they report on a three-area postwar model of the world economy. Rhomberg made further reports on the model at meetings of the Econometric Society in September and December of 1962. A Brookings Institution study (*The United States Balance of Payments in 1968*, by W. S. Salant, *et al.*, Washington, 1963) develops a projection of world merchandise trade and the U. S. balance of payments, using a three-region analytic model of interdependence similar to Rhomberg's.

the ability to buy or lend depends upon success in selling or borrowing. Countries generally have limited reserves of gold or convertible currency and must watch their economic policies to ensure that losses of reserve are quickly stemmed. Conversely, though a gain of reserves is less of a constraint than a loss, few countries would wish to accumulate idle reserves indefinitely. Countries are linked in a network of trade and financial relations which makes one country's credit another's debit. As private and governmental decisions of countries respond to changing international economic circumstances, the effects ramify out through the network of international trade and finance and may return to affect the original country.

Because of its essentially interdependent nature, the network of international transactions is worth studying. This book presents a record of transactions, by main types, between world areas over a particular period of time. The aim has been to comprehend the full range of exchanges entering into the balance of payments—merchandise, services, unilateral transfers, capital and gold movements, and multilateral settlements. In setting out to compile and analyze this record, we hoped to accomplish objectives of three kinds—statistical, descriptive, and analytical.

The statistical objective was to locate data that measured transactions between world areas or that could be used to make such measurements where the data did not exist, to design a set of accounts which could be fitted together in a reasonably consistent record covering all countries, to construct such a record by compiling, adjusting, and supplementing accounts of different countries, and to assess its limitations and usefulness for different purposes.

The second objective was to study the record to observe the nature of the interrelationships for the period—the nature of international specialization in trade, financial interrelations, and the nature of interdependence. The third and more theoretical objective was to use the record to test hypotheses about the operation of the world economy.

This book will treat primarily the statistical objective, presenting the data prepared on transactions between world areas, namely, two-valued matrixes of transactions of all major types compiled for each of the five years 1950-54. In addition, the book seeks to assess the limitations of the data for descriptive and analytic uses. The accuracy of statistics cannot, of course, be evaluated apart from the uses to which they are put. Insofar as observations about trade and payments relations are made in this book, the data can be assessed in relation to those findings. They can also be related to a number of other questions we have explored and touched upon but do not go into in this book.

B. NATURE OF THE RECORD AND PLAN OF THE BOOK

Table 1 illustrates the kind of record considered in this book. It is a summary set of matrix tables showing transactions for the single year 1954 between four parts of the world—Western Europe, Other Eastern Hemisphere countries, the United States, and Other Western Hemisphere countries.[5] The table is divided into four parts. Part I gives gross goods and services transactions, with line A for the export of the area in the stub matching, on line B, the comparable measure of the same transaction carried in

[5] Table 1 is a consolidation of the more elaborate matrixes in Appendix B. Western Europe (WE) is the sum of United Kingdom (UK) and the Continental countries of the Organization for European Economic Cooperation (Cont. OEEC), and also includes the European Payments Union (EPU). Other Eastern Hemisphere (OEH) is the sum of the Rest of the Sterling Area (RSA), Continental Overseas Territories (Cont. OT's), and Other Countries. Other Western Hemisphere (OWH) is the sum of Canada, Latin America, and International Organizations (IO). These and other abbreviations used in this book are explained in the glossary.

the account of the importing area in the caption.[6] Part II gives net goods and services transactions between the four world areas; Part III gives net unilateral transfers, capital and gold transactions; and Part IV gives the residual, balancing matrix of net multilateral settlements and error. In each case the

[6] In all of the matrix tables of the book (i.e., tables showing transactions of a given type between world areas) the exporting area, or area credited, is listed in the stub and the importing area, or area debited, is given in the caption. Where two values are shown, as in the tables of Appendix A, line A denotes the record of the area credited and line B denotes the record of the area debited. Where the two entries of the record are not paired off on lines A and B, as in the tables of Appendix B, the area of report is the area in the stub unless it is clear from the language used in the table headings that it is otherwise. (E.g., in the case of Table B-1 on goods and services credits, the figures shown are as carried in accounts for the exporting area in the stub; in the case of Table B-2 on goods and services debits, the figures shown are the transactions of the importing area in the caption; but in the case of Table B-3 on net goods and services, the figures are the balances in accounts of the area in the stub.)

TABLE 1
Transactions Between Four World Areas, 1954
(*million U.S. dollar equivalents*)

Area Credited \ Area Debited		All Areas	Unallo-cated	Western Europe	Other Eastern Hemisphere	United States	Other Western Hemisphere
I. GROSS GOODS AND SERVICES							
All areas	A	100,902	1,332	40,304	29,037	15,551	14,678
	B	100,810	—	39,667	28,948	16,346	15,849
Unallocated	A	—	—	—	—	—	—
	B	1,389	—	455	506	—	428
Western Europe	A	41,454	534	18,871	14,189	4,724	3,136
	B	41,071	—	18,316	14,369	4,897	3,489
Other Eastern Hemisphere	A	26,080	491	12,972	7,798	3,644	1,175
	B	25,932	—	13,042	7,586	4,098	1,206
United States	A	18,550	—	4,802	4,845	—	8,903
	B	18,249	—	4,515	4,503	—	9,231
Other Western Hemisphere	A	14,818	307	3,659	2,205	7,183	1,464
	B	14,169	—	3,339	1,984	7,351	1,495
II. NET GOODS AND SERVICES							
All areas		92	−57	−767	3,105	−2,698	509
Unallocated		—	—	—	—	—	—
Western Europe		1,787	79	555	1,147	209	−203
Other Eastern Hemisphere		−2,868	−15	−1,397	212	−859	−809
United States		2,204	—	−95	747	—	1,552
Other Western Hemisphere		−1,031	−121	170	999	−2,048	−31
III. NET UNILATERAL TRANSFERS, CAPITAL, AND GOLD							
All areas		113	688	1,735	−2,440	1,394	−1,264
Unallocated		—	—	—	—		
Western Europe		−1,188	320	93	−684	−640	−277
Other Eastern Hemisphere		2,308	321	844	−18	1,035	126
United States		−2,382	—	251	−1,536	—	−1,097
Other Western Hemisphere		1,375	47	547	−202	999	−16
IV. NET MULTILATERAL SETTLEMENTS							
All areas		−205	−631	−968	−665	1,304	755
Unallocated		—	—	—	—	—	—
Western Europe		−599	−399	−648	−463	431	480
Other Eastern Hemisphere		560	−306	553	−194	−176	683
United States		178	—	−156	789	—	−455
Other Western Hemisphere		−344	74	−717	−797	1,049	47

SOURCE: Appendix B.

NOTE: For Part I, entries on line A are from the accounts of the area credited (in the stub) and entries on line B are from the accounts of the area debited (in the caption); for Parts II–IV, the entries are from the accounts of the area in the stub and the comparable partner record is given (with opposite sign) on the partner area's line in the appropriate column.

For a definition of the areas included here, see footnote 5 and the glossary.

record is two-valued but lines A and B have not been entered in the net transactions matrixes of the table (Parts II-IV) since the balances as shown by each partner can be readily identified and compared (e.g., Western Europe's balance with the United States should be the same as the U.S. balance with Western Europe but with the opposite sign).[7]

Each dimension of Table 1 is elaborated in the basic record given in Appendix B. The geographic scheme of recording transactions between world areas is elaborated into eight country groupings and three special accounts; the items are elaborated into merchandise, five different types of services, and separate accounts for unilateral transfers, capital, and gold; the time dimension is elaborated by adding more years. Altogether twenty-eight matrix tables are presented in Appendix B for each of five years, 140 in all, and in general for each interarea transaction there are two entries to be compared.

This mass of data can be viewed from many different angles. Taking the time dimension, one can look at experience over the whole five years, year-to-year changes, or changes from 1950 to 1954. From the viewpoint of items, one can look at the record for each type of transaction in turn over these periods of time and make comparisons between different types of transactions. The regional breakdown of transactions invites the study of each area's account in turn, examining its item composition vertically for different time periods and comparing it with other areas' accounts. We have not undertaken here any of these systematic reviews of the material, but have followed each approach to some extent in focusing on certain aspects of the record of particular significance.

Before the record is presented, Chaper 2 describes the method of developing the two-valued matrixes for 1950–54. Following this explanation, Chapter 3 examines the over-all totals of all countries with all countries, carried in the corner box of the matrix tables for each type of transaction (e.g., figures like the $100,902 million of goods and services credits and $100,810 million of debits traded between countries in 1954 and the −$205 million net over-all error in the multilateral settlements account shown in Table 1). These totals are important as measures of the magnitude of world trade in merchandise and the several types of services for which data on gross transactions are available. They also show the over-

[7] See note to Table 1.

all divergence between credit and debit records of world trade, which, conceptually, should be equal. For net transactions matrixes, of course, *world* totals should be zero, and the entries in the corner box of the net transactions matrixes provide insight into the systematic nature of errors in the whole set of accounts. Chapter 3 also reviews the country composition of the over-all balance of all countries with all countries in the residual matrix of multilateral settlements and error. This review shows the extent of offsetting errors in the set of country accounts and focuses on the country accounts with the largest (net) errors and omissions.

The next two chapters consider the interarea record of goods and services transactions (Chapter 4) and the record of net financial flows (Chapter 5). In each chapter, first the patterns given by the record for the whole five years are examined and then the annual matrixes.

The main conclusions from this study of world trade and payments are given in Chapter 6, which also includes some reflections on the usefulness of this type of record. The use of five-year totals in analyses of experience over the whole five years is, of course, equivalent to working with average annual experience, the average being weighted by each year's transactions.

Appendix A gives consolidated figures for the whole five-year period showing the gross and net goods and services matrixes (Tables A-1, A-2, and A-3) and the net transactions of each account from merchandise to net multilateral settlements and error (Table A-4). The matrixes in Appendix A differ from the basic annual matrixes in Appendix B in that the former have been adjusted to allocate all transactions and in certain other ways explained in Chapter 2.

Appendixes C and D elaborate some points discussed in the text, notably the effect on the set of matrixes of redirecting petroleum trade transactions and the divergence in the goods and services matrix.

Appendixes E and F are concerned with two problems encountered in adjusting payments accounts that warrant further explanation, namely, valuing merchandise imports f.o.b. and estimating sales of marine bunkers.

Notes on the adjustment or preparation of the seventy-eight country accounts underlying the matrix tables are on file on microfilm at the National Bureau.

2

CONSTRUCTING THE RECORD

A. DESIGN OF THE RECORD

An international transaction consists of the transfer of ownership of something of value between two parties residing in different countries at some point in time. To be useful and meaningful, a comprehensive record of such transactions must employ principles for consolidating transactions according to the attributes mentioned, and in constructing such a record a decision must be made on the principles to be followed.

The International Monetary Fund's *Balance of Payments Manual* (hereafter cited as the *Manual*), which embodies much past experience and thinking, has been extremely useful and has made it possible to avoid considering here every problem of balance-of-payments accounting and to concentrate instead on those offering some particular difficulty.[1]

Moreover, the task of preparing a record of transactions between world areas has been greatly facilitated by the regionally elaborated accounts which countries publish or file with the International Monetary Fund and by the compilations of merchandise trade statistics by the United Nations, the IMF, and the Organization for European Economic Cooperation (OEEC). Our record was designed with an eye to using these official accounts and trade statistics with a minimum of adjustment.

One basic principle that should be followed need only be stated: To achieve comparability of paired entries in a comprehensive two-valued matrix, it is necessary that the countries party to a transaction should record it alike—give it the same value, call

it the same kind of transaction, allocate it to the same time period, and identify it with the same national or residential characteristics.[2]

The problems of designing a matrix of international transactions may be considered according to the following attributes, or dimensions, of an individual transaction: (1) geography, (2) item, (3) time, and (4) currency.

1. The Geographic Dimension

The geographic dimension poses several problems. First, how are boundaries to be drawn around different parts of the world so as to permit transactions with domestic and foreign residents to be distinguished for every place? Then, for each country we must secure a record of all of the transactions of residents with foreigners. This problem of coverage is partly a matter of ensuring an accounting for all places in the world and partly a matter of ensuring that every account covers all transactions. There also arises a problem of direction: the residence of partners to a transaction must be properly identified and consistently given. A particular phase of this problem is the difficulty arising from transactions that remain unallocated by partner area in some of our country accounts. A final problem concerns the grouping of countries into a manageable number of combinations suitable for analysis.

---

[1] The problems were discussed more fully in my paper "On the Elaboration of a System of International Transaction Accounts" in *Problems in the International Comparison of Economic Accounts*, Studies in Income and Wealth 20, Princeton for National Bureau of Economic Research, 1957. The second edition of the *Manual* (1950) was the one relied upon here; a third edition was issued in 1961.

[2] On the surface this basic principle seems plain enough, but it is frequently violated when systems of classification are adopted under which a given transaction can be viewed differently by countries whose residents are party to it. Thus, gold may be current production to one country, while it is a monetary reserve to another; bank balances may be regarded as official reserves by the country of ownership but be treated as a private short-term liability by the country in which the balance is held; commodities may be merchandise exports to the selling country but "government" purchases to the buying country.

Defining Country Boundaries

It is desirable to divide the world into statistical reporting units—countries or groups of countries— so as not to obscure important features of the world economy, double count, or leave gaps in the record. This might seem to be a straightforward task. Disputes arise, however, about some boundaries and areas and become touchy subjects politically. What is East Germany's relation to West Germany for purposes of recording international transactions? Is Southwest Africa a part of South Africa?

The IMF *Manual* met this difficulty by laying down an explicit definition: "A reporting country is defined as the economic unit delimited by a customs area and a single currency system, or by similar unifying economic arrangements. A separate schedule should be completed for each reporting country. In particular a schedule for a country with dependencies should cover only the metropolitan area." [3]

The language permitted the United Kingdom, Belgium, and the Netherlands to report one way and the United States, France, and Portugal another. The U.K., at least some of whose dependencies had distinct currencies and their own customs systems (and were on the way to Commonwealth status), [4] reported the external transactions of the British Isles only, and these included transactions between the metropolitan territory and dependencies overseas. Belgium and the Netherlands did likewise. The United States has a unitary customs area and a single currency within that area; it reported transactions of the customs-currency area with the rest of the world and excluded from consideration in its external payments accounts transactions within the area. [5] France reported for the franc area, and Portugal for the escudo area. The Union of South Africa treated Southwest Africa as

[3] *Manual*, 2nd ed., p. 9. Member countries with colonies or dependencies are requested to fill schedules for each one or for appropriate groups.
[4] The political status of territories is not static. Countries are grouped here according to their status in the early 1950's; though, since the study was undertaken, most of the British, French, and Belgian territories in Africa and Asia have become independent.
[5] The IMF also receives an account of Puerto Rican transactions with the U. S. and the rest of the world, apparently out of regard for its special "commonwealth" status in relation to the U. S. However, in contrast to, say, French Overseas Territories, Puerto Rico has not pressed for autonomy as have the larger African and Asian territories of France.

part of its internal economy, including transactions of Southwest Africa with other countries and excluding transactions between the Union and Southwest Africa. West Germany likewise excluded transactions between West and East Germany, considering these as internal transactions, but it did not cover East Germany's transactions with other countries.

The treatment followed here in constructing a set of accounts has been to consider all European overseas dependencies as reporting units, but to consider U.S. overseas dependencies as part of the U.S. economy and Southwest Africa as part of the Union of South Africa. East Germany has been considered as part of the Soviet Bloc in Europe. Accordingly, at least partial accounts have been constructed for European Overseas Territories, including transactions with their Own Currency Area, and for the Soviet Bloc with the free world, but not, however, for transactions of West Germany with East Germany. All told, we have worked with, adjusted, and, in some cases, constructed seventy-eight country accounts as the basis for our matrixes of international payments.

Securing Coverage

A number of places recognized as independent countries did not publish international payments accounts at the time we developed our record, and one problem was to identify the omitted countries and to devise means of constructing the fullest account possible of their transactions by partner area. The IMF compilation of total world merchandise trade was of considerable aid in spotting countries not reporting balance-of-payments statistics to the IMF. In due course totals were built up for world merchandise transactions which, as can be seen in Table 2, differ from totals for world merchandise exports compiled by *International Financial Statistics* by less than 0.1 per cent of the five-year totals. This comparison suggests that the list of countries included in the present compilations is about as complete as it possibly could be. As will be noted later in this chapter, however, the coverage of merchandise trade is much more complete that that of other payments transactions.

Trial-run matrixes for each type of transaction, which were cast up from an initial compilation for 1951, provided leads on nonreporting "countries" and also on certain important unreported transactions. The trial-run matrix of merchandise transac-

TABLE 2

Comparison of Total Merchandise Credits
in International Payments Statistics with
IFS Export Totals, 1950–54
(*million U.S. dollars*)

	1950	1951	1952	1953	1954	1950–54
World merchandise exports, f.o.b., payments statistics[a]	57,364	76,808	73,411	72,521	76,994	357,098
Less Soviet Bloc exports to free world[b]	−1,386	−1,599	−1,461	−1,419	−1,566	−7,431
Total, adjusted	55,978	75,209	71,950	71,102	75,428	349,667
Free world merchandise exports, f.o.b., *IFS*[c]	56,730	76,535	73,837	74,715	77,237	359,054
Less U.S. military aid exports[d]	−282	−1,065	−1,988	−3,511	−2,255	−9,101
Total, adjusted	56,448	75,470	71,849	71,204	74,982	349,953

[a] Table B-4.

[b] Country account for Soviet Bloc, NBER files.

[c] *International Financial Statistics* (*IFS*); the issue for July 1958 shows somewhat revised figures as follows: $56,680 million for 1950; $76.557 million for 1951; $73,860 million for 1952; $74,830 million for 1953; $77,662 million for 1954. The last revision brings the *IFS* total very close to the merchandise credit total for that year.

[d] *Economic Indicators*, March 1955, March 1954, and March 1953.

NOTE: Custom records, which frequently provide the basis for preparing the merchandise account in a country's international payment statistics, usually have to be adjusted to bring them more into conformity with the accounting principles underlying transactions accounts. Recorded goods movements not involving transfer of ownership must be excluded; unreported transfers (e.g., smuggled goods or some kinds of merchandise transactions abroad) must be added; the record of goods movement must be adjusted, or offset in the capital account, to approximate the time of change in ownership; the recorded values may be more or less arbitrary and need to be adjusted; and the direction of movement may not show the residence of the partner to the transaction. (For a more complete analysis of the problems involved in preparing merchandise transactions from recorded trade, see Walter Gardner's article, "Merchandise Trade in the Balance of Payments," in *International Trade Statistics*, edited by R. G. D. Allen and J. Edward Ely, New York, 1953, and the IMF *Manual*, pp. 21–28.) The IMF *Balance of Payments Yearbook* usually shows for each country as much information as the country supplies on the adjustments made to total merchandise trade.

The adjustments to conform to payments account usage sometimes augment and sometimes reduce the recorded trade total of the country. Except for the revaluation of imports c.i.f. to f.o.b., they tend to subtract out. The net effect of adjustments to trade was modest as can be seen in this table by comparing total merchandise credits from the matrix of merchandise transactions in Appendix Table B-2 with the total of world exports according to *IFS*.

IFS trade totals include U.S. "special category" exports, some of which were military aid items, while the U.S. payments account entering into our merchandise transactions matrix excludes military aid. Moreover, our transactions matrix includes an account for exports of the Soviet Bloc to the free world which the *IFS* trade totals exclude. To make the comparison, it is necessary to adjust the two series so that U.S. military aid exports and Soviet Bloc exports to the free world are excluded from both.

tions pointed to the necessity for including a report for Soviet Bloc transactions with non-Soviet Bloc countries (i.e., an account with the Soviet Bloc as a reporting area rather than as a partner area). The trial run for transportation indicated the need to include a report for fleets flying the flags of Panama, Honduras, and Liberia (hereinafter referred to as the PHL fleet), which are considered nonresident both by the countries owning the vessels and by the countries of registration.[6] Auditing trial-run matrixes of

[6] The U. S. reports transactions of foreign-flag vessels operated by residents of the U. S., but this is only a part of these fleets (*Survey of Current Business, Balance of Payments Supplement of 1952*, p. 31). In consolidating accounts for the eight-area matrix, we have treated the PHL account as a Latin American reporting "country," although partner countries may have shown transportation transactions with the Liberian fleet in Other Countries. It

official transfers and capital flows showed the necessity of including accounts for the International Organizations located in the United States (U.N., IMF, and International Bank for Reconstruction and Development), which provided a channel for a substantial amount of grants and loans to countries, and for the European Payments Union, which served as a short-term lending agency and clearing house for countries participating in that organization. While countries report their own transactions with the international agencies, no country has the responsibility of reporting for them.

The audit of trial-run matrixes pointed out not only the need to add some new "country" accounts but also the omission of items from accounts of reporting countries. Oil-source countries and the United Kingdom generally did not report gross transactions on oil company operations. In order to have a merchandise matrix in which exporting country accounts would match importers' records of goods received, it was decided to follow an accounting convention of entering petroleum on a trade record basis, directing the payment for petroleum imports to the country which the importer counts as the country of provenance. This required using trade records to adjust the direction of petroleum in the merchandise debits of countries entering these debits according to purchase records or exchange control records (U.K., France, West Germany, India, New Zealand, Norway, and Greece). (A similar decision was made to adjust Mexican cotton, recorded as sold to the U.S., to a final-destination basis.) The oil-source account thus needed to be credited with the f.o.b. value of petroleum exports. This value was estimated for each of six oil-source countries and then allocated back to local expenditures, including royalties due the local government, and investment income (including reinvested earnings) due British and American companies, in proportions appropriate to the participation of each in local production. The U.K. account then needed to be credited for the investment income of British and British-Dutch companies from the six oil-source countries, marketing earnings on the Continent, and earnings from participation in Shell (U.S.). It also needed to be debited for earnings accruing to the Dutch interest in the

Royal Dutch-Shell group and for American oil company earnings in the United Kingdom.

Just as it was necessary to create an account for the transactions of the PHL fleet, so it was necessary to develop and introduce into the U.K. statement an account of tanker transactions of British and British-Dutch oil companies; allowances also had to be made for transactions of vessels registered in Greece which were introduced into the Greek statement on the principle that the ships could properly be identified with that country, even though not effectively controlled by Greek exchange regulations. Both the U.K. and Greece gave only net transactions of these fleets (and Greece gave only the net exchange realized by the authorities). We, of course, wanted gross transactions. The Greek dry cargo transactions also had to be estimated.

Bunker sales, which of course are usually by British, British-Dutch, or American oil companies, were not always included in transportation although petroleum exports to bunkering stations were included in merchandise exports from oil sources and frequently were in merchandise imports of the bunkering country. To remedy this, a special calculation was made of bunker sales by country (the results of which are reported in Appendix F).

Establishing Direction

Even after handling these questions of coverage, there remained the problem of direction, that is, securing a consistent treatment of the residence of the parties to a given transaction, particularly for goods and services sold by international companies operating in several different countries.

Broadly speaking, there are three methods for recording direction of imports and exports: first, to identify the country of origin for imports and the country of final consumption for exports; second, to identify the country of consignment for imports and exports; and third, to identify the country of purchase for imports and the country of sale for exports. The last most clearly conforms to the definition of the direction taken by international "transactions." The three approaches do not differ when goods are sold by residents of the country of origin and consigned directly to purchasers in the country of ultimate consumptions, which is the case for most of world trade. Only about 15 per cent of merchandise appears to come under the control of residents of countries other than the originating and consuming

---

would have been better to divide the PHL fleet account so as to be able to combine the reporting of Liberian flag transactions with Other Countries, but the underlying estimates were not prepared in such a way as to permit this.

countries. But this 15 per cent will be differently treated by different countries depending on which of the three concepts of direction they employ. Or, if they rely on exchange control records, they may enter transactions according to the currency of contract and thus introduce a fourth variant.

Petroleum accounts for about one-third of the merchandise trade in this category, and for almost all of petroleum trade we have been able to present the record on both an origin-destination or consignment basis (whichever countries use in their trade statistics) and a purchase-sales basis, channeling the trade through the accounts of the United States and the United Kingdom. Thus the effects on the pattern of gross trade, net trade, and net settlements of following one approach or the other can be observed. This exercise is presented and discussed in Chapters 4 and 5 and Appendix C.

As for the rest of world trade that passes through middlemen, it is only possible to speculate on the direction which a similar adjustment would require.

The problem of the consistent treatment of the direction of transactions is not limited to merchandise; it may also apply to some services, particularly freight. Where countries report merchandise import transactions c.i.f. (making the regional elaboration according to customs records without any special adjustment), clearly the direction of freight is not consistently reported unless the country supplying the goods also happens to supply the shipping services. In view of the prominence of Norwegian and Greek shipping in world trade, this is frequently not the case. Where we have deducted freight from merchandise imports valued c.i.f., we have had to allocate the freight payments to the partners supplying shipping; and, for want of a better basis, we have used the flag of vessels calling at the importing country's ports or unloading tonnage there. Some countries are known to have employed the same device in their estimates. Yet the flag of a vessel does not necessarily denote the residence of the person operating it and receiving the freights paid. Vessels may be chartered under various arrangements, some of which make the charterer the operator (e.g., bareboat and long-time charters). The residence of the operator may not be known to statisticians making the payments estimates; hence inconsistencies may arise in the transportation account about the direction of freight payments and also, of course, about

that of receipts from port charges and other ship disbursements.

Some other services and financial transactions pose difficulties in recording direction. For instance, there may be no good guide to the source of tourist receipts. Investment income may be paid to parties of uncertain residence, as when individuals doing business in several different countries are the recipients of earnings from foreign investments, and of course the related capital flows are equally ambiguous.

Allocating Unallocated Transactions

It will be noted in Table 1 and in the related tables of Appendix B that a small part of the transactions of some areas remain unallocated by partner area. After studying the patterns of divergence between paired entries in the matrix tables for each type of transaction, we thought it might be possible to improve the agreement on figures by reviewing each country account and allocating these unallocated amounts, bearing in mind the country in whose account they appeared, the nature of the unallocated transactions, and the record of partner areas. The result of this effort is included in the five-year consolidated matrixes of *net* transactions in Table A-4.

As an illustration, consider the $2,309 million of unallocated merchandise debits over the five years 1950-54 in Table B-5. These arose mainly in the accounts of Continental OEEC countries, Latin America, and Other Countries.[7] Detailed examination showed that $1,056 million of the total (including all the unallocated amounts in the Continental OEEC account) represented the import of marine bunker oil (usually imported in bond) to be supplied to ships bunkering at ports in the importing country. The method of allocation followed here was to distribute these imports by source according to the pattern of all petroleum imports over the five years established for each importing area in the special study of petroleum trade (see Table C-1).

Another $837 million of the unallocated merchandise debits arose in the account of a single country, Lebanon, and represented imports for re-export. Correspondingly, there was in the merchandise credit matrix in Table B-4 $947 million of unallocated Lebanese exports. Allocating this Lebanese middleman trade required guessing its pattern, and, on the basis of quite limited evidence drawn partly from

[7] See following section on grouping of countries.

partner trade records, half the unallocated Lebanese imports was attributed to the U.S., 5 per cent to Canada, 10 per cent to the Middle East (Other Countries), 15 per cent to the U.K., and 20 per cent to the Continental OEEC countries. The heaviest allocations were made to sources of manufactures on the grounds that they accounted for most of the goods flowing through Lebanon to nearby countries, but the 10 per cent figure for the Middle East allowed for some imports from Syria for re-export to world markets. As exports, these Syrian goods were allocated 5 per cent to the Continent, 3 per cent to the U.S., and 2 per cent to the U.K.; and of the remaining unallocated exports, one-third was allocated to the Rest of the Sterling Area (Iraq and British Arabian States) and two-thirds to Other Countries (including Saudi Arabia).

After the disposal of unallocated bunker oil imports and Lebanese middleman traffic, the remaining unallocated merchandise debits fell $61 million in the account of the Continental Overseas Territories, $258 million in the Latin American account, and $96 million in the account of Other Countries (mostly in the Korean account). The unallocated imports of the Continental Overseas Territories were distributed about equally among the Rest of the Sterling Area, Latin America, and Other Countries on the grounds that they were mostly imports by African colonies from small partner countries. For lack of any better basis, the unallocated imports of Latin America and Other Countries were distributed in proportion to allocated imports.

In the merchandise credit matrix, the unallocated exports over five years totaled $2,035 million, almost half of which was the Lebanese exports discussed above. Another $471 million of unallocated exports arose in the accounts of the Netherlands Antilles and Venezuela in the form of unallocated exports of petroleum. In support of the hypothesis that these exports were sales to government, the government transactions matrix in Tables B-19 and B-20 was found to show sizable U.S. debits to Continental Overseas Territories (which includes the Netherlands Antilles) that were not matched by any corresponding credit entry of the latter group. Similarly, the government account for Latin America shows receipts on government account from the U.S. that are much below U.S. government debits to Latin America. Accordingly, it was judged that, for com-

parable treatment, these $471 million of merchandise debits should be transferred to the services account in Table A-4.

In reviewing the unallocated transactions in the various matrixes of Appendix B in relation to the pattern of interarea divergence, we also observed a number of other differences for which the appropriate remedy, for the purposes of Table A-4, seemed to be to introduce offsetting entries in certain of the accounts. In the investment income account of the United Kingdom with nonsterling EPU countries, there were large debit entries not matched in the Continental OEEC account with the Sterling Area. In constructing our account for the U.K. we had entered $1,052 million of debits for the Dutch share of Royal Dutch-Shell group earnings, and we observed only $188 million of investment income over the five years from the Sterling Area in the Netherlands account. Most of this ($181 million) was accounted for by dividends declared by the Royal Dutch-Shell group to the Dutch parent. Evidently, the reinvested earnings of the Royal Dutch Petroleum Company in the Royal Dutch-Shell group were omitted from the Dutch account, and, accordingly, we increased services credits and capital debits of Continental OEEC countries with the U.K. by $871 million in the five-year consolidated figures in Table A-4.

Unallocated U.K. transportation credits and debits were tanker transactions related to oil exports of British companies (Table C-1) unallocated by destination. As with the unallocated oil exports of Venezuela and the Netherlands Antilles, we considered that these were oil sales to military vessels, in this case to the British military, and, accordingly, the transportation credits and debits were considered domestic transactions and deducted.

Large unallocated travel credits and debits in the Latin American account came in the accounts of Venezuela and Mexico. To judge from the larger partner entries, the unallocated debits should count partly as expenditures in the U.K. and the Continent. However, raising Latin American debits up to the larger partner credits did not dispose of more than $88 million of the $609 million unallocated. Possibly part of the rest was spent in Latin America itself (thereby helping to account for part of the unallocated credits), but since the unallocated debits also came in the accounts of Venezuela and Mexico and the unallocated credits came in the Mexican account, this is also unlikely. From conversations with government officials we understood that the Mexican travel account was grossly overstated. Rather arbitrarily, we reduced unallocated credits and debits by $465 million and $313 million, respectively, in moving from the Appendix B tables to Table A-4.

The unallocated miscellaneous services credits and debits in the U.K. account were in the nature of an error term, and in Table A-4 these credits and debits were charged to the multilateral settlements and error account.

Finally, it should be mentioned that the allocation of unallocated gold transactions and the reconciliation of net credits with net debits in that account resulting in the gold entries in Table A-4 involved a rather complicated piece of guesswork. Net gold sales in the unadjusted gold matrix (Table B-27) consistently exceeded net gold purchases each year. It is not possible to infer the purchaser from the selling side since large amounts of sales are unallocated. To effect a reconciliation in the account and to allocate the unallocated gold sales, we proceeded for purposes of Table A-4 as follows. First, we raised the total of (net) gold purchases over the five years to equal total (net) sales. This meant adding $1,708 million of net gold purchases to the accounts of some areas. On the basis of fragmentary information on the probable pattern of gold hoarding, we allocated one-third to each of the Rest of the Sterling Area, the Continental OEEC countries, and Other Countries.[8] We then constructed the matrix of interarea

gold sales on the following assumptions: that each area met its demand for gold first out of the unallocated gold sales of countries in the area; that Other Countries secured their residual gold purchases from Latin America; that the balance of gold sales by Latin America and Canada went to the Continent; and that the rest of the Continent's needs were met by the U.K.

Clearly other matrixes could be constructed assuming different patterns for unreported net gold purchases and for the allocation of unallocated gold sales. The particular allocation we made has a considerable element of arbitrariness in it both in the way over-all gold disappearance was allocated by partner area and the fairly simple assumptions made about the flow of unallocated gold sales into the hands of purchasers. It does, however, preserve all that has been reported about the destinations of gold sales and of itself does not change the direction of net multilateral settlements between Latin America and Other Countries or between Latin America and the Continent from the pattern observable in the unadjusted matrix of multilateral settlements (Table B-28). While it does not alter the pattern of net settlements between the Continent and either the U.K. or the Rest of the Sterling Area, it does result in a Sterling Area credit balance with the Continent in contrast to the deficit shown in the unadjusted annual tables.[9]

The effect of all of these adjustments to allocate the unallocated transactions was in general to reduce the extent of divergence in the set of accounts and also to alter some of the measures of total trans-

[8] The gossip in the bullion reports of gold brokers and the existence of premium gold markets indicate that Tangier, Lebanon, Saudi Arabia, Egypt, Thailand, Indonesia, and Communist China were likely places among Other Countries for gold to be hoarded. Disappearance into India and the British protectorates on the Persian Gulf, among sterling countries, and into private and sometimes unreported government holdings in France, Switzerland, and other Continental countries is also a common presumption.

Writing on Indian gold, Arthur H. Taylor (*Gold and Its Price*, New Delhi, 1954, p. 17) says: "It is alleged that gold is smuggled in [to India] from Kuwait via Goa and Pondichery and in dhows along the coast. It is said that the gold is bought in Kuwait from the international markets, Switzerland, France, Hong Kong, Macao and Bangkok, against dollars. . . . I have heard it from a reliable source that between 1¼ and 1½ million ounces [$50–$60 million] are smuggled into India annually." Taylor is Vice Chairman of John Taylor and Son, Ltd., which operates the Kolar gold mine in India.

Samuel Montague and Company's *Annual Bullion Review*, 1951, states: "We estimate that during the year under review the net absorption of gold by the free markets

of the world for non-monetary purposes [was] . . . 40% . . . by European markets, 30% in the Middle East and the balance [30%] in the Far East." Montague's review for 1952 carried the observation (p. 3) that the "main support of the free market [in 1952] was the French hoarding demand."

Two entertaining accounts of the shady activities involving gold are an article by H. R. Reinhardt in *The Reporter* (July 22, 1952), entitled "Trailing Illicit Gold Across a Hemisphere," and Joachim Joesten, *Gold Today* (New York, 1954).

[9] The reporting of partner information about gold transactions is very spotty. As with foreign aid, reinvested capital, and investment income, the statistical offices of other countries have frequently resorted to the use of published U. S. records to fill their accounts, and where official country accounts do not provide an entry, we have sought to fill in the record. Consequently, many of the paired entries in the unadjusted gold matrix actually are from one side only. For this reason it has not been thought useful to study the divergence between paired entries in Table B-27 in Chapter 5.

actions. In consequence, totals obtained from summing the annual matrixes of net transactions in Appendix B will differ from the corresponding figures given in the consolidated matrixes of net transactions in Table A-4.[10]

The net excess of merchandise credit transactions of all areas with all areas in the adjusted Table A-4 ($5,112 million) is less than the $5,583 million of net merchandise credits summed up from the unadjusted matrixes of Table B-6, given below in Table 3; and the net excess of services debits in the adjusted table is −$8,209 million compared with −$8,951 million. Likewise, the over-all net excess of capital credits, ($2,419 million in the adjusted matrix in Table A-4) is less than the $3,290 million obtained from the unadjusted matrixes of Appendix B and shown in Table 4 below. However, largely because the gold account is reconciled and balanced out to zero, the over-all balance in the residual multilateral settlements and error account rises from −$29 million in the unadjusted settlements matrix of Appendix B to $2,279 million in Table A-4.

We have not carried these adjustments to allocate the unallocated transactions back into annual matrixes because, for the most part, they are rather speculative, but they do suggest that the agreement in the annual accounts could be improved with more work than has been possible here.

Grouping Countries

The final geographic problem was to decide what groupings of partner countries to keep in each country account. The IMF *Manual* asks for a twelvefold division of the world: [11]

> United States
> Canada
> Latin America
> Continental OEEC
> United Kingdom
> Rest of Sterling Area: Europe
> Rest of Sterling Area: Far East
> Rest of Sterling Area: Elsewhere
> Eastern Europe
> Middle East
> Far East
> Rest of World

However, inspection showed that this scheme was

[10] Note that the gross and net goods and services transactions matrixes given in Table A-1 are *not* so adjusted and represent a simple consolidation of the annual lines of Tables B-1, B-2, and B-3; while adjusted matrixes have been prepared for gross goods and services transactions, they are not given in this book.

[11] 2nd ed., Table A.

not followed by some important countries, particularly those participating in or affiliated with the Organization for European Economic Cooperation. These countries followed a format, worked out in connection with the European Recovery Program, to facilitate the operation of the European Payments Union (EPU) and to illuminate the problems of the Sterling Area. In their scheme, Continental Overseas Territories were generally combined with the metropolitan territory, and Continental OEEC accounts showed the Sterling Area as a combined group. Similarly, in accounts of Sterling Area countries, transactions with Continental OEEC countries and with their Overseas Territories were usually combined, and the U.S. was combined with Canada, but transactions with the U.K. and the Rest of the Sterling Area were usually shown separately. The U.S. followed the OEEC definitions in distinguishing the U.K., other European sterling countries, British dependencies, and other Sterling Area, Continental OEEC countries, and their Overseas Territories. The countries participating in the OEEC frequently did not distinguish the U.S. as a partner but combined it with Canada or with an even broader dollar area.

Faced with this multiplicity of practices and with three objectives in mind—first, to keep as close as possible to the framework of each country's own report; second, to employ the *Direction of International Trade* and OEEC records of merchandise (which were tabulated in the common numéraire) to distribute more aggregate groupings; and, third, to respect the importance of the United States, the United Kingdom, and Continental OEEC countries as economic centers—we determined the following eight areas for our two-valued matrixes:

> United States
> Canada
> United Kingdom
> Rest of Sterling Area
> Continental OEEC Countries
> Continental Overseas Territories
> Latin America
> Other Countries

These eight areas were augmented by the addition of columns and rows for transactions with International Organizations and the EPU and columns and rows in the accounts of the Continental OEEC countries and of their Overseas Territories for transactions with their own currency area. The Organization for European Economic Cooperation had found it necessary to distinguish transactions within the currency areas of particular countries from transactions between currency areas. Only the latter were cleared through the European Payments Union. In order to provide a record which would be useful for studying the financial history of the period, we have respected, and maintained, the distinction. The International Organizations and the EPU were quite unimportant for goods and services transactions but of some importance for the financial accounts—transfers, capital, etc.

In general we employed all available evidence on transactions of each reporting country to elaborate its payments account according to this eight-area scheme. Where we developed accounts ourselves, we distinguished the eight areas and the supplementary rows and columns.

To obtain an elaboration of the U.K. transactions with the dollar area, we compiled the record of partner transactions with the United Kingdom, consolidated countries according to the U.K. definition of dollar area, entered the partner record as an allowance, and attributed the balance to the U.S. as a partner. Thus our account of the U.K. transactions with Canada is as reported by Canada; that with Latin America includes a component reported by fourteen dollar Latin American Republics and by our PHL fleet account; and that with Other Countries includes a component reported in the accounts of Liberia, Saudi Arabia, and the Philippines. For transactions of the Rest of the Sterling Area as a whole with the U.S. and Canada, the same procedure was followed. Transactions reported by all the Rest of the Sterling Area countries with the U.S. and Canada were allocated to Canada (and International Organizations) according to the report of the partner area and the balance attributed to the U.S.

The elaboration of transactions reported by the component EPU areas with partner areas within the EPU could not be made by this method. However, in the matrix for each type of transaction we did have, on the one hand, reports of transactions by the U.K. and the Rest of the Sterling Area with the nonsterling EPU area and, on the other hand, reports by the Continental OEEC countries and their Overseas Territories with the Sterling Area as a whole. We subdivided these totals into components by assuming that both the Rest of the Sterling Area and U.K. transactions with the nonsterling EPU area were distributed between the Continental OEEC countries and their Overseas Territories in propor-

tion to the totals which the Continent and their Overseas Territories reported with the Sterling Area, and similarly that transactions of the Continent and their Overseas Territories were distributed within the Sterling Area subdivisions in the proportions indicated by the transactions of the U.K. and the Rest of the Sterling Area with the whole nonsterling EPU area. A similar procedure was used to distribute the transactions of Continental OEEC countries and of their Overseas Territories with the nonsterling EPU area. Estimates obtained by use of partner data have been entered in parentheses in the two-valued matrix tables. This method was applied to goods and services as a whole and to merchandise, and the distribution of services was derived by differences. Only in the case of services transactions between the Rest of the Sterling Area and Continental Overseas Territories does the method result in nonsense.[12]

The eight-area grouping used in the country accounts has thus been taken for the sake of convenience and to minimize adjustments to published accounts, but we are not confined to it. Since our record has been developed country by country, it is possible to consolidate the country accounts in different groupings to produce asymetrical matrix tables of transactions with the eight standard partner areas. Most of the transaction relations among countries grouped by Hilgerdt's criterion can be established in this way.[13] One can observe transactions between countries grouped by principle trading interest or any other criterion one might wish to examine, as, for example, the pattern of the balance over the five years with the U.S., the U.K., and Continental OEEC countries for a given type of transaction.

2. *The Item Dimension*

In designing the format for items to be distinguished in the accounts, we have been guided in the main by the detail which the International Monetary Fund generally carries in its *Yearbook*. The only

---

[12] This could have been avoided and a better result obtained had the method been applied to services directly. The allocation of merchandise transactions could better have been made from trade records which are usually available. The method described was modified somewhat in distributing net transfers and capital where a presumption exists that transactions were with the Continent and the U.K.

[13] Hilgerdt's criterion was employed in *The Network of World Trade,* League of Nations, Geneva, 1942.

major departure arose from the need to show a given transaction as the same type in the accounts of both the area credited and the area debited. For this reason, nonmonetary gold has been omitted from the goods and services account (where it is normally placed by the IMF) and combined with monetary gold in the section of financial accounts.[14]

Merchandise has been kept separate and valued f.o.b. in all accounts. Where there was evidence (as in the case of certain petroleum sales) that some merchandise export was counted in the U.S. or U.K. account as government purchases, the sale has been entered in the government services line. Otherwise, in general government purchases of merchandise (e.g., in the Indian account) have been shown as merchandise imports.

Most countries report merchandise imports valued c.i.f. As noted above, these accounts had to be adjusted to an f.o.b. valuation to permit a separate entry in the accounts for freight and insurance payments abroad, and these payments had to be allocated by countries. These adjustments had to take account of the differing commodity composition and origin of each country's imports and entailed substantial work which is described more fully in Appendix E.

In making these adjustments, it was convenient to keep the allowance for insurance on imported goods in with freight charges. Consequently, where the marine insurance item was distinguished, we have included it in transportation.

We did not keep the full detail on services transactions provided for in the IMF *Manual* and *Yearbook* but considered that five types would be sufficient for most analytic purposes and about the most that would be generally reported.

We have included reinvested earnings in both investment income and capital accounts whenever possible, notably in the accounts of and with the U.S., Canada, and oil-source countries.

In worksheets we sought to distinguish private from official unilateral transfers, and this distinction is made in the consolidated five-year matrixes of Table A-4. Where the annual accounts are given, as in Appendix B, private and official transfers are combined. We also sought to compile gross credits and debits for unilateral transfers, but many countries evidently give only net transfers. Agreement between paired entries in the net transfer matrixes was somewhat better than in the gross matrixes; hence we have found it better in general to work with the former.

We prepared trial-run matrixes for private and official, long- and short-term capital, net, but to distinguish these categories would have taken much supplementary work. One problem is the conceptual difficulty already mentioned that capital which is official on one side may be private on the other; then too, countries do not always keep to a common criterion for distinguishing short- from long-term capital. Walther Michael has undertaken a searching examination of these questions.[15] In this volume we do not attempt to subdivide our matrix on capital movements, but in Section B of Chapter 5 we do make a partial segregation of liquid assets on the basis of information for the two principal reserve centers, the United States and the United Kingdom.

We thus came to distinguish eleven main items: merchandise valued f.o.b., five types of services, private and official transfers, capital, gold, and the residual net multilateral settlements and error. For the goods and services accounts, credits and debits have been kept as well as the net of the two; for the financial accounts, only net transactions with

[14] The IMF includes nonmonetary gold movements in goods and services. Such a treatment of newly produced gold is particularly useful and appropriate in analyses relating a country's balance of payments to its domestic production and income, but not at all appropriate in relating a country's payments account to transactions reported by others. Newly produced gold sales are nonmonetary to the selling country but usually monetary to the buying country. There are only a few countries to which newly produced gold is important; for most countries gold transactions are monetary. The simplest, and I believe the most useful, treatment of gold is the one followed here. One must, however, bear in mind the availability of newly produced gold in some countries to cover goods and service deficits or add to reserves. New gold production by country is regularly tabulated in *International Financial Statistics*. It is of prime importance (amounting annually to several hundred million dollars) only to the Union of South Africa (and hence to the Rest of the Sterling Area). It is of substantial importance (over $100 million annually) to Canada and of only minor importance (less than $50 million annually) to Australia, the British Colonies, and a few other countries. It is also of importance in some years in the account for the Soviet Bloc. For a fuller discussion of this problem, see Poul Høst-Madsen's comment on my preliminary paper, "Transactions between World Areas in 1951," in *Problems in International Economics* (Supplement to the *Review of Economics and Statistics*, February 1958, pp. 23 ff.) and my reply (pp. 33 ff.).

[15] "International Capital Movements: The Experience of the Early Fifties, 1950–54," unpublished Ph.D. dissertation, Columbia University, 1965.

partner areas have been kept. This format was largely dictated by the available data. An elaboration of the merchandise account into components was started in a special investigation by C. Dwyer of petroleum transactions; therefore petroleum can be presented in the merchandise matrix both on a trade records basis and on a purchase-sales basis, and the nature of the adjustments needed to go from one basis to the other can be observed (Appendix C).[16]

The Residual Item: Net Multilateral Settlements and Error

In such a system of accounts as we have developed, interest tends to focus on the pattern of final net multilateral settlements and error, which it is desirable to consider at some length.

First of all, it should be noted that for most of our accounts the net settlements and error line has been obtained as a residual. Conceptually, of course, the final balance with all partners in this account should be zero for any reporting country or area. In general it is not, and the over-all balance represents *net* error in the sense that all errors of omission, valuation, timing, etc., in the various items balance out to an amount which must be offset by the net error term. When it is large, the over-all net error term indicates a large error; but when it is small, it may be that large errors are offsetting.[17] Thus, the over-all net error term in country accounts is not a measure of error, but is still a magnitude which should be examined.

The regional elaboration of net settlements in a

country's account, conceptually, should represent the element of multilateralism in its trade and payments relations with partners; and our accounts have been designed so that, apart from errors producing the over-all net error term and apart from error of direction, the balances offset by the last line represent balances to be settled by multilateral transfers between partner areas. They represent, in principle, the net on the bilateral transactions between the reporting country or area and each of its partner areas after all types of exchanges are entered—i.e., the net in each case, which has to be compensated by earnings from other areas or by payments to other areas. Apart from errors, therefore, the multilateral settlements matrix consists of settlements between areas on account of all exchanges—whether of goods for goods, goods for assets (including money and gold), or assets for assets (including money and gold). Shifts from assets held in one area to assets held in another area give rise to multilateral settlements, just as merchandise trade involving purchases and sales in different areas does. Both kinds of settlement are in the matrix, gold being considered as an asset. The significance of the record of multilateral settlements and error is considered at some length in Chapter 5.

3. The Time Dimension

Like any operational accounting statement, a record of transactions between world areas must be related to some definite time period, and every account in the system should relate to that period. These are elementary considerations but do pose some practical problems. The use of the Gregorian calendar year is not universal. Moreover, a strong argument can be made in favor of another accounting period, notably, the fiscal year ending June 30, which more nearly approximates the agricultural crop year.[18] But most countries use the calendar year ending December 31, and we have sought to adjust accounts of countries to that basis when they were reported otherwise.

The *Manual* [19] provides a criterion for establishing the time referent for a transaction: "when the goods are sold and the services rendered." The change in ownership is the crucial question. Changes in asset

---

[16] It should be noted that, although our goods and services account is primarily composed of newly produced goods and services, in fact it includes some "movables" that are not part of the current production of the supplying country. Countries quite generally include in their merchandise transactions account all movable goods changing ownership. The presumption is that international trade in movables draws either on current production or "stocks." Actually, art works, antiques, used ships and aircraft, second-hand articles generally, and scrap move in international trade and are a part neither of current production nor of the stocks which are normally replaced in the conduct of business. Transfers of war surplus and used ships on occasion have been large, and there is a continual business in scrap. Our goods and services category is only approximately a measure of trade in currently produced goods.

[17] In a few accounts (usually with a zero net over-all error), the net capital account is made the balancing item on the ground that the largest omitted transactions are capital movements. In such cases, coverage and valuation errors are netted out in the capital account rather than in the final settlements account.

[18] For a fuller discussion of the time dimension, see my paper in *Problems of the International Comparison of Economic Accounts.*

[19] 2nd ed., p. 4.

positions and liabilities should, in principle, also be based on the time of a change in ownership. In practice, various expedients are used to approximate the timing of transactions; and, as these expedients are not always consistent, errors of timing are introduced which give rise to divergence between paired entries in the two-valued matrixes.

Countries seem to make more of an effort to maintain a "vertical" consistency in the timing of transactions of different kinds in their own account (e.g., between trade and finance) than to maintain a "horizontal" consistency with partner areas in the timing of transactions of the same type. This seems to be one important source of the tendency for the divergences in two-valued matrixes to be offsetting between transactions of different types. We have not been able to go very far in correcting differences in timing, but have resorted instead to consolidating accounts over the five-year period when observing structural relationships. The longer the time period taken, of course, the less important are the horizontal inconsistencies in timing.[20]

4. The Currency Dimension

Every international transaction is valued in some currency and may also be related by a specified exchange rate to a second currency. Third-country currencies may be used. The many international transactions expressed in different currencies must be converted into a single unit of account if the world matrix is to have any meaning at all.

In general each country compiling a payments statement expresses the transactions in local currency units; these must then be converted into a unit common to all countries. For 1951, thirty-two countries submitted statements to the IMF in their own currency while twenty-eight used U.S. dollar equivalents.[21] The choice of a unit of account for the 1950's thus offered little problem—U.S. dollar equivalents was the most convenient unit.[22]

For the conversion from local currency into dollar equivalents, we have generally used the conversion rates given by the IMF in its *Yearbook*. Only in the accounts of Argentina, Lebanon, and Syria were there serious problems and these were dealt with by special techniques described in the notes on those countries. Countries with conversion difficulties characteristically sacrifice comparability with their internal accounts in order to maintain the comparability of their external accounts with those of other countries.[23]

Another aspect of the currency dimension of great practical importance during the period under study was the difficulty that countries (notably Western European ones) had to maintain a tenable equilibrium in the foreign exchange market at the established rates of exchange. Discriminatory trade and exchange controls were used to defend overvalued currencies in the belief (since proved well founded in many cases) that the difficulties were temporary and would be overcome with recovery from wartime dislocation and devastation. Because many countries had a "dollar problem," it would have been desirable to distinguish transactions according to the international currency actually employed. A number of countries sought to do this directly; others used geographic groupings as an approximation; but the most we have done is to use combinations of the eight areas or special groupings of countries to cast some light on the nature of the demand for and supply of currencies widely used in international trade.

B. PREPARING THE RECORD

The opportunity to compile a set of accounts such as we present here arose because of the great effort government and central bank statisticians all over the world, following the lead of the IMF, have expended in preparing regionally elaborated payments accounts. The Secretariat of the Monetary Fund hospitably afforded us access to their unclassified files of statements supplied by countries, and these materials provided the basic core of data. Each country ac-

---

[20] It is well to remember that vertical errors in timing do exist because, for example, merchandise export credits may be measured by the time that customs records are tabulated, while short-term capital debits may be measured by the time papers are sent air mail to correspondent banks.

[21] The IMF asks countries to render an account in "some convenient unit of the domestic currency" but where multiple currencies are in force, also in "some fixed currency unit . . ." (*Manual*, 2nd ed., p. 9).

[22] This has not always been the case: Hilgerdt found it necessary in the *Network* study to express 1928 data both in "new gold" and "old gold" dollars.

[23] Earl Hicks noted this in his article, "Exchange Conversion," in *International Trade Statistics*, pp. 108–109.

count was reviewed in terms of the geographic structure and itemization desired and, where possible, was adjusted to the format employed. Where our special studies indicated the need, the accounts were modified appropriately. We also developed accounts for transactions not reported on by countries to the IMF.[24]

We worked out the method of compiling the accounts in stages, first concentrating on all the country accounts for 1951 (the latest year available at the time) to develop a trial-run matrix for merchandise, transportation, other services, and finally the financial accounts. Then we went back and did all accounts for all types of transactions for the years 1950 and 1952–54. Walther Michael conducted the phase of this work which drew on IMF files and, with several assistants, prepared most of the country accounts. It was not until we had two-valued matrixes for all types of transactions for 1951 that we could identify many of the problems of adjustment and supplementation.

1. Special Studies

Petroleum and transportation provided peculiarly challenging difficulties to the construction of a matrix of transactions between world areas. Special studies were consequently planned for these topics. Cornelius Dwyer undertook the study of petroleum transactions, Herman Karreman the study of transportation, and Carmellah Moneta the tasks of estimating freight and insurance on imports valued c.i.f. and the value of bunker sales. Since a substantial part of the landed cost of petroleum is transportation, since bunkers are largely petroleum bunkers, and since the adjustment of merchandise valuation was a corollary to the construction of an adequate transportation matrix, these three studies were closely meshed. They contributed also to a fourth special study, made by Robert Lichtenberg, which focused on the problems of adjusting the record of merchandise transactions to a purchase-sales basis.

The study of petroleum transactions was not limited to trade. Rather, the comprehensive compilation and estimation of trade in petroleum between world areas which Dwyer prepared for 1951–54 provided a basis for examining a "verticle slice" out of the whole set of accounts. The transactions of petroleum

companies not only represented 10 per cent of all goods trade, they were also prominent in the transportation sector—tanker freights comprising 30 per cent of all freight payments;[25] prominent in the investment income account—making up nearly a third of international payments of this type over the five years; and prominent in the capital account—representing about 30 per cent of all U.S. direct investment abroad (including reinvested profits) over the five years.

The special knowledge Dwyer brought to the study made it possible to develop accounts for nonreporting oil-source countries and to treat petroleum transactions in the merchandise account in two ways, as discussed in Chapter 4 and Appendix C. Dwyer also supplied much of the expertise entering into the preparation of accounts for tanker transactions for the U.K. and PHL fleets, especially the underlying assumptions about the chartering and employment of the world's tanker fleet by British and American companies.

In contrast to the "vertical" study of petroleum, the transportation study was conceived as a "horizontal" study of a single component of the whole set of accounts. It has been fully reported on in Karreman's technical paper.

2. Some Deficiencies in the Record

In spite of our efforts to adjust published country accounts and to introduce accounts where none was published, the record presented in Appendix B is still deficient in a number of important respects. Some of these deficiencies have been discussed in connection with the effort to allocate the unallocated transactions and reconcile the gold account. While the country coverage is reasonably complete, for certain countries adequate information is not available on all types of transactions. Most notably, our account for Soviet Bloc transactions with the free world lacks all types of transactions except merchandise (f.o.b.) and gold. We could find no adequate basis for estimating Soviet services, transfers, or capital transactions. Our accounts for transactions between European countries and associated Overseas Terri-

---

[24] Adjustments of official accounts are described for each country in the country notes on file at the National Bureau.

[25] According to Dwyer's calculation, tanker freights were $1.35 billion in 1953 out of the $4.53 billion total freight payments compiled by Karreman (*Methods for Improving World Transportation Accounts, Applied to 1950–1953*, Technical Paper 15, New York, NBER, 1961, Table A-9).

tories are also extremely deficient in the coverage of services and financial flows. Particularly lacking are allowances for services (except transportation), unilateral transfers (private and official), and capital flows between France and her Overseas Territories, between Portugal and her Overseas Territories, and Spain and Spanish possessions. Accounts for oil-source countries in the Middle East (which we constructed outright or modified substantially) fail to explain the disposition of the large oil royalties and local oil company expenditures received by local governments. These deficiencies result in some large residual error entries (see Section D of Chapter 3).

In addition to not measuring completely all types of transactions by all countries, we have met with numerous difficulties in treating transactions uniformly according to type. The most notable such deficiency arises from the category "government transactions" in the U.S. account, which includes goods and transportation and thus cuts across the more conventional classification. There is also a ten-dency in a number of accounts to lump private unilateral transfers with miscellaneous services. The recording of gold transactions leaves a great deal to be desired.

These and lesser deficiencies are discussed in succeeding chapters as they affect the comparability of paired entries in the set of accounts and as they affect the usefulness of the record for measuring international transactions. The extent to which paired entries in the two-valued record differ is examined for the light it sheds on the statistical limitations of the accounts. Complete success in reconciling accounts would have given an agreed record in which world balances for each type of transaction equal zero. The observable differences that remain indicate uncertainties of measurement on one side or the other or both, the extent of the problem depending on the magnitude of the difference. Where paired entries differ little, it is still possible that both records err. The user of the record must be particularly alert to the possibility of omissions on both sides.

3

WORLD TOTALS

In the matrix tables of Appendixes A and B the entries in the upper left-hand corner provide world totals for the several types of transactions. In this chapter the record of these totals will be examined for what they tell about the course of world trade and its composition and for the light the paired entries shed on the nature of error in the accounts. To set the statistics in proper perspective, the salient historical developments of 1950–54 should be briefly recalled.

The five years were marked by the following events: the outbreak of a "small war" in Korea on June 25, 1950, the threat of a "big war" later in the year when Communist China intervened, the emergence of a military stalemate in mid-1951, the conclusion of a truce in mid-1953, and the subsequent readjustment to a period of eased tension. Throughout most of the period 1950–54, civil war between Communist nationalists and French forces disrupted life in Indochina. Stepped up after the Korean truce with the redeployment of Red Chinese forces, this war ended, shortly after the defeat of French forces at Dien Bien Phu, with the conclusion of an armistice at the Geneva conference in mid-1954. France was also pressed by unrest in North Africa throughout the period. Communist-led revolts during the early 1950's threatened governments in the Philippines and Malaya. Not all the disturbances could be attributed to the Communists. Of considerable significance to world trade and the British payments position was the nationalization of Iranian oil (March 1951), which interrupted the flow of Iranian oil from mid-1951 to late in 1954 and prompted the British to rely on alternative sources.

By 1950 most of the countries of the free world had pretty well recovered from the disruptions and actual devastation of World War II. Our former enemies, Germany and Japan, lagged behind partly because Allied policy aimed at giving their European and Far Eastern rivals a head start at rehabilitation; and the problems of the newly independent countries of the Far East were increased by the disruptions accompanying the establishment of new governments and by Communist-led revolts. The currencies of Western European countries and of the countries trading principally with them had been realigned in September 1949 with a sharp devaluation against gold and the U.S. dollar, thereby placing European countries in a stronger position to compete for markets.[1] The devaluation came just as the force of the first postwar recession in the United States was spent, so that, in addition to benefiting from the devaluation, Western Europe benefited from the revival of U.S. demand. Then, after the outbreak of fighting in Korea, governments in the West launched new programs of military rearmament, and they as well as private business everywhere engaged in a wild scramble for raw materials, with prices skyrocketing.[2]

A. THE COURSE AND COMPOSITION OF WORLD TRADE IN 1950–54

As a consequence of the above developments, world trade in goods and services rose sharply from 1950 to 1951, as can be seen in Chart 1. Subsequently, the

military situation in Korea stabilized and Western governments proceeded with plans to revitalize the common defense, governments modified their stock-

[1] "Countries accounting for 65 per cent of world imports devalued their currencies, most of them by about 30 per cent" (J. J. Polak, "Contribution of the September 1949 Devaluations to the Solution of Europe's Dollar Problem," *International Monetary Funds Staff Papers*, September 1951, p. 1).

[2] *World Economic Report, 1949–50*, United Nations, New York, 1951, p. 8; and *World Economic Survey, 1955*, U. N.,

New York, 1956, pp. 21 ff. Bert G. Hickman (*The Korean War and U. S. Economic Activity, 1950–1952*, NBER, Occasional Paper 49, New York, 1955) describes the anticipatory buying waves in the U.S. immediately after the outbreak of hostilities and again after the intervention by Red China. He observes that the subsidence of this speculation coincided with the actual increase in military expenditures later in 1951.

CHART I

The Course of World Trade: Goods and Services Credits and Debits
by Type of Transaction, Annually, 1950–54
(million U.S. dollars)

——— Credits   - - - - - Debits

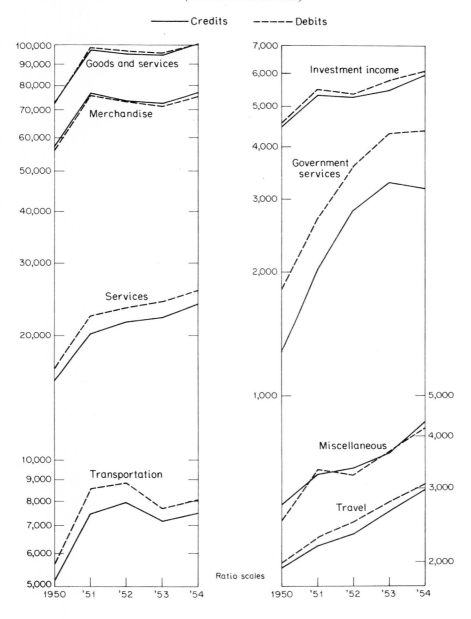

Ratio scales

Source: Appendix B.

piling policies, and private expectations reflected renewed confidence in the future. The "extraordinary inventory cycle" prompted by the outbreak of the Korean War gave way to liquidation and slackening demand in international markets.[3] World trade receded moderately in 1952 and 1953, the last year being affected also by the U.S. recession which began in the second quarter of 1953. World trade in goods and services expanded again from 1953 to 1954 under the stimulus of continued growth in Western Europe and revival in the United States. Over the five years 1950–54 the current dollar value of world trade in goods and services rose by 38 per cent, with most of the increase from 1950 to 1951. Both total credits and debits show the growth and a cyclical swing. Compared with the movement of world trade, the difference between the credit and debit records is evidently minuscule.

The contribution of merchandise and the several types of services to total world trade can be seen in Table 3, which gives the credit and debit totals for each type of transaction from two-valued matrixes. These totals have also been plotted in Chart 1.

As measures of total world trade and its division into goods and various types of services, the figures given in Table 3 suffer from the omissions mentioned in the previous chapter. Services transactions are probably understated but, in spite of deficiencies, the figures are more comprehensive and provide a better basis than anything hitherto available for judging the relative importance of goods and services.

As can be seen in Table 3, the six categories do not represent an equal division of all goods and services transactions. Merchandise accounts for more than three-fourths of the total, whether credits or debits. Transportation, the largest of the five types of service, represents no more than 8.4 per cent of either credit or debit totals over the five years and about 10 per cent of merchandise f.o.b.; investment income was a little smaller; and travel, government, and miscellaneous were much smaller, running from 2.6 to 3.7 per cent of all goods and services depending on the item and on whether credits or debits are used. The smallest category, travel, was only about a third the size of transportation.

Although the proportions of merchandise and the several types of services transactions in total world

[3] *World Economic Survey, 1955,* p. 21.

trade varied somewhat from year to year and over the five years, these variations were small compared with the great differences in order of magnitude between these categories.

However, the several types of trade did not experience the same growth over the period or the same year-to-year variation. The rise, decline, and revival of world trade in the period 1950–54 characterized merchandise separately and some services, but not all. Total services rose without interruption throughout the five years although more rapidly from 1950 to 1951 and from 1953 to 1954 than from 1951 to 1953 (see Chart 1). Transportation, investment income, and miscellaneous services (debits) show the cyclical rise-fall-rise, with declines either in 1952 or 1953, but the strong upward surge of government services and travel expenditures throughout the period smoothed out the combined services total.

Whereas all trade grew 38 per cent over the five years, merchandise increased 34 per cent and services rose by more than 50 per cent and grew as a proportion of all goods and services (Table 3). Growth was most pronounced in government services, which more than doubled from 1950 to 1954, mainly as a reflection of expanding U.S. military expenditures abroad. Travel and miscellaneous services increased by about 50 per cent. Transportation transactions rose relatively from 1950 to 1952 but then declined, ending up at about the same proportion of all goods and services in 1954 as they were in 1950. Investment income tended to rise and fall with merchandise, but not as pronouncedly, and represented a smaller proportion of all goods and services in 1952 than in 1950 or 1954. It was evidently the cyclical movement in the merchandise account which set the pattern for the cyclical variation in total trade including services (Chart 1).

Again, both credit and debit records show the broad movement in world trade for each type of transaction and the difference between records generally is small relative to the variation in the series over time. However, in two instances when year-to-year movements were small, the credit record shows a different direction of movement from that of the debit record: miscellaneous debits declined slightly while credits rose slightly from 1951 to 1952 and government services credits declined while debits rose slightly from 1953 to 1954.

TABLE 3

The Course and Composition of World Trade in 1950–54

CREDITS (million dollars)

	1950	1951	1952	1953	1954	1950–54
Goods and services	72,980	97,001	95,083	94,706	100,902	460,672
Merchandise	57,364	76,808	73,411	72,521	76,994	357,098
Services	15,616	20,193	21,672	22,185	23,908	103,574
Transportation	5,195	7,428	7,915	7,155	7,492	35,185
Travel	1,938	2,188	2,328	2,635	2,970	12,059
Investment income	4,464	5,304	5,262	5,473	5,944	26,447
Government	1,278	2,028	2,818	3,292	3,193	12,609
Miscellaneous	2,741	3,245	3,349	3,630	4,309	17,274

CREDITS (per cent)

	1950	1951	1952	1953	1954	1950–54
Goods and services	100.00	100.00	100.00	100.00	100.00	100.00
Merchandise	78.60	79.18	77.21	76.57	76.31	77.52
Services	21.40	20.82	22.79	23.43	23.69	22.48
Transportation	07.12	07.66	08.32	07.55	07.43	07.64
Travel	02.66	02.26	02.45	02.78	02.94	02.62
Investment income	06.12	05.47	05.53	05.78	05.92	05.74
Government	01.75	02.09	02.96	03.48	03.16	02.74
Miscellaneous	03.76	03.35	03.52	03.83	04.27	03.75

DEBITS (million dollars)

	1950	1951	1952	1953	1954	1950–54
Goods and services	72,775	98,210	96,727	95,518	100,810	464,040
Merchandise	56,142	75,774	73,239	71,309	75,051	351,515
Services	16,633	22,436	23,488	24,209	25,759	112,525
Transportation	5,766	8,556	8,846	7,695	8,070	38,933
Travel	1,991	2,383	2,489	2,784	3,068	12,715
Investment income	4,553	5,490	5,353	5,772	6,079	27,247
Government	1,814	2,691	3,577	4,306	4,374	16,762
Miscellaneous	2,509	3,316	3,223	3,652	4,168	16,868

DEBITS (per cent)

	1950	1951	1952	1953	1954	1950–54
Goods and services	100.00	100.00	100.00	100.00	100.00	100.00
Merchandise	77.14	77.16	75.72	74.66	74.45	75.75
Services	22.86	22.84	24.28	25.34	25.55	24.25
Transportation	07.92	08.71	09.15	08.06	08.01	08.39
Travel	02.74	02.43	02.57	02.91	03.04	02.74
Investment income	06.26	05.59	05.53	06.04	06.03	05.87
Government	02.49	02.74	03.70	04.51	04.34	03.61
Miscellaneous	03.45	03.38	03.33	03.82	04.13	03.63

DIVERGENCE[a] (million dollars)

	1950	1951	1952	1953	1954	1950–54
Goods and services	205	-1,209	-1,644	-812	92	-3,368[b]
Merchandise	1,222	1,034	172	1,212	1,943	5,583[b]
Services	-1,017	-2,243	-1,816	-2,024	-1,851	-8,951[b]
Transportation	-571	-1,128	-931	-540	-578	-3,748
Travel	-53	-195	-161	-149	-98	-656
Investment income	-89	-186	-91	-299	-135	-800
Government	-536	-663	-759	-1,014	-1,181	-4,153
Miscellaneous	232	-71	126	-22	141	406

SOURCE: Appendix B.

[a] Credits less debits.

[b] The adjustments described in Chapter 2 to allocate the unallocated transactions reduced the net over-all discrepancies to $5,112 million and −$8,209 million, respectively (Appendix Table A-4), mainly because of the transfer of $471 million of unallocated oil sales to the government account.

B. DISCREPANCY IN TOTAL CREDITS AND DEBITS FOR GOODS AND SERVICES

Conceptually, the purchases and sales of all areas from all areas for any given type of transaction should be equal, i.e., credits should equal debits. But in fact we do not find this to be so, and the pattern of divergence between credits and debits, both between different types of transactions and over time, provides some insight into the nature of errors in the accounts.

Divergences between total credits and debits for goods and services together are shown in Table 3 and are plotted in Chart 2 below. Certain features are striking. First, over the five years as a whole, the balance was negative with an excess of debits over credits. Second, the excess arose mainly in the middle years of greatest uncertainty in world affairs. The divergences at the beginning and end of the period were exceptionally small and opposite to the five-year total.

The over-all balance for each year, obtained by summing net goods and services (excluding major nonmonetary gold transactions) in the sixty-eight summary statements or full country accounts available in the International Monetary Fund *Balance of Payments Yearbook,* shows much the same magnitude and movement over the period 1950–54 as the over-all divergence in our goods and services account

(Table 4 below). Evidently, the tendency for debits to be reported in excess of credits in a period of world-wide uncertainty shows up in the combined accounts of the most important trading countries on which IMF regularly reports and is not greatly affected by the adjustments we have made or the accounts we have added for omitted countries.[4] This time pattern cannot be readily explained by rising trade coupled with a lag in reporting debits, although such a lag may have had some influence.[5]

The pattern of divergence between total credits and debits, which can be observed for the different types of goods and services transactions (Table 3 and Chart 2), reflects a persistent bias in the record. Merchandise credits exceed debits each year; debits for each type of services (except miscellaneous) exceed credits. It is because the excess of service debits exceeded the excess of merchandise credits that the goods and services account as a whole shows excess debits. The swing (decline-rise) in divergence observed for all goods and services over the five years also characterized divergences between total credits and debits for merchandise, transportation, and travel. In contrast, the divergence tended to mount in the government account and to move erratically in the account for miscellaneous services.

[4] This should not be surprising since added accounts usually include credits and debits with the world of much the same order of magnitude, and when we are ignorant of transactions (as in the case of services and financial flows between France and French Overseas Territories) we cannot include them on either side.

[5] When customs records are used to measure merchandise trade flows, the supplying of goods tends to be reported in advance of their purchase. The influence of the rising trend of trade and its cyclical variation on the agreement between credit and debit reports can be judged by calculating

the hypothetical excess of merchandise credits that would result from a lag of one month (more exactly, a lag of a third of a quarter) in reporting.

Consider the unadjusted fourth-quarter totals for world merchandise exports from *International Financial Statistics.* The divergence (measured as an excess of credits) which would result from a one-month lag in reporting the debiting of these goods can be calculated and compared with the observed excess of credits in the merchandise matrix for 1950–54 (in million dollars):

	Fourth-Quarter Exports f.o.b. (1)	One-Third Change (2)	Excess of Merchandise Credit (3)	Col. 3 Minus Col. 2 (4)	IMF Account, Net Goods and Services (5)	Col. 5 Minus Col. 2 (6)
1949	12,700					
1950	17,052	1,450	1,222	− 230	163	− 1,290
1951	19,479	810	1,034	220	− 1,398	− 2,210
1952	18,320	− 390	172	560	− 1,653	− 1,260
1953	19,087	260	1,212	950	− 362	− 620
1954	20,350	420	1,943	1,520	169	− 250

Col. 1: *International Financial Statistics* with some supplementation.

Col. 3: From Table B-6 and Table 3.
Such a time lag would result in an excess of merchandise

The fact that the errors in reporting merchandise and services tend to offset each other can be traced, at least in part, to accounting difficulties, such as the treatment of government transactions. Purchases and sales by government are usually counted by most countries as merchandise, transportation, etc.; however, government transactions reported by the United

credits each year except 1952, amounting over the five years to $2.5 billion, which would explain a part of the excess of merchandise credits in years of rising trade. However, the remaining "unexplained" merchandise matrix divergence (col. 4) tends to mount with time; the "unexplained" IMF net balance (col. 6) still shows a cyclical swing, but now with 1951 as the year of greatest "unexplained" deficiency in credits.

It is also possible that the lag in reporting may have increased over the five years. If it were as short as one-sixth of a quarter in 1950 and 1951 and increased to one-third of a quarter in 1952, to two-thirds of a quarter in 1953, and to a full quarter in 1954, most of the cyclical swing in the excess of merchandise credits would be explained. Such an increasing lag would also largely explain the year-to-year differences in movement in credit and debit totals for merchandise. There are reasons to suspect that the reporting lag may have increased: over this period the European middleman was being freed from rigorous exchange control, and as middleman trade increased, more of world trade was "in transit" or passed through bonded warehouses of processing plants for subsequent re-export. Presumably the lag would not go on increasing indefinitely, but it is possible that inventories in bond, in process, and in transit might expand and contract with swings in world trade.

The effect of the hypothetical increase in the reporting lag would be as follows (in million dollars):

	Excess of Credits	Lag	Effect on Divergence Between Credits and Debits	Unexplained
1950	1,222	⅙ Q	730	490
1951	1,034	⅙ Q	400	630
1952	172	⅓ Q	−390	560
1953	1,212	⅔ Q	520	690
1954	1,943	1 Q	1,260	680
Change				
1950–51	− 188		− 330	140
1951–52	− 862		− 790	70
1952–53	1,040		910	130
1953–54	731		740	− 10

It is clear from these calculations that the time sequence of the merchandise trade and reporting lag may well have produced a cyclical excess of merchandise credits, but, with a fixed reporting lag, there remains an unexplained residual which mounts with time; moreover, a fixed reporting lag only modifies and does not fully explain the cyclical swing in net goods and services, nor all the chronic deficiency of goods and services credits. However, it is possible that mounting excess credit error in merchandise was associated with an increasing lag in reporting. It could also be related to the mounting excess of net transfer debits (Chart 2 below) and/or net government debits (Chart 1).

States and the United Kingdom—by far the largest part of the total—are not given by the usual types of transactions. The government account as now reported by the U.S. and the U.K. cuts across the conventional categories and answers the question "who" rather than "what." Consequently, the government debit transactions in Table 3 include some purchases of goods, transportation, travel, and miscellaneous services (but both the U.K. and the U.S. include government interest transactions in investment income). According to the method we have followed in adjusting country accounts, we have kept these as government debits and, where possible, have adjusted the credits in the partner account consistently (e.g., those of oil sources supplying military purchases). But this adjustment has not been made in all suppliers' accounts, notably not in accounts of European suppliers, and we suspect that over the five years nearly half a billion dollars worth of unallocated petroleum exports by the Netherlands Antilles and Venezuela were sales to government.[6]

Consequently, the excesses of credits in the merchandise and miscellaneous services account and of debits in the government account very likely arise partly from the different classification of government purchases by the U.S. and the U.K. If the more conventional approach of distinguishing transactions by type had been maintained by the U.S. and the U.K., we might have arrived at larger totals for merchandise debits.

The division of transactions between merchandise and transportation is also somewhat uncertain because of the possible errors introduced by the adjustment of imports valued c.i.f. to an f.o.b. valuation. Our study of freight cost in relation to the value of merchandise leads us to believe that the countries making such adjustments themselves may have overstated the cost of freight and insurance on merchandise, thus understating merchandise imports f.o.b. and overstating transportation debits. Karreman found that gross freight payments (debits) in 1950–53 persistently exceeded receipts.[7]

In addition to these sources of systematic and offsetting divergence, some other sources of error can be identified. We have sought to include reinvested earnings on foreign investments in the investment

[6] See p. 11.

[7] Herman Karreman, *Methods for Improving World Transportation Accounts, Applied to 1950–1953*, NBER, Technical Paper 15, New York, 1961, Table A-9.

income matrix wherever possible and have succeeded for the U.S. and Canadian records and for the accounts we have prepared on transactions of petroleum source countries. But partner accounts may not always include such earnings either as debits or as credits, e.g., omission from the Netherlands account of reinvested oil company earnings in the U.K. mentioned in Chapter 2.[8] The gross totals for investment income debits and credits are both probably understated. We have reached the totals in Table 3 for transportation and investment income only by adjusting the U.K. account extensively to add in gross petroleum company transactions.

The excess of transportation debits may partly reflect the inclusion of marine insurance on the paying side of many accounts and its absence from our transportation accounts for the United States and the United Kingdom. Finally, we suspect that the excess of travel debits is largely the result of omitted credits in the accounts for France and Italy, which did not come under the control of the official exchange agency on whose records the accountants re-

lied. In the case of France, it has been estimated that total travel receipts were understated by $120 million in 1950 and $150 million in 1951.[9]

It is also possible that the chronic excess of merchandise credits (see footnote 5 above) was partly related to a tendency for the account of unilateral transfers to show a chronic excess of debits. This is discussed in Section C below.

The two-valued matrix for goods and services together appears, from the closer agreement between over-all credit and debit totals, to be a more reliable account than either merchandise alone or the account combining goods, services, and transfers. The goods and services matrix is not entirely free of classification problems, but it is free from errors that arise in compiling the subclasses and that cancel out in the aggregate.[10] This feature of the record provides a good statistical reason for preferring to work with the records of goods and services transactions, reinforcing the analytical advantages of comprehensiveness where that is important.

C. OVER-ALL ERRORS IN THE FINANCIAL ACCOUNTS

The financial accounts display a pattern of over-all divergence that indicates continuing structural error. The persisting excess of net transfer debits augmented, and the persisting excess of capital and gold credits offset, the tendency for all goods and services debits to exceed credits. Over the years 1950–54 the residual, uncompensated error (i.e., "net errors and omissions") fluctuates, sometimes widely, around zero, and over the five-year period it was close to zero. It must be understood, therefore, that the over-all net error in the final multilateral settlements and error matrix only measures the balance of errors in the system of accounts not offset by compensating errors.

The balances (i.e., over-all discrepancies) in the financial accounts of all areas with all areas for 1950–54 are given in Table 4 and Chart 2.

A very small over-all net error of $29 million emerges for the five-year period. It does not mean that the error in the accounts is small, but rather that errors tend to offset each other between types of transactions, over time, and (we shall see in the next section) between countries. The underlying

country distribution reveals large debit errors in several accounts, particularly those for oil-source countries. These might well represent unreported capital transfers and gold purchases since the sheikhs of the Persian Gulf are known to have invested part of their oil royalties in other countries and wealthy people in these lands like to hold gold. If the disposition of Arabian oil royalties were known, the over-all excess of reported net capital and gold credits might be smaller and the net error for all accounts might show a sizable credit balance.

The broad pattern of divergence in the balances for different types of transactions supplies prima-facie evidence that, over the five-year period, countries made current disbursements into the world (the excess of goods and services debits) which disappeared into

[8] See p. 11.

[9] H. C. Eastman, "The Role of Speculation in French Foreign Exchange Crises," *Journal of Political Economy,* June 1953, pp. 209, 218.

[10] More is at issue than the well-known statistical proposition that the standard error of a sum of components subject to independent errors is less than the standard error of the individual components. Here there is evidence that the errors in the components are *systematically* related by virtue of classification inconsistencies in the accounting by the two countries party to certain types of transactions.

TABLE 4
Balances of All Areas with All Areas from the Two-Valued Matrixes
and of Sixty-Eight Countries with All Areas, 1950–54
(*million U.S. dollars*)

	Net Goods and Services[a]	Net Transfers	Net Capital	Net Gold	Net Capital and Gold	Net Error
TWO-VALUED MATRIXES						
1950	205	−261	306	132	438	−382
1951	−1,209	−218	1,067	489	1,556	−129
1952	−1,644	−299	778	397	1,175	768
1953	−812	−373	869	397	1,266	−81
1954	92	−450	270	293	563	−205
1950–54	−3,368[b]	−1,601	3,290[b]	1,708	4,998	−29
SIXTY-EIGHT COUNTRIES[c]						
1950	+163	−352			201	−12
1951	−1,398	−604			1,422	580
1952	−1,653	−568			674	1,547
1953	−362	−693			977	78
1954	+169	−700			336	195

SOURCE: Appendix B and IMF *Yearbook*.
NOTE: Conceptually all entries should be zero.
[a] Excludes nonmonetary gold.
[b] The adjustments described in Chapter 2 to allocate the unallocated transactions reduced the net over-all discrepancies for net goods and services to − $3,097 million and for net capital to $2,419 million (Table A-4), mainly because of the addition of $871 million of Royal Dutch Petroleum Company reinvested earnings to the Continental OEEC account.
[c] IMF accounts.

unreported capital reserves and gold purchases. Over that period unreported purchases of capital assets and gold, measured by the excess of reported credits over reported debits for capital movements and gold transactions, amounted to approximately $5 billion—a figure close to half as large as the increase in gold and foreign exchange reserves reported by countries outside the United States in the period.[11]

Evidence for such a disappearance of exchange earnings into hidden reserves is not given in the over-all error term of the two-valued settlements matrix, but is to be inferred from the effort to strike a balance between total debits and total credits for the different types of transactions in the accounts of all countries with all countries and from an examination of the pattern of over-all errors in individual country accounts.

We have seen that the goods and services debit balance over the five years is composed of large net credits for merchandise valued f.o.b., offset by even larger net debits for services. This pattern does not fit in with the widely held view that capital flight was effected through undervaluing exports (and taking the unreported part of the true value in unreported earnings held abroad) or overvaluing imports (and remitting the excessive part of the value abroad to be held to the importer's account). To judge from the over-all excess of service debits over credits, it does seem likely that unreported purchases of gold and unreported capital debits were fed in good part from unreported service credits. Opportunities for unreported transportation and tourist earnings to move into capital accumulation and gold hoarding seem to have been particularly good.[12]

[11] *International Financial Statistics* (June 1955 and January 1957) shows gold and foreign exchange reserves of countries outside the U.S. rising from $26,290 million at the end of 1949 to $36,460 million at the end of 1954.

[12] The reader should bear in mind the possibility that part of the excess of services debits may represent classification errors against merchandise, but if *all* net excess of merchandise credits were explained thus, there would still remain a net excess of services debits (see also the explanation in footnote 5 above). The reader should also bear in mind

CHART 2

Over-All Discrepancies in Trade and
Financial Accounts, Annually, 1950–54
(balances of all areas with all areas)
(billion U.S. dollars)

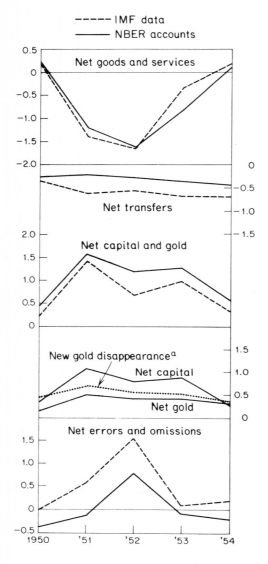

SOURCE: Table 4 and footnote 14 in this chapter.

ᵃ New gold production plus Russian gold sales less change in official gold reserves.

There are similar tendencies to err in the combined accounts of sixty-eight countries with the world given in Table 4 and Chart 2. Compared with our matrix accounts, there is, however, a greater excess of net transfer debits, a smaller excess of net capital

and gold credits, and a persisting tendency to require a net credit coverage in the over-all error account. Evidently, our efforts at supplementation and adjustment for 1950–54 have, on balance, reduced the discrepancies in accounting for transfers but have produced a greater discrepancy in accounting for capital and gold than appears from the sixty-eight accounts.[13]

In Chart 2 the Bank for International Settlements series for gold "disappearance" (which is measured by new production plus Russian gold sales less additions to official reserves in the free world) shows a continuing balance which in most years can be attributed largely to private hoarding but in 1954 was about equally divided between private hoarding and industrial use.[14]

The cyclical swing which we marked in the excess of goods and services debits, with large divergences characterizing times of great uncertainty in world affairs, was matched by a compensating swing in gold disappearance, unreported capital outflow, and net error. The swing in this last item, the residual, lends support to the thesis that the whole set of accounts has been influenced by periods of uncertainty which prompted funds to go into hiding.

The matrix of transfers (Table B-25) is primarily a record of official aid given by the U.S. and U.K. governments (mostly the former). The over-all discrepancy in the net transfers account is, therefore, very largely a difference in American (and British) accounts of aid extended and partner accounts of aid received. Perhaps the excess of transfer debits is related to a failure of some aid recipients to include in merchandise the debits for aid goods imported and in unilateral transfers the offsetting credits for dona-

---

our suspicion that unreported gold purchases and capital debits were met to some extent from the balances in nonoil sectors of oil-source country accounts which are represented by large error terms in those accounts (see pp. 32–33).

[13] The U.S. account included in the IMF series is from the *Survey of Current Business* without adding reinvested earnings, whereas our matrix account includes such reinvested earnings both in the U. S. account and in partner accounts. This difference, however, does not explain the difference in the *over-all* divergence in the two series for net capital and gold since it affects both creditor and debtor accounts.

[14] The Bank for International Settlements (in its *Twenty-Eighth Annual Report*) places gold use in industry in 1950–54 at $140 to $190 million annually. The difference between new supply of gold (production plus Russian sales) and additions to official reserves, as reported by the Bank in its annual reports, is as follows (in million dollars) for 1950 through 1954: 435, 665, 535, 505, and 345.

tions received. We have audited every country account against the record of U. S. foreign aid to ensure that every recipient country includes some record of aid received—though it may not be the same as the U.S. record. Still, areas generally show smaller aid received from the U.S. than the U.S. records of aid extended; over five years the difference came to about $450 million, and more than half the difference was in the U.S. account with Continental OEEC countries. This seems too much to be accounted for by the (questionable) inclusion in the U.S. record of the services of U.S. foreign aid missions (which involves a corollary understatement of government services debits by aid recipients).

Net transfer debits tended to increase over the five years covered by the two-valued matrixes. This excess tends to augment rather than offset the goods and services debit excess, and the account for net goods, services, *and* transfers tends to show a larger over-all net excess of debits than the net goods and services account, along with a tendency for the excess of debits to mount with time. Moreover, the growing excess of transfer net debits seems unlikely to reflect a time lag in reporting (say, with U.S. debits recorded ahead of recipient country reports of credits) since the aid program was not rising; it declined from 1950 to 1952 and then held fairly steady. Rather, the explanation seems to lie either

in poor reporting in the accounts of the sixty-eight countries or in the tendency for more aid to go to countries not covered.

Divergences between credits and debits in the goods and services account and balances in the financial accounts, while not large relative to gross trade, were sizable relative to the balances of areas and between areas. Comparisons with the level of gross trade can be made directly with the aggregates given in Table 3. Over the five years, the net excess of goods and services debits was only 0.73 per cent of all trade, and the net excess for merchandise was 1.56 per cent of goods trade; the net excess for services was larger, 8.28 per cent of all services traded. The excess of capital and gold transactions together over the five years amounted to little more than 1 per cent of all goods and services trade.

However, compared with totals of *net* transactions of countries, the excesses of credits or debits for different types of transactions were large. For each type of transaction, Table 5 shows, in column 1, the combined balances of countries with all partners for the five years 1950–54 and, in columns 2 and 3, separate totals for countries with net credits over the period and for countries with net debits. A comparison of column 1 with columns 2 and 3 provides an idea of the size of the persisting errors. The excess of capital credits represented nearly a third of the net

TABLE 5

Balances of All Areas with All Areas Compared with Total
Net Credits and Debits of Countries with All Areas, by
Type of Transaction, over the Five Years 1950–54

(*million U.S. dollars*)

	Balance (discrepancy) (1)	Combined Balance of Countries with[a]		Ratio of Col. 1 to Mean of Cols. 2 and 3[b] (per cent) (4)
		Net Credits (2)	Net Debits (3)	
Net merchandise	5,583	32,022	−26,439	19.1
Net services	−8,951	16,116	−25,067	43.5
Net goods and services	−3,368	21,892	−25,260	14.3
Net transfers	−1,601	13,307	−14,908	11.3
Net capital	3,290	11,941	−8,651	32.0
Net gold	1,708	6,152	−4,444	32.2
Net error	−29	7,307	−7,336	0.4

a From country accounts (NBER files) with error in the account for the Netherlands Antilles offset against error in the Venezuelan account. In Table 6 these two countries have been kept separate, resulting in the larger figures for total net credit error, $7,511 million, and debit error, $7,540 million, shown in that table. The two were combined here because their opposite error terms are thought to reflect the single uncertainty attached to the valuation of Venezuelan oil exports to the Netherlands Antilles.

b Col. 1 multiplied by two and divided by the sum of cols. 2 and 3.

TABLE 6
Net Error in Country Accounts, 1950–54
(*million U.S. dollars*)

	1950	1951	1952	1953	1954	1950–54
Total of All Areas	−382	−129	768	−81	−205	−29
Sum of plus error	1,308	1,965	2,571	1,778	1,700	7,511[a]
Sum of minus error	−1,690	−2,094	−1,803	−1,859	−1,905	−7,540[a]
Sterling Area	204	−387	−156	−201	−257	−797
United Kingdom	71	−279	69	45	−122	−216
Rest of Sterling Area	133	−108	−225	−246	−135	−581
British Arabian oil sources	−5	−10	−124	−130	−145	−414
India	−59	−116	−145	−5	16	−309
Iraq	−7	−38	−35	−5	10	−75
Burma	5	−12	−6	4	−43	−52
Pakistan	−30	1	−5	—	−1	−35
Union of South Africa	−7	−10	−6	−4	14	−13
Iceland	−3	1	1	−1	−1	−3
Jordan	−2	−3	3	—	—	−2
So. Rhodesia (C.A. Fed.)	—	—	—	—	—	—
British Colonies	—	—	—	—	—	—
Libya	1	3	1	—	1	6
Ceylon	4	14	9	2	−5	24
New Zealand	−5	−24	36	20	2	29
Ireland	18	7	17	16	5	63
Australia	223	79	29	−143	12	200
All Nonsterling EPU Area	−194	−100	735	320	289	1,050
Continental OEEC countries	−844	−948	−498	−469	−450	−3,209
France	−517	−808	−844	−594	−441	−3,204
Germany	−34	−70	32	−50	−118	−240
Italy	−185	12	52	14	−23	−130
Belgium	43	−13	−11	−51	−81	−113
Netherlands	−4	−39	−1	−52	36	−60
Greece	1	−37	−22	−8	24	−42
Turkey	−97	−23	−14	104	—	−30
Sweden	1	1	1	−4	4	6
Denmark	—	10	37	8	−8	47
Norway	−9	−40	44	40	25	60
Switzerland	−46	14	107	−6	12	81
Austria	−39	−17	63	28	48	83
Portugal	42	62	58	99	72	333
Overseas Territories (excl. Netherlands Antilles)	487	844	1,109	797	720	3,957
French	508	843	1,098	845	739	4,033
Belgian	−4	28	5	−7	−5	17
Surinam	—	−2	−1	—	—	−3
Portuguese	−17	−25	7	−41	−14	−90
Netherlands Antilles	64	56	43	−5	46	204
EPU countries	99	−52	81	−3	−27	98
U.S., Canada, and IO	−34	471	507	298	175	1,417
U.S.	−33	472	509	296	178	1,422
Canada	−1	−1	−2	2	−3	−5
International Organizations	—	—	—	—	—	—

(continued)

TABLE 6 (concluded)

	1950	1951	1952	1953	1954	1950–54
Latin America and PHL Fleet	−145	−19	−145	−182	−341	−832
Venezuela	−79	−139	−204	−145	−295	−862
Argentina	−68	−13	45	33	−78	−81
El Salvador	−11	−8	−4	−6	−6	−35
Cuba	5	1	15	−22	−29	−30
Dominican Republic	−13	−4	3	10	−13	−17
Ecuador	—	−3	−1	−10	5	−9
Honduras	1	−3	−1	−3	1	−5
Guatemala	−6	1	2	—	−2	−5
Paraguay	2	—	−2	−5	2	−3
Columbia	−11	22	−12	18	−19	−2
PHL fleet	—	—	—	—	—	—
Haiti	—	−2	7	−5	3	3
Nicaragua	—	1	6	−1	−2	4
Uruguay	—	5	9	−2	−5	7
Peru	3	1	−1	3	3	9
Bolivia	4	2	−6	11	3	14
Chile	6	—	−16	5	22	17
Brazil	−14	121	−41	−108	61	19
Mexico	18	−24	23	30	−25	22
Costa Rica	7	8	13	2	—	30
Panama	11	15	20	13	33	92
Other Countries	−213	−94	−173	−316	−71	−867
Saudi Arabia	−163	−65	−151	−239	−315	−933
Soviet Bloc	16	−8	−61	−145	22	−176
Philippines	−83	5	−11	−33	—	−122
Indonesia	−9	−13	−29	−3	−31	−85
Iran	−74	−26	−5	11	43	−51
Taiwan	−4	−11	−7	−12	−10	−44
Egypt	3	−6	−9	−6	−4	−22
Yugoslavia	−9	−4	—	−1	−5	−19
South Korea	—	—	−2	−2	2	−2
Sudan	2	—	−5	3	−1	−1
Ethiopia	—	1	−1	1	2	3
Japan	−14	10	−3	3	9	5
Liberia	4	—	3	7	−1	13
Finland	3	1	26	−3	−9	18
Syria	15	23	20	−2	1	57
Thailand	18	17	−14	5	47	73
Lebanon	49	17	17	13	28	124
Spain and possessions	−28	−146	60	72	169	127
Israel	61	111	−1	15	−18	168

SOURCE: Country accounts, NBER files.

a Vertical sum. Horizontal sums are $9,322 million and −$9,351 million. The smaller vertical sum reflects intertemporal offsetting of error in some country accounts.

capital flow out of capital-exporting countries into capital-importing countries; and the excess of gold credits represented about a third of the net gold transactions of countries selling or buying gold. The excess of transfer debits (mainly official American and British transfers) was more than 10 per cent of the net transfer flow out of and into countries; and the goods and services debit balance was 14.3 per cent of the trading balances of countries over the five years. The residual net error in the final settlements account, which appears as 0.4 per cent of the

sum of plus and minus error, must be interpreted differently. Because it is small and because there are evidently substantial errors in the other accounts, it signifies that an important feature of the record is the compensating nature of omissions—either entries omitted from both partner records or offsetting entries of different types omitted from individual country accounts.

Table 5 also gives some idea of the relative size of net financial flows between countries over the five-year period. Whereas net capital flows into and out of countries were on the order of $12 billion (taking the larger of the net credit and net debit totals), net gold sales were about half that size and net unilateral transfers were substantially larger than net capital flow. The sum of credit and debit error in the country accounts over the five years was larger than net gold movements between them. Totals such as those in columns 2 and 3 of Table 5, of course, greatly understate the *gross* asset flows between countries, es-

pecially since long-term outflows from the United States and the United Kingdom are known to have been offset by short-term capital inflows (see Table 8 below). Walther Michael's calculations indicate an increase in internationally held assets and liabilities of about $25 billion over these years.[15] The understatement of gross transfers, in contrast, is much less since reverse transfers received by the principal donor countries were comparatively small.

D. DISTRIBUTION OF NET ERROR BY COUNTRY

Further light on the nature of error in the matrixes can be obtained by examining the country distribution underlying the over-all net error in the residual settlement matrix (Table 6). Over the whole five-year period, the net error in all accounts balanced out to a tiny −$29 million, but this was the result of offsetting positive errors aggregating $7,511 million and negative errors aggregating $7,540 million in the individual accounts.[16] A good part of these aggregate errors lay in a few country accounts, the

[15] "International Capital Movements: The Experience of the Early Fifties, 1950–54," unpublished Ph.D. dissertation, Columbia University, 1965.

[16] The totals for the five-year period are smaller than the sum of annual totals for the five years (see note a to Table 6) because of intertemporal offsetting of error in some country accounts over the five years.

[17] Since our accounts were prepared, a somewhat better record of transactions between France and her Overseas Territories has been published in the French national accounts and reported, with some rearrangement, in the IMF *Balance of Payments Yearbook*, Vols. 9 and 10, notes to area statements, beginning with 1953. Through 1954, these accounts show a much reduced error, but the error subsequently mounted with the political difficulties in Algeria.

IMF area statements for 1953–54 give the following balance for France with the rest of the franc area (in million dollars):

	1953	1954
Net goods and services	− 80	− 80
Economic aid	—	—
Capital, other donations, and monetary movements	− 80	− 20
Net error and settlements	160	100

For comparison, the balance on goods and services (transportation only) of France with the rest of the franc area in our account was $540 and $478 million in 1953 and 1954, respectively. It would thus appear that net French outlays for travel, investment income, government, and miscellaneous service in the Overseas Territories (items which we were unable to include) were well over half a billion dollars in both 1953 and 1954. The IMF secretariat suggests that the net error and settlements figures represented

largest in the accounts for France and her Overseas Territories because of the partial nature of our accounting for transactions between them.[17] For the five years, nearly half the total of minus error was in the French account and more than half the plus error was in the account of French Overseas Territories. As we have no measure of transactions between France and her Overseas Territories except merchandise and an estimate of transportation, we understate the magnitude of payments in either direction for travel, government expenditures, investment income, and miscellaneous services. Since, however, both metropolitan and territorial accounts are in error, the omission does not affect the over-all discrepancy in the services account for all countries. It is not clear how the transfer and capital accounts between France and her Overseas Territories would be altered by better information; but here again the over-all discrepancies would not be affected since the lack of a debit entry on one side is offset, in the world totals, by the lack of a credit entry on the other.

A similar instance of related compensating error exists in our accounts for Portugal and her Overseas Territories, although the error is not as large. Portugal has a credit error term, her Overseas Territories have a debit error term, and undoubtedly the omitted transactions were investment income earnings or other other services earnings of Portugal in her colonies.

Three oil-source accounts—Saudi Arabia, Venezuela, and British Arabia—show a persisting year-to-year excess of credits for which a debit error entry is required; and Iraq, a fourth oil-source country,

largely an unaccounted-for return flow of private capital back to France, which more than offset known capital and transfer outflows to the Overseas Territories.

TABLE 7
Summary of Error Term in Country Accounts over
the Five Years 1950–54
(*million U.S. dollars*)

Credit Error		Debit Error	
United States	1,422	Five oil-source countries and	
France and Overseas Territories, net	829	Netherlands Antilles, net	-2,080
Portugal and Overseas Territories, net	243	Other countries with debit error:	
Other countries with credit error:		India and United Kingdom	-525
Israel, Spain and possessions,		Germany, Belgium, Italy	-483
and Lebanon	419	Soviet Bloc	-176
Five Sterling Area countries	322	Philippines	-122
Five nonsterling EPU countries and EPU	392	Five Sterling Area countries	-105
Ten Latin American countries	217	Four nonsterling EPU countries	-135
Six other countries	169	Nine Latin American countries	-187
Total	4,013	Seven other countries	-224
		Canada	-5
		Total	-4,042

SOURCE: Table 6.

also shows a debit error entry in most years. Our account for the Netherlands Antilles shows the opposite tendency, probably because of the method of valuing Netherlands Antilles oil imports from Venezuela; the errors for these two countries are offsetting and both appear to reflect the problem of distributing the value of oil back through the stages of production.[18]

For the five oil-source countries together, our accounts show large foreign exchange earnings not offset by known imports of goods and services, purchases of gold, or outflow of capital. In the case of Venezuela, the error may lie in the valuation of oil exports, but it may also lie in either investment income or capital.

The debit error terms in the accounts for British Arabia and Saudi Arabia arise entirely in the nonoil sector, since in constructing accounts for the oil sectors we made investment income the balancing item. The sizable and rising excess of credits accruing to these countries reflects our ignorance of the disposition of the oil royalties accruing to the local economies. Possibly some of the error concerns merchandise imports or services purchases, but, as noted above, most of it probably represents capital out-

[18] Hence it is useful to think of the two accounts in combination. Our calculation of the value of Venezuelan oil exported exceeds the value included in the official balance-of-payments account published in the IMF *Yearbook,* to which the oil company investment income and capital entries in the Venezuelan account are related.

flow or gold purchases. There is no record of the net gold purchases by these countries, although it is known that Saudi Arabia for a long time took its oil royalties in gold coin, and it may well be that the unknown debits in its account were partly gold purchases. Because of the limited opportunity for the productive use of funds locally, it is also to be expected that these Middle East oil sources invested their surpluses wherever there were opportunities for return and security.

Table 7 summarizes the error terms in the country accounts so as to net out the related and partially offsetting errors which have been noted. There remains a sizable plus error for France and her territories, after consolidation, though much smaller than that for the U.S. The consolidated minus error for the oil-source countries stands out very prominently. Among others with relatively large minus error are India, the U.K., three Continental countries—Belgium, West Germany, and Italy—and the Philippines and the Soviet Bloc.

The last calls for special comment. We have only two types of transactions entered in the Soviet Bloc account—merchandise (f.o.b.) and gold sales. The cumulative net debit results from an offsetting of credit error entries in 1950 and 1954 by larger debit error entries in the intervening years. Services and capital flows for the Soviet Bloc over the whole period appear to have been debit entries. As the Soviet Bloc enjoyed substantial transfer credits according to the Finnish account,[19] the magnitude of the omitted debits is probably greater than indicated by the error term.[20]

The error term in the accounts of Australia, India, and the U.K. also requires special comment. The Australian account has a large credit error in 1950 which may reflect an imperfect meshing of the extraordinarily large wool sales late in the year with short-term capital movements. The Indian account has sizable earnings in the first three years of the period not balanced by known debits, and in view of the well-known disposition for India to absorb gold, gold purchases may have been the true offset to these net credits. The over-all error in the official U.K. account arises in good part from the lack of adequate information about private capital movements but may also lie in the goods and services accounts, according to the IMF.[21]

Error terms in country accounts, of course, represent the inability of a country's statisticians to account for credits and debits equally, but not all country accounts carry error terms. Thus in the account of Canada, the balancing entry is regularly combined with the capital item. Not only do some countries not show error terms but, even for those which do, any error shown is net and does not reflect the compensating types of error arising from the omission of matching credit and debit entries (as, for example, the smuggling of goods compensated by related unreported capital or gold movements). Although the error terms in published country accounts are not an exact measure, they may give some idea of the location and order of magnitude of error. As they persist from year to year or swing from debit to credit, they provide clues as to the nature of the error. Error terms persisting in one direction are likely to indicate bias in the statistical techniques employed, whereas error terms fluctuating from plus to minus may result from difficulties in matching the timing of the debit and credit aspects of transactions.

E. CONCLUDING OBSERVATIONS

Examination of world totals for the several types of transactions has provided a useful introduction to the record for two reasons. First, they furnish new measures of the magnitudes traded internationally including services. Second, the over-all discrepancies in the two-valued record give an indication of the nature and extent of error in the accounts.

For gross trade, credit and debit totals are found to have differed by only small percentages, and the extent of agreement is better for goods and services than for individual components. Internal evidence in the accounts affords little reason to think that the trade totals are greatly in error; external evidence, however, indicates that total world transactions (notably services) are probably understated because of known omissions.

Differences between total credits and debits for merchandise and services and the net over-all discrepancies in financial accounts, while small in relation to total world trade, are sizable in relation to the five-year net position of countries, especially for services, capital, and gold accounts. Internal evidence in the accounts thus indicates that matrixes of net transactions and especially of capital and gold flows are subject to considerable error. Cumulative errors in these accounts are found to be large in relation to the reported accretion in gold and foreign exchange reserves of countries outside the U.S. over the period.

The pattern of over-all discrepancies for transactions of different kinds persisted over the period and exhibited a movement related in time to the swing in world confidence associated with the Korean War. Its nature suggests that the flow of funds into hidden capital and gold holdings was fed mainly by unrecorded services transactions. Individual country accounts show sizable net credit or net debit error positions over the five years. In the face of this and the over-all discrepancies in trade and financial accounts, the over-all error for all accounts is practically zero. Clearly, more is to be learned about the nature of unrecorded transactions from a study of the whole record than can be observed from an examination of country accounts individually.

[19] Finnish official donations to Eastern Europe were $34 million in 1950, $54 million in 1951, and $36 million in 1952, a total of $124 million.

[20] In assessing the balance of Soviet Bloc trade with the West, one should not disregard freight on imports. A trade balance between derived bloc exports c.i.f. and derived

Bloc imports f.o.b. has sometimes been used, but such a balance overstates Bloc earnings unless all the trade both ways is carried on vessels operated by the Soviet Bloc, and even then port charges and charter fees would be incurred. (See *The Banker*, February 1957, p. 96, for an example of such a doubtful use of unadjusted trade statistics to show the trade balance of the Soviet Bloc with the Sterling Area.)

[21] See IMF *Yearbook*, Vol. 8, comment on the U. K.

4

GOODS AND SERVICES TRADE

Whereas the last chapter dealt mainly with two dimensions of the record—items and time—this chapter introduces the third, spatial, dimension. We can thereby observe not only the course and composition of trade but also the nature of specialization by countries and areas and the orientation of trade. While we do not have much to add to the stock of knowledge about trade between areas in merchandise, our record of services transactions is unique and warrants special comment (Section C below).

One may ask, first, whether the two-valued matrix accounts consistently measure the *magnitude* of inter-area transactions for the five years as a whole and for each year separately; second, whether they consistently measure the *movements* from year to year and over the five years. These questions may be applied to the record of both gross and net transactions, for uncertainties in reporting and errors of estimation may be compounded or offset in balances. We shall proceed by examining the structure of trading shown for the five years as a whole in the two-valued matrixes, gross and net, and then the structure and movement of trading as shown by the annual matrixes.

A. THE GEOGRAPHIC STRUCTURE OF TRADING OVER THE FIVE YEARS

1. Gross Transactions in the Two-Valued Matrix

When the annual two-valued matrixes are aggregated for the five years 1950–54 (Table A-1), credit and debit records are obtained in which the errors of reporting introduced by time leads and lags and erratic errors can offset each other. Divergence between paired entries is thus reduced. However, divergences of a continuing nature in the annual matrixes will tend to cumulate in the five-year aggregates. In examining the consistency of reports in the five-year matrix, therefore, we necessarily focus upon the structural, persisting reporting differences.

That slightly more than 1 per cent of credits and debits are not allocated by area is immediately apparent. In spite of this defect, the two-valued matrix shows that our country accounts are broadly consistent. The percentage distribution of the world's debits and credits (the first column in Part I and the first line in Part II of Table A-3) is measured the same to the nearest 1 per cent of the total whether sellers' or buyers' records are used.[1] The interarea distribution of sales or purchases by each area to or from partners is measured the same to the nearest 1 or 2 per cent of the total from buyers' or sellers' records with few exceptions (and some of these would be reduced to within 2 per cent of the total if the unallocated transactions were spread out).

If areas are ranked on the basis of the 1950–54 data as suppliers of goods and services or as buyers (including intra-area trade), the same sequence is found using credit or debit records and, as it turns out, viewing the areas as buyers or sellers:[2] (1)

[1] The effort to allocate the unallocated transactions described in Chapter 2 on the whole improved agreement between paired entries in the matrix of gross goods and services as measured by the sum of the differences without regard to sign. We have not reproduced this matrix for the five years with all transactions allocated, but the net effect is carried in Table A–4 and can be observed by comparing net goods and services in that table with line A of Table A–2.

[2] How an area is ranked, of course, reflects the particular grouping of countries employed. While it is of some interest to observe the ranking and participation of the several areas in world trade, the result of primary interest here is the quality of measurement. Both records give the same result for rankings and much the same result for percentage distributions.

Continental OEEC countries, (2) United States, (3) Rest of Sterling Area, (4) United Kingdom, (5) Other Eastern Hemisphere, (6) Latin America, (7) Canada, and (8) Continental Overseas Territories. About a quarter of world imports were supplied, and a quarter of world exports taken, by the Continental OEEC countries; not quite a fifth of world imports were supplied by the U.S., and not quite a sixth of world exports went to the U.S.; the U.K. supplied about an eighth of world imports and took a little less than an eighth of world exports; and other Sterling Area countries supplied a little more than an eighth and took about a seventh. The share of these and other areas in world trade in goods and services is indicated by the percentage distributions in Table A-3.

It is also evident that particular interarea, or intra-area, relations in the matrix would rank about the same whichever record was used as the measure. Trade among Continental OEEC countries as given in Table A-1 was the largest and nearly twice the next largest—U.K. exports to other Sterling Area countries; this was followed by U.S. exports to Latin America, Rest of the Sterling Area exports to the U.K., Latin American exports to the U.S., and U.S. exports to Canada. (These were all the interarea flows which amounted to $20 billion or more over the five years.)

The structure of trading reflected in the distribution of an area's credits and debits appears much the same from partners' records. The U.K. trade was heavily concentrated on the Rest of the Sterling Area (38–39 per cent of imports and 46–47 per cent of sales), and vice versa (41 per cent of imports and 36–37 per cent of sales). More than half of the latter's trade was with the Sterling Area as a whole. An important part of U.K. trade (but less than 30 per cent of imports or exports) was with the Continent and the Continental Overseas Territories; the proportion of trade by the Rest of the Sterling Area with the Continent was smaller than that of the U.K.

The trade of both Canada and Latin America was concentrated on the United States while U.S. trade was concentrated on the Western Hemisphere. Trade of the Continental Overseas Territories was concentrated on the associated metropolitan area while that of the Continental OEEC countries was concentrated on trade within the group. The group "Other Countries" was not a dominant market nor source of supply for any area.

The trade of particular areas evidently does not spread over partner areas in proportion to the latters' importance in all world trade. Rather it exhibits a systematic departure.[3] The trade of peripheral countries tends to focus on one of the three more advanced central areas—the U.S., the U.K., and the Continent—and the same concentration is found in the reverse direction. Trading thus tends to radiate out from the centers, but this radial system of trade is only suggested by the structure shown in our matrixes since the countries were not grouped according to a trading orientation criterion. Our arrangement, largely determined by the nature of the available data, results in a dispersed pattern of trade by Other Countries, some of which trade principally with the U.S., some principally with the U.K., and some with the Continent.

The pattern of divergence in paired entries in Table A-1 shows that the records, while exhibiting a high measure of agreement, are subject to systematic rather than random errors (this would be even more evident if the unallocated transactions were distributed). The most striking systematic divergence is the tendency for the U.S., Canada, and Latin America to report larger transactions both ways with Eastern Hemisphere areas than the latter report. Apart from this, the Continental OEEC countries tend to report smaller sales and larger purchases than partners report for them. There are a number of instances in which a divergence in accounts with the Rest of the Sterling Area is offset by an opposite divergence in accounts with the U.K., and similarly divergences with Continental OEEC countries and their Overseas Territories tend to offset each other.

These systematic tendencies seem to reflect several reporting inconsistencies in the accounts. One is the practice followed by some countries of reporting some transactions, particularly minor services, on a net basis. Another stems from the fact that the merchandise transactions have been developed in good part from customs records and some countries use a "general trade" record system and others a "special

---

[3] See my "Observations on the Structure of World Trade and Payments," *World Politics,* July 1956. Trading ties of individual countries are even more pronouncedly with centers when measured by their gross goods and services transaction account than when measured simply by merchandise because service transactions tend to be more concentrated on the principal center of a country than merchandise.

trade" system. Also the differences between customs practices in identifying countries of provenance and destination may contribute systematic discrepancies.[4] Transactions involving intermediary countries may not be recorded alike in all the countries concerned.[5] The wonder is that, given the many possible sources of difference, the pattern and magnitude of gross goods and services transactions seem to be measured more or less the same from either side.

2. *The Effect of Redirecting Petroleum Trade and the Influence of Middlemen on the Trading Pattern*

One reason for the extent of agreement between paired entries in Table A-1 is that the country accounts were adjusted to place petroleum (and Mexican cotton) on a trade records basis. Each movement of petroleum across customs boundaries was considered a transaction whether or not its ownership changed. An alternative method would be to treat oil originating in free world sources outside the U.S., the U.K., and Continental OEEC countries and entering into international trade as though it were sold by the producing country to enterprises in the U.S.

or the U.K. and distributed by the U.S. and the U.K. to the countries of refining or ultimate consumption.[6] To consider the effect of a different treatment of petroleum transactions, such an adjustment is presented in Appendix C. It, of course, increases the amount of world trade to the extent of the value of the oil considered moving through the U.S. and U.K. That part of petroleum trade for which the adjustment was made adds 5 per cent to merchandise trade and 4 per cent to goods and services trade.

The general effect of adjusting petroleum transactions to a purchase-sales basis is to increase the proportion in which nearly every area trades with the United States, and most areas also show larger proportions traded with the U.K. The Rest of the Sterling Area shows a higher proportion of its trade, both purchases and sales, with the U.K., but curiously enough the proportion traded by the U.K. with the Rest of the Sterling Area is somewhat lower because the added oil trade of the U.K. is out of proportion with the added oil trade with the Rest of the Sterling Area. The Continental Overseas Territories show greater proportions traded with the U.S. and the U.K. because of the redirection of Netherlands Antilles trade. The middleman activity in the oil trade tends also to disperse the trade of the U.S. and U.K.[7]

The modifications introduced into the pattern of interarea trade from placing petroleum on a purchase-sales basis are considerably greater than the rather minor differences in pattern shown by credit and debit records and hence are of greater importance for structural analyses. Yet the orientation of trade toward three centers indicated by the unadjusted country accounts would still hold if the individual country accounts could be adjusted to place

---

[4] For a discussion of the peculiarities of customs records which may affect the comparability of merchandise trade in the balance of payments, see R. G. D. Allen and J. Edward Ely, eds., *International Trade Statistics* (New York, 1953), Chapter 9 by Walter R. Gardner. Systems of reporting are discussed in detail in Chapter 3 and country classification in Chapter 7.

The two-valued matrixes of merchandise transactions in Tables B-4, B-5, and B-6, which are unique in presenting paired entries both valued f.o.b., provide an unusual basis for studying the extent of agreement in measuring interarea merchandise transactions. These exhibit a systematic pattern of divergence, with Western Hemisphere areas generally showing greater debits than partner areas acknowledge receiving. A large excess of credits in intra-Continental trade persisted. Indeed, every area shows more exported to the Continent than it reports importing. Altogether, over the five years areas showed over $5 billion of exports more than the amounts the Continent acknowledged importing. This difference in reports was of considerable significance to the staff analysis of the American foreign aid program for Europe. Commodity analysts working from a historical record derived from exporters' records f.o.b. continually arrived at larger European import bills than country analysts who were working with merchandise debits in payments accounts. While the difference was only about 5 per cent, translated into the need for American aid it implied a difference of $1 billion per annum.

[5] Robert Lichtenberg's paper *The Role of Middleman Transactions in World Trade* (NBER Occasional Paper 64, New York, 1959) was undertaken in an effort to establish whether or not this particular difficulty could be remedied.

[6] I considered various alternative ways of accounting for petroleum transactions in my paper "On the Elaboration of a System of International Transaction Accounts," in *Problems of International Comparison of Economic Accounts,* Income and Wealth 20, Princeton for NBER, 1957. I have not redirected the oil refined on the Continent since most of it was sold for EPU currencies by subsidiaries of American and British companies resident on the Continent and the European governments in question controlled the foreign exchange proceeds.

[7] A similar adjustment for countries grouped according to trading orientation had the general effect of showing stronger trading ties between outlying countries and their associated center, at the expense of their secondary trading ties with other areas, and of dispersing slightly the trade of the two centers conducting this world-wide business.

petroleum on a purchase-sales basis. Such an adjustment would probably provide additional supporting evidence in certain cases (e.g., Saudi Arabia and the Netherlands Antilles) where we have otherwise looked to foreign investment interest rather than to the movement of goods for an indication of the country's trading orientation.[8]

Although petroleum is the most important of the internationally traded items channeled through middleman countries, it is not the only one. Rubber, coffee, cocoa, tea, nonferrous metals, cotton, wool, cereals, fats and oils, and most other bulk items are also subject to middleman control.[9] Lichtenberg's estimates indicate that in 1952 international trade in products other than petroleum handled by middlemen amounted to about 10 per cent of all merchandise trade (hence about 8 per cent of goods and services).[10] His data show that large proportions of the exports of European Overseas Territories, Southeast Asia, the independent outer Sterling Areas countries, and Canada passed through the control of middleman countries, notably the U.K. and its Asian outposts (Hong Kong and Singapore), the Netherlands, Belgium, and the U.S. Lichtenberg's observations on the record of trade in coffee, rubber, and cotton give some clues to the nature of the adjustment necessary to place the record of interarea goods and services transactions on a purchase-sales basis. The broad effect would be to increase the sales of affiliated countries to their principal trading partner and to increase purchases by the centers from each other. Trade between the centers would be much more concentrated in basic foods and raw materials than customs records show.

It is difficult, however, to say how great an adjustment would have to be made to put trade in items other than petroleum on a purchase-sales basis. The redirected petroleum transactions represented 4 per cent of world trade in goods and services. It seems unlikely that the adjustment for other items would be as much as twice the petroleum adjustment since some countries basing their accounts on exchange control records already carry merchandise transactions approximately on a purchase-sales basis. We can be reasonably sure that the adjustment for items other than petroleum would not be so highly concentrated on the U.S. and the U.K. as middlemen since Continental countries are involved to a considerable extent in some trades, especially as sellers to other Continental countries.

3. Net Transactions in the Two-Valued Matrix

The systematic differences in reporting gross goods and services (Table A-1) fortunately tend to reduce rather than augment the divergences between paired records of the interarea balances (Table A-2). Although these differences are sometimes sizable in relation to the balance, as may happen when the net is close to zero, in no case do the two measures of interarea balances differ in direction.[11] The only paired entries in Table A-2 that differ in sign are all those for intra-area balances and those of Latin America and Continental OEEC countries for balances with all areas. The former discrepancies are clearly in error since trade within an area should balance out. The latter appear related to the former; the two values recorded for balances with all outside countries agree on the surplus of Continental OEEC countries and the deficit of Latin American countries. This circumstance suggests that in these two cases the proper adjustment to balance out the intra-area trade would correct the disagreement in the over-all balances.

Not only do the paired entries in Table A-2 agree on the direction of the balances between areas, but in nineteen out of twenty-nine instances they also agree on the amount of the balance to within 25 per cent of the mean of the two measures, and in all but two of the remaining instances they agree to within 50 per

---

[8] We were not in a position, however, to carry out the oil adjustment in the basic country accounts, for this would have required information on the imports of oil by each country by source and the market share enjoyed by U.S. and British companies, respectively, in each country in each of the five years. Data on oil imports by source could be obtained for most countries, but information on market shares by country is not available. We were prepared to estimate U.S. and British company shares in the broad grouping employed in the eight-area tables, which could be checked out against information on sales in company reports, refining capacity, etc.

[9] Lichtenberg, *Role of Middleman Transactions*, Table 2, pp. 12 and 13.

[10] *Ibid.*, pp. 34–38 and 73. The figure of 10 per cent is obtained after allowing for that part of all middleman trade which was in petroleum.

[11] The two records of trade of areas with International Organizations are not sufficiently independent to provide a test of the direction of the net; both records are based on the account we have developed for International Organizations.

cent, which I would count as agreement on the "order of magnitude." [12] The two instances of wider divergence involve the small balances of Continental Overseas Territories with the U.S. and Canada, which are known to be deficient in our accounts for the Overseas Territories.

In Table A-2 small amounts (net) remain unallocated in several area accounts. The allocation of the unallocated transactions described in Chapter 2 reduced the divergence in gross transactions but widened the divergence in balances between the areas; it did not, however, increase the differences enough to alter the general nature of our observations on the agreement of direction and magnitude of interarea balances (see footnote 1 above).

Patterns of Net Trade

Over the five years the three central areas ran trade surpluses with the world while each of the peripheral areas ran over-all deficits; the U.S. was the main surplus area.

Table A-2 suggests that the goods and services balances of countries outside the economic centers follow a symmetrical pattern in which each group of affiliated countries ran deficits with the economic center with which it traded principally. Thus, the Western Hemisphere groups were in deficit with the U.S., the Rest of the Sterling Area in deficit with the U.K., and Continental Overseas Territories (if transactions are combined with their Own Currency Area and with other Continental countries) were in deficit with Continental OEEC countries. The group Other Countries was also in deficit with the Continental OEEC countries.

In contrast to these deficits with their principal trading partner, the affiliated areas seem to have had surpluses from one or both of the other two centers. Thus, Canada ran surpluses with the U.K. and the Continent, the Rest of the Sterling Area ran surpluses with the Continent (but a deficit with the U.S.), and Continental Overseas Territories ran surpluses with both the U.K. and U.S., but both Other

Countries and Latin America were in deficit with all three centers.

The net trade orientation of countries is, of course, imperfectly shown in the two-valued matrix tables of Appendixes A and B since there the countries (and particularly Other Countries) are not grouped by trading interest or by trade balances.

The basic trading pattern in the eight-area matrix becomes rather complicated to diagram. It has, therefore, been reduced to a six-area scheme by consolidating Canada, Latin America, and International Organizations into Other Western Hemisphere and combining Overseas Territories with Other Countries to give a grouping of nonsterling countries of the Eastern Hemisphere outside the OEEC.[13] Chart 3,

CHART 3

Combined Goods and Services Balances Between World Areas over the Five Years 1950–54: Six-Area Consolidation of the Two-Valued Matrix
(arrow points from area debited to area credited; figures are placed adjacent to area of report)
(million U.S. dollars)

A. With Petroleum on a Trade Record Basis

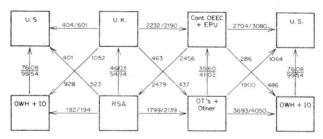

B. With Petroleum Channeled Through U.S. and U.K.

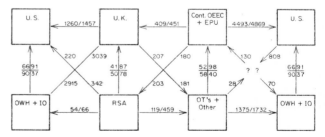

SOURCE: Tables A-2 and C-1.
NOTE: Unallocated transactions have not been allocated.

[12] If two numbers and their mean are in the relationship of 7:8:9, the relative divergence will be 25 per cent of the mean; if the relationship is 3:4:5, the relative divergence will be 50 per cent of the mean; if the relationship is 1:2:3, the relative divergence will be 100 per cent of the mean. There is a sense in which even the last, relatively wide divergence can be said to represent "agreement on order of magnitude," but in general I have used the term to refer to agreement within 50 per cent of the mean.

[13] Anyone who wishes to draw the distinctions between patterns for the component areas of Other Western Hemisphere and between Overseas Territories and Other Countries can do so readily from the data in Table A–2.

Part A, shows the direction of balances and paired entries from the two-valued matrix consolidated into the six areas. The three central areas are placed at the top of the diagram and three peripheral areas below them with the Rest of the Sterling Area under the U.K., Other Western Hemisphere under the U.S., and Overseas Territories and Other Countries under Continental OEEC.[14]

It can be seen from Chart 3 that the three economic centers ran surpluses with the areas beneath them, which were largely composed of countries trading principally with them, and deficits with peripheral areas on the diagonal, which were largely composed of countries trading principally with one of the other centers. There are, however, two exceptions to the last rule: the surpluses of the U.S. with both groups of peripheral Eastern Hemisphere countries. The Other Western Hemisphere area, however, ran surpluses with both Eastern Hemisphere centers, and the Overseas Territories and Other Countries ran a surplus with the Rest of the Sterling Area. Oil movements contributed heavily to this pattern, and, to a lesser extent, so did the inclusion of International Organizations in Other Western Hemisphere.

Evidently, there was a general tendency for balances between centers and areas placed in the chart under another center to be small and for balances between centers and areas placed under them to be large. This tendency is more pronounced when petroleum transactions are placed on a purchase-sales basis (Part B of Chart 3).

Petroleum Trade, Middlemen, and the Pattern of Net Trading

The changes in gross merchandise and goods and services transactions between world areas required to channel petroleum transactions through the U.S. and the U.K. to reflect purchases and sales were discussed above and are given in Appendix C (see Table C-1).

Channeling petroleum transactions through the U.S. and the U.K. has the effect of directing to those centers the net debits which consuming areas previously directed toward the oil sources and the net credits which the oil sources previously directed toward the consuming areas. The amounts redirected are large relative to some of the interarea balances in Table A-2. In eight instances the petroleum adjustment reverses the direction of the balance previously shown by both sides, and in two more instances it reverses the direction of one of the two records so that they no longer agree on direction. In seven other instances the adjustment reduces the balance between the paired areas without changing its direction. In ten other instances, however, it works to increase the balance previously shown. The adjustment does not affect balances with International Organizations.

Most strikingly altered is the pattern of net trading between the U.K., the Continent, and the Rest of the Sterling Area. The U.K.'s previous deficits with the Continent and its Overseas Territories are more than offset by British petroleum company earnings, and the Rest of the Sterling Area's surplus with the Continent is reduced to small proportions. Striking reversals from deficit to surplus appear in the relations of Other Countries with the U.S. and the U.K. and of Latin America with the U.K. The Latin American deficit with the U.S. is substantially reduced; the Rest of the Sterling Area's deficits with the U.K. and the U.S. are also improved modestly. The larger Latin American surplus from Continental Overseas Territories, which reflected the refining of oil in the Netherlands Antilles, is wiped out by the adjustment and is replaced by a small, ambiguous net position.

Trade by middlemen in commodities other than oil is less heavily concentrated on the U.S. and the U.K. than oil, as was observed above, and many items are dealt in by Continental traders and toll processors. The trade most heavily controlled by middlemen is that of countries politically or economically closely associated with an economic center—the Overseas Territories of Western Europe, former colonies like Indonesia, the sterling Commonwealth, Chile, and other Latin American countries in which the U.S. has invested heavily. The economic centers, on a purchase basis, are likely to control more of the produce exported by countries trading principally with them than the latter's export record indicates and to supply more of their imports. In the case of U.S.-oriented countries, the U.S. role as a middleman in marketing produce very likely was consider-

---

[14] The figure is conceived as a cylinder split down one side and laid out flat. To carry out that sense of circularity, the U.S. and Other Western Hemisphere areas are entered on both sides of the figure. Note that in this type of diagram (which also will be employed in the next chapter) the arrow points in the direction of the net payment to be made from the area in deficit to the area in surplus.

ably more important than its role as a middleman in supplying imports originating in other countries.[15] Hence, on a purchase-sales basis the deficit of U.S.-oriented countries with the U.S. was probably less than indicated in Chart 3 even after being reduced by a petroleum adjustment, but in view of the size of the deficit its direction would probably not be reversed.

In the case of countries oriented toward the U.K. and the Continent, particularly colonial territories, one may wonder whether the middleman role of the centers is more important in the marketing of exports than in the supplying of imports. Since, however, the exports of these countries are concentrated on specialities and the food and raw materials which account for most middleman trade, it seems likely that, even for the colonial territories, middlemen of the associated center would be more important factors in handling exports than imports. Hence, we would expect that an adjustment to a purchase-sales basis, if that were possible, would increase sales in relation to purchases in a peripheral area's trade with its

principal trading center and would produce the opposite effect in its trade with other centers.

It is difficult to guess how balances between centers would be altered: I suspect that British sales in the United States of wool, rubber, nonferrous metals, and beverages (cocoa, coffee, tea) from Sterling Area sources more than offset U.S. sales to Britain of sugar, cotton, flour, and nonferrous metals from Other Western Hemisphere sources, and that such sales by both the U.S. and the U.K. to the Continent exceeded Continental sales to the U.S. and the U.K. of Congo minerals, tropical fats and oils, North African phosphate rock, and Russian furs. I would therefore suppose that the U.S. and the U.K. earned more from the Continental OEEC countries and the U.K. more from the U.S. than Chart 3 shows.

It seems likely that the intervention of middlemen tended to reduce the extent to which areas of the world offset trade deficits in one direction by trade surpluses in another. Surpluses of centers with affiliated areas were probably smaller and deficits with the affiliated areas of other centers also smaller.

B. THE ANNUAL MATRIXES

In Appendix D the differences between paired credit and debit records in the eight-area matrix have been examined to judge the agreement on the size of the gross and net trade between areas, on the direction and magnitude of year-to-year change in trade, and on changes over the five years. Despite the fact that in the annual accounts trade among parts of the sterling and nonsterling EPU areas has been esti-

[15] See the Commerce Department study by Samuel Pizer and Frederick Cutler, *U. S. Investments in the Latin American Economy*, Washington, 1957. Reporting on the activities of many of the most important U.S.-controlled foreign subsidiaries in Latin America, the authors observed export sales by these enterprises of $800 million in 1955 to countries (including other Latin American republics) other than the U.S. and imports by these enterprises from countries other than the U.S. of $140 million (*ibid.*, pp. 9–10). These enterprises include the principal U.S. firms producing petroleum, sugar, bananas, nonferrous metals, meat products, locally distributed manufacturers, and utility services. They would account for the bulk of the Latin American exports controlled by U.S. enterprises (Mexican cotton and Brazilian coffee are notable exclusions) and probably also for the bulk of Latin American imports from sources outside the U.S. controlled by U.S. companies. The U.S. trading and distributing concerns that were not included probably did not deal to any great extent in products originating outside the U.S.—apart from products produced by Canadian affiliates.

mated (see Chapter 2, Section A-1) and fairly large transactions remained unallocated by area, the divergence between paired entries is not such as to impair the usefulness of the record for most descriptive and analytical purposes. From the detailed examination of the divergence, we conclude the following.

Most of the magnitudes traded between paired areas were measured alike to within 10 per cent, though in a few cases, mainly involving the trade of peripheral areas, only the order of magnitude (see footnote 12 above) was agreed. In most of the latter cases there were good reasons for preferring one record to the other.

In most cases paired records of gross trade exhibited year-to-year movements in the same direction and differed by no more than 10 per cent absolutely or relatively (Appendix Table D-2). Many times when movements were in opposite directions, they were so small as to represent virtual stability by either record. Moreover, most cases of significant divergence in direction of movement involved the trade of peripheral countries and could be resolved in favor of one side or the other.

Similarly, the movements of the paired records over the five years agreed in direction and, for the most part, agreed closely also in magnitude. Peripheral areas were mainly involved in instances of large divergence, but Continental European and U.K. sales to the U.S., while agreeing with the U.S. record in direction, showed a cumulative divergence amounting over the five years to more than 10 per cent.

In most cases paired records agreed on the direction of the balances between areas in each year, and disagreement arose mainly when balances were very small. Where disagreement on direction of the balance was sizable, a basis existed for preferring one partner's record to the other. Paired records usually agreed also on order of magnitude of the balance; two-thirds of the time they diverged by no more than $100 million or no more than 10 per cent of their mean. In over half the cases the divergence was not more than $50 million or not more than 10 per cent. The worst cases of large absolute and relative divergence in the balance were the U.S. with Latin America and with the Continent.

In most cases paired entries for net trade showed year-to-year movements in the same direction; in about two-thirds of these cases the paired records also agreed on the order of magnitude of the movement. Differences in direction of change of the balance were most frequent in 1951–52 and 1953–54 when trade tended to reverse direction. Notable instances of large differences in direction as measured on the two sides came in U.S. transactions with Latin America and Canada in 1951–52 and seem to reflect time lags in reporting.

Agreement on the direction of change in balances over the five-year period was somewhat better; in about half the cases they agreed on the relative change to within 25 per cent of the mean. Only a quarter of the trade balances showed agreement in direction but diverged by more than $50 million in the amount of the change or by more than 50 per cent of the mean of the two figures. In four cases the direction of change was not agreed.

This review shows that at certain points the record is subject to considerable ambiguity and it is well to have the full account from both sides as a check on the magnitudes of and changes in trade.

C. THE NATURE OF SPECIALIZATION IN TRADE: THE SERVICES MATRIXES

We have stated that the trade of nations in the early 1950's tended to focus on three economic centers—the United States, the United Kingdom, and the Continent—for nearly every country could be identified as trading primarily with one of these centers. Most countries also had important trade ties with either or both of the other centers, and close trade relations were common among neighboring countries.

Much has been written about the product content of world trade, especially by the U.N. in its annual *World Economic Report* and the Secretariat of the General Agreement of Tariffs and Trade in its annual review of *International Trade*. The particular contribution we can make to an understanding of international specialization lies in the record (given in Appendix Tables B-7 through B-24) of services transactions.

1. The Nature of Trade in Services

On balance, services are supplied by the centers and bought by the peripheral areas.[16] This pattern reflects the role of the centers in supplying capital for international investment, ocean transportation, and special skills. At the same time the centers make large net payments for travel and military expenditures.

The share of the centers in world services credits was relatively larger than in merchandise credits, and they also incurred relatively more services debits. For peripheral areas services credits were generally small compared with their part in merchandise credits, but services debits were usually proportional to merchandise debits. There were some notable exceptions among peripheral area countries for which services credits were high in proportion to merchandise.

The maritime nations, especially those with tonnage in excess of domestic needs, are mainly countries of the North Atlantic, and fleets registered elsewhere are largely owned by the economic centers. The cen-

[16] For annual matrixes on services, see Table B–7 through B–24.

ters realized 80 per cent of all transportation credits, including those earned by the PHL fleet, close to 90 per cent of gross freights, and (on a purchase-sales basis) almost all bunkers. The U.K. and the Continent particularly earned a disproportionate amount from transportation compared with merchandise.

Countries tend to employ the transportation services of the center with which they trade principally, but the U.S. fleet is in a weak competitive position compared with the European fleets in carrying the trade of Other Western Hemisphere countries.

In spite of large differences in the paired records (which suggest an underreporting of credits by the Continental OEEC countries and, possibly, a general overstating of debits), the pattern of net transportation transactions between world areas is generally agreed as to direction and rough order of magnitude. Each of the three centers earned from each peripheral area; the U.S. paid the U.K., which paid the Continent, which (over the five years but not the last two years of the period) paid the U.S.

Travel expenditures mainly originated in and were spent in the more developed countries. The heaviest expenditudes were by Western Hemisphere countries and the U.K. (the U.S. being the largest spender). The Continent was the largest earner followed by Western Hemisphere areas. Travel balances tended to flow from the Western Hemisphere to the Eastern Hemisphere; the U.K. and Rest of the Sterling Area tended to run deficits with the nonsterling areas of the Eastern Hemisphere.

Seven countries—the U.S., the U.K., Canada, France, the Netherlands, Belgium, and Switzerland—received 90 per cent of all investment income, including some reinvested earnings; [17] the U.S. earned not quite half of all investment income; nearly 30 per cent was earned by the U.K., including the estimated earnings of British petroleum companies.

Peripheral countries incurred the bulk of total investment income debits. The largest were by the Rest of the Sterling Area and Latin America and their debits went mainly to the U.K. and the U.S., respectively. The direction of flow points to the concentration of foreign investments by principal trading interest and to a substantial exchange of investments between the three centers. The largest sources of investment income were: countries that were themselves large earners of investment income, oil-supply-

ing countries, and the larger countries in the outer Sterling Area and in Latin America.

Each of the centers had a surplus on investment income with each of the five peripheral areas. The U.S. ran a surplus with the other centers as well. Divergence in the two-valued matrix of investment income appears not to impair its usefulness for observing the main flows of investment income.

The U.S. made nearly two-thirds of all government expenditures and, together with the U.K., made 80 per cent. The pattern of interarea government transactions was largely set by the expenditures of these two countries. The U.S. spent heavily in Other Countries and the Continent; the U.K. spent heavily in the Sterling Area. These three partner areas realized most of the government debits. The U.S. and the U.K. ran over-all deficits; other areas surpluses. The U.S. ran a deficit with all areas, the U.K. ran a deficit except with the U.S. and Canada, and the Continent ran a surplus with the Anglo-American areas. Military necessities rather than commercial interests evidently set the pattern of government expenditures.

Miscellaneous services, like investment income, tended to follow the principal trading interests and to flow heavily between the centers. With some exceptions, balances tended to flow from peripheral areas to the centers.

2. Further Comment on the Services Matrixes

The foregoing observations drawn from an examination of the services matrixes require qualification because of the limitations of the record mentioned in Chapter 2.

The record of transport transactions (Tables B-10, B-11, and B-12) is subject to considerably more relative error in both level and direction of transactions than the merchandise matrix. Altogether the estimates we have made add considerably to the account of transportation transactions, raising the totals in published country accounts for 1951 by about 40 per cent.[18]

It must be remembered that the PHL fleet was owned mainly by residents of the United States, the United Kingdom, and the Continent, and that bunker oil sales were almost entirely by American and British-Dutch companies. Thus, the extent to which transportation credits and debits came under the

---

[17] See Chapter 2, Section A–2.

[18] Herman Karreman, *Methods for Improving World Transportation Accounts, Applied to 1950–1953,* NBER Technical Paper 15, New York, 1961.

control of residents of the centers is somewhat understated by the accounting conventions followed, notably by the reliance upon the flag of a vessel to give the direction of transactions.[19]

A noteworthy feature of the transportation account is that partner areas in deficit with the Continental OEEC countries showed larger net payments to the Continent than the Continent reported receiving (Table B-12). In the case of sterling transactions the comparison is between nonsterling EPU and Sterling Area records. We disregard the balance within Continental currency areas which we calculated from merchandise trade records and which, consequently, shows a close agreement. The records of net payment by Sterling Area, Latin America, and Other Countries, in particular, showed large differences from the Continental records. This suggests that not all the foreign exchange earnings of Continental shipping companies came under the control of European exchange authorities.

Since travel is a small item in many country accounts and is difficult to distinguish in some respects from miscellaneous services and remittances, travel transactions appear to suffer from general underreporting of credits. Every area showed greater payments than partner areas (especially Eastern Hemisphere) showed receiving. Even so, the over-all excess of debits reported was about 5 per cent of the mean of total travel debits and credits, a smaller proportion than for transportation and government services but larger than for investment income and miscellaneous services (see Chart 1).

Because of the persisting tendency for travel credits to be less well reported than debits, the two-valued record of balances (Table B-15) is subject to somewhat more disagreement of direction than either the merchandise or the transportation matrixes.

The direction of net investment income flows between areas was generally agreed upon between paired entries in the matrix (Table B-18). Disagreements of direction were all small flows between peripheral areas, not more than $20 million each over the five years. This general agreement is perhaps not surprising since 70 per cent of the investment income payments originated in the peripheral areas, 90 per cent was earned by the centers, and the flows were mainly to centers.

The flow of international investment income, in-

cluding a good deal of reinvested income, came to about $27 billion over the five years, with the record of payments exceeding the record of credits by 3 per cent. The total includes investment income for the United Kingdom ($7.8 billion for 1950–54) nearly double the figure for investment income reported in the official U.K. balance-of-payments statement, which places interest profits and dividends over the five years at £1,461 million—$4.01 billion.[20] The published figure "excludes overseas earnings of U.K. insurance, shipping, and oil companies." It "represents for the most part total earnings remitted for the payment of interest and dividends, taxation and management expenses in the U.K. and for later reinvestment, but to some extent also reinvested profits not remitted."[21] The excluded earnings are sizable, and the true investment income position of the U.K. is much greater than the published $4 billion.

American oil companies earned $4,525 million on their foreign investments in the five years 1950–54.[22] Despite losses arising from the dispute over Iranian oil, which interrupted operations during most of the five years in Iran, British oil companies, with a worldwide business comparable in scope to American companies,[23] must have realized earnings of a comparable order of magnitude—although these earnings may have been reinvested in good part. Our direct calculation of U.K. oil company "income," including reinvested earnings abroad and that part of the gross margin over sales used to cover home office expense, came to $3.72 billion for the five years.[24]

[19] The U.S. transportation account does not include Panama Canal tolls which are carried as miscellaneous government services.

[20] *United Kingdom Balance of Payments, 1946–1957*, London, 1959. In the official account net current transactions of oil companies were counted among miscellaneous services.

[21] *United Kingdom Balance of Payments, 1946 to 1954* (No. 2), Command Paper 9430, London, 1955, p. 49, item 10.

[22] *Survey of Current Business*, August 1956, Table 9, p. 22.

[23] *The International Petroleum Cartel* (U.S. Senate Select Committee on Small Business, Staff Report to the Federal Trade Commission, Washington 1952, pp. 24–25) shows the crude production and refining capacity of the seven largest international companies, two British and five American.

[24] Income from petroleum transactions was only the largest category of investment income counted in the British official accounts in miscellaneous. Profits from the overseas operations of British shipping and insurance companies were also put (net) into miscellaneous. With one of the worlds largest dry cargo merchant fleets and one of the most highly developed insurance businesses in the world, both operating widely outside the British Isles, the U.K. must have realized substantial earnings from those overseas operations, too. Thus, our estimates may even understate British investment income.

Altogether, investment income from petroleum company operations accounts for a very sizable part of all investment income over the period. If we add to the oil company income earned by the U.K. the $4,525 million earned by American oil companies from all sources, we arrive at a five-year total of $8,247 million, which is 31.5 per cent of total investment income credit. This tends to understate the proportion of the total contributed by petroleum operations since it excludes income earned by Continental interests in foreign oil concerns (notably Dutch, Belgian, and French).

The agreement between investment income credits and debits in the Sterling Area account arises because transactions of the British colonies with the U.K. were estimated as those that balanced the intra-Sterling Area investment income account. We do not have an independent report on service transactions of British colonies including Hong Kong and petroleum company transactions.

If we could include reinvested earnings in the table where they are not now entered, this would reduce the U.S. fraction of the total but it would still be the largest part.

The degree of concentration of foreign investments in the hands of a few countries indicates that a study of international capital movements can concentrate on a few suppliers and would be greatly facilitated if the governments concerned were to provide a complete accounting of public and private, long-term and short-term capital transactions by partner with some industry detail. If the analyst were to have from five European governments—the U.K., France, Switzerland, the Netherlands, and Belgium—the kind of information published by the U.S. and Canadian governments, his understanding of world capital flows in the early 1950's would be greatly enhanced.[25]

With debits totaling $16,762 million and credits $12,609 million for the five years 1950–54, the government transactions matrix (Tables B-19, B-20, and B-21) shows a large divergence in the over-all total, the largest divergence for any of the goods and serv-

ices matrixes. This reflects the fact, discussed in Chapter 2, that the U.S. and the U.K. report a substantial part of their transactions not in the conventional categories but rather in a category that has the government in question as one party to the transaction. While partner countries are instructed by the IMF to report the transactions of their residents with foreign governments, it is plain from the large discrepancies in amounts reported on both sides that the payments which the U.S. and the U.K. report as "government debits" are not similarly reported by partners as government credits. Over the five years the U.S. reports government payments to the world totaling $10.8 billion, but partners only account for $7.6 billion with the U.S.[26] The U.K. account shows government payments totaling $3.2 billion while partner accounts show only $1.9 billion credited.[27] Thus, approximately $5.5 billion of U.K. and U. S. government debits do not appear in partner records as government transactions, though they may show up in accounts for a different category.

Comparing the U.S. balance of payments for 1951 given by the Commerce Department in 1952 with a revision the following year, one can infer that the Commerce Department once counted as "merchandise" more than $400 million of military purchases in 1951 which it later put into the government account. Any ocean freight payments to foreigners on these purchases likewise now go into government rather than into transportation.[28] Partners might well have counted these transactions, as the Commerce Department once did, as merchandise and transportation credits.

Similarly, U.K. government debits in 1951 included $340 million of "overseas expenditures of U.K. military forces, including f.o.b. value of food

[25] U.S. investment income and capital transactions are reported in *Survey of Current Business,* August issues. Canadian transactions are reported in *Canada's International Investment Position, 1926–1954,* Dominion Bureau of Statistics, International Trade Division, Balance of Payments Section; and *The Canadian Balance of International Payments and International Investment Position,* Annual Report, Ottawa, 1956. In the middle 1960's one might need to add Germany and possibly Italy and Japan to the list of principal capital suppliers.

[26] The $7,929 million of transactions with U.S., Canada, and International Organizations less transactions by Canada and International Organizations with the world.

[27] This assumes that the debits of the Rest of the Sterling Area with nonsterling EPU countries were with the Continent. The close agreement between the U.K. and the Rest of the Sterling Area entries for the latter's credits arises from using U.K. records on both sides. (The slight discrepancy shown comes from rounding.) The excess of the Rest of the Sterling Area debits to the U.K. over U.K. credits from the Rest of the Sterling Area arises in the country accounts and could not be reconciled by introducing more debits by British colonies.

[28] Compare the corresponding adjusted merchandise import figures of the revised balance of payments in the *Survey of Current Business* (July 1954, Table 3, p. 10) and in the 1952 supplement (*Balance of Payments of the U. S., 1949–1951,* Table 1, p. 118).

and oil purchased and consumed overseas." [29] To the extent that these purchases involved consumption in a country different from the one supplying the goods, the transaction might well have been entered into the partner's merchandise account or, if it were bunker oil, into its transportation account.

The U.S. government account also includes a variety of other transactions which partners might put into a miscellaneous category, not knowing that the U.S. government was party to the transaction. These include expenditures of government personnel abroad and expenditures for government travel, wages and salaries of foreign employees, purchases of lands and buildings not of an income-producing character, and troop pay disbursed abroad. [30] Thus, it is not surprising to find that miscellaneous receipts of certain areas from the U.S. exceed payments recorded as "miscellaneous" by the U.S. France, Italy, and Germany in particular show large miscellaneous receipts from the U.S. not matched in the U.S. account.

The matrix of miscellaneous services is the only one of the services accounts to show an excess of credits. This was a slight one—only 2.6 per cent on gross transactions of around $17 billion. However, this close apparent agreement emerges only after the rather substantial adjustments (previously described) to the U.K. miscellaneous services accounts to transfer petroleum transactions to the shipping and investment income accounts and after a further adjustment which consisted of entering into the U.K. account with each partner area the partner's account of *gross* miscellaneous transactions with the U.K. Thus in the two-valued matrix the entries for the U.K. are the same on both sides. [31] One further feature of this adjustment should be noted. A balancing entry to maintain the over-all net miscellaneous services total remaining after all other adjustments was introduced into the U.K.'s unallocated column as a credit or debit depending on the sign needed. The over-all net services total in the U.K. account thus is that shown by the White Papers. The entries, gratifyingly, were usually small and less than $100 million except in

1954. [32] Besides the net overseas transactions of British petroleum companies, the net miscellaneous account of the U.K. includes (net) overseas transactions of dry cargo shipping companies, insurance companies, and the net profit of merchandise transactions not involving passage of goods through the U.K. customs territory. The fact that the balancing entry tended to rise over the period undoubtedly reflects the growing participation of British middlemen in world trade.

The treatment we have given to the U.K. miscellaneous services account also has the effect of excluding from the miscellaneous account (and from the net goods and services account) the interarea transfers implied in the official account by the inclusion of net profits from overseas merchandise transactions.

By following this procedure we arrive at a matrix which describes the main transactions for miscellaneous services apart from the profits on middleman trade. The method does not provide an estimate for British net miscellaneous transactions with British colonies, which are therefore excluded. Since we also lack any estimate of miscellaneous services transactions between France, Portugal, and Spain and their respective Overseas Territories, the totals shown in the matrix table, both around $17 billion, are probably somewhat understated.

3. The Contrasting Patterns for Merchandise and Services

Economic centers tended to run services surpluses while almost all peripheral countries ran services deficits, and, in contrast, peripheral countries tended to run merchandise surpluses while the economic centers in Europe were mostly in merchandise deficit. This contrast can be readily seen in panels i and ii of Chart 4. [33] Areas composed predominantly of countries trading principally with the U.S. and the Sterling Area were in merchandise surplus while the Overseas Territories and Other Countries together

[29] *Balance of Payments Yearbook*, IMF, Vol. 5, U.K. section, p. 5.

[30] See *Balance of Payments, Supplement, 1952*, pp. 6 ff.

[31] U.K. net miscellaneous service transactions with non-sterling EPU countries were obtained by subtracting the Rest of the Sterling Area transactions with nonsterling EPU countries from the nonsterling EPU transactions with the Sterling Area.

[32] They were $40 million credit in 1950; $97 million debit in 1951; $74 million credit in 1952; $25 million credit in 1953; and $225 million credit in 1954.

[33] Panel iii of Chart 4 is a repetition of Chart 3 but with values appropriate to the adjusted net goods and services table (Table A–4) in which unallocated transactions are spread out. Comparison of the two diagrams will show that the adjustment has not altered the pattern nor the order of magnitude of the interarea balances; although some paired entries are brought closer together, the over-all effect is to increase the divergence.

(and separately) were in deficit. The two European centers were in goods deficit while the U.S. had a goods surplus. The over-all balances of areas on services account show the marked contrast between the surpluses of centers and the deficits of peripheral areas previously noted.

CHART 4

A Comparison of Merchandise and Services Balances Between World Areas over the Five Years 1950–54: Six-Area Consolidation of the Two-Valued Matrix (arrow points from area debited to area credited; figures are placed adjacent to area of report; entries in boxes are the area's over-all balances)
(million U.S. dollars)

i. Net Merchandise

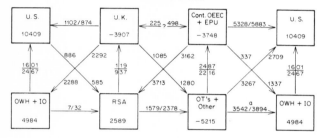

ii. Net Services

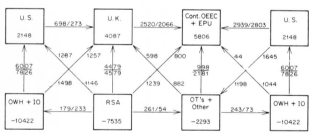

iii. Net Goods and Services

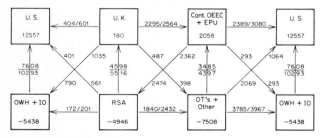

Source: Table A-4.

Note: In contrast to Chart 3, unallocated transactions have been allocated. This figure is continued in Chart 5 in the next chapter.

ᵃ Venezuelan exports to the Netherlands Antilles were $3049 million.

In spite of the merchandise deficits of European centers, each center ran goods surpluses with the areas entered in Chart 4 directly below it and composed mainly of countries trading principally with it, and each center ran goods deficits with the areas placed under the other principal centers—except for Overseas Territories and Other Countries which were in deficit with the U.S. The U.S., in fact, had a merchandise surplus with each of the five partner areas except the Rest of the Sterling Area.[34]

The services balances, in most cases, ran contrary to goods balances between the six areas diagramed. The economic centers earned net services from the peripheral areas in every instance but one—the U.S. made net services payments, largely because of military expenditures, to Overseas Territories and Other Countries (payments accruing to each). The Continent—which had goods deficits with the U.S., Other Western Hemisphere countries (Canada, but not Latin America according to the Continental accounts), and possibly the U.K.—enjoyed a services surplus with every partner; the U.K. ran services surpluses with every partner but the Continent.

A comparison of net merchandise and net goods and services (panels i and iii in Chart 4) shows that services not only tended to offset net merchandise but sometimes more than offset the balance of the goods account. The most marked such reversal came in the balance between U.S. and the Rest of the Sterling Area which, after taking account of services, favored the U.S. The small balance between the Rest of the Sterling Area and Other Western Hemisphere coun-

[34] The goods balance between the U.K. and Continental OEEC countries is ambiguous in that *each* side shows a surplus. It will be recalled that the balance between these areas was obtained by allocating U.K. transactions with the nonsterling EPU area between components, using partner reports as a guide, and by allocating Continental OEEC transactions with the Sterling Area by a similar method. The assumption was made that the U.K. distributed its goods sales and purchases to the Continent and Overseas Territories in proportion to the purchases and sales by the latter to the whole Sterling Area. Quite possibly a disproportionate part of the trade was conducted with the economic centers; if this were the case, it would seem more likely that several hundred million dollars of the Continent's net deficit with the Rest of the Sterling Area were incurred with the U.K. than that equal amounts of the Overseas Territories' much smaller surplus with the U.K. and other sterling countries was earned by the Continent. The balance in any case appears to have been small in relation to the large trade between the areas, and perhaps the most we can infer is a rough balance between the U.K. and the Continent.

tries was also reversed and came to favor the latter. In addition, reversals appear in the more detailed eight-area table in the balances of U.K. with Latin America and Other Countries and in the accounts of the last two areas with the Continent. The amount of the services surplus of the Continent with the U.K. was so large as to overshadow the uncertainty attaching to the goods balance, and the combined goods and service net was clearly in favor of the Continent (on the accounting principle used for directing petroleum transactions). Where net services and net merchandise were augmenting, combining the two together produced sizable balances, e.g., between peripheral areas and the center of principal interest. In contrast, where net services offset net merchandise, the result was to reduce the balance in favor of the peripheral area substantially, e.g., between centers and the areas composed of countries trading principally with another center. The net goods surplus of the U.S. with the Overseas Territories and Other Countries also was substantially offset by U.S. net services payments (mainly on government account).

D. CONCLUDING OBSERVATIONS

Can the two-valued record of goods and services transactions be used to observe the structure of trading? The answer is a qualified yes. For gross interarea trade, the broad structure is recorded very similarly by both creditor and debitor areas and it is much the same whether based on customs records or adjusted to a purchase-sales principle. Indeed, the differences introduced by different accounting principles are more important in modifying the view obtained of the structure of trade than the divergences between paired records in the two-value matrixes.

For net interarea trade, differences in accounting concept obviously loom larger. An even approximately complete adjustment to a purchase-sales matrix could not be made. The partial one given was sufficient, however, to indicate that its results could very well be different in pattern and magnitude.

Can the two-valued record of goods and services transactions be used to observe the direction and magnitude of changes in gross and net trade from year to year and over a five-year period? The answer to this question is also a qualified yes. When the two values do not agree well, the one from the partner with the more complete record can usually be adopted, but disagreement indicates the usefulness of a two-valued record as a check.

By including services in the trade account, we obtain a more complete picture of the nature of specialization among countries, and we see that in a number of interarea relationships the net services trade is sufficiently important to offset (or more than offset) net goods trade. Thus, it is apparent that one should not seek to discuss the pattern of net trade between world areas without taking into account trade in services as well as merchandise.

5

FINANCIAL FLOWS AND
MULTILATERAL SETTLEMENTS

Each country's goods and services balance with all areas of the world, if measured without error, must be compensated by some combination of private or official unilateral transfers, capital movements, and gold transactions. With any individual partner area, a country may also cover a deficit with surpluses realized from other areas (i.e., by multilateral settlements). It is convenient to refer to all of these offsetting categories as "financial transactions," and we do so without implying anything at all about the direction of causation between the offsetting transactions and the goods and services balances with which they are associated in time.

The pattern (i.e., direction) of net financial flows between world areas for the five-year period 1950–54 can be read from Table A-4 (in which private unilateral transfers are distinguished from official). Annual flows are given in Tables B-25 through B-28. We start in Section A by examining the consolidated five-year record to see the extent of agreement on measurement between paired records and the way in which financial flows compensate trade balances.

The matrix of capital flows given in the tables is comprehensive and includes (but does not distin-

guish) changes in official reserve funds and other liquid capital assets. For many purposes it would be desirable to segregate these flows of liquid capital from other capital movements, to consider their role, along with that of gold, in international settlements, and, in particular, to examine their relation to multilateral settlements as defined above. We discuss this subject using supplementary materials in Section B.

The pattern of balances met by multilateral settlements is of particular interest since it reflects all other exchanges and helps one to judge the extent of "multilateralism" in world trade and payments. The concept of multilateralism has been widely employed in discussions of international trade, and in Section C we examine this concept, the problem of measuring multilateralism, and the meaning of our final matrix of multilateral settlements.

The annual matrixes are examined in Section D to see whether annual patterns deviate seriously from the five-year average, whether paired entries in the annual matrixes are consistent, and whether the record of multilateral settlements shows systematic variation from year to year.

A. THE PATTERN OF FINANCIAL FLOWS, 1950–54

Chart 5, made up from Table A-4, shows interarea flows between the six areas previously employed in Charts 3 and 4 in Chapter 4 and can be considered an extension of those charts. Panel i of Chart 5 repeats panel A of Chart 4; panels ii, iv, and vi of Chart 5 are for net unilateral transfers, capital, and gold; panels iii, v, and vii are the balances between areas after taking account successively of transfers, capital, and gold. Panel viii is like vii but with petroleum transactions channeled through the U.S. and the U.K.

1. Unilateral Transfers, Capital, and Gold

The record diagramed in Chart 5 is two-valued except for the gold matrix. All transactions have been allocated by partner area and the gold matrix has been reconciled as explained in Chapter 2, Section A-1. Examination of panels ii and iv shows that the paired records of transfers and capital were generally in agreement on direction and order of magnitude. The consistency of paired records of annual financial flows is examined below in Section D and

CHART 5

Financial Balances Between World Areas over the Five Years 1950–54:
Six-Area Consolidation of the Two-Valued Matrix
(arrow points from area debited to area credited; figures are placed adjacent to area of report; entries in boxes are the area's over-all balances)
(million U.S. dollars)

i. Net Goods and Services

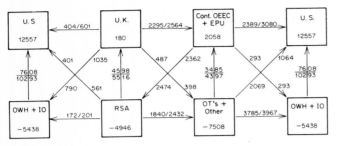

v. Net Goods, Services, Transfers, and Capital

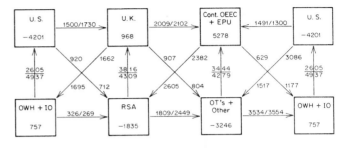

ii. Net Transfers

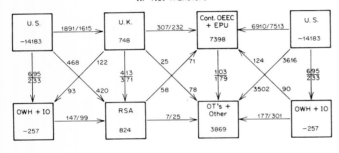

vi. Net Gold (single-valued)

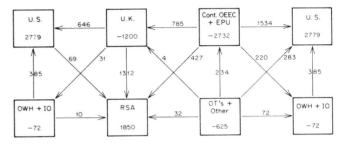

iii. Net Goods, Services, and Transfers

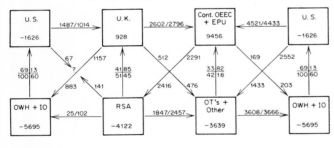

vii. Balances to Be Settled Multilaterally (v + vi)

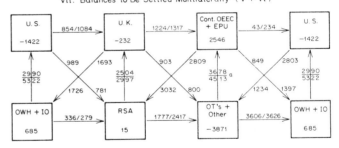

iv. Net Capital

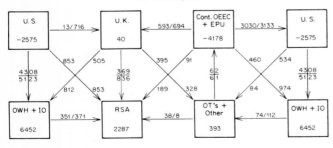

viii. Balances to Be Settled Multilaterally Adjusted for Petroleum[b]

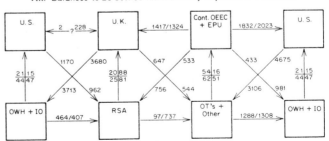

SOURCE: Table A-4.

NOTE: Balances adjusted to allocate unallocated transactions and reconcile the gold account.

[a] Of which 3542/3996 million dollars were balances to be settled in the direction shown within Continental currency areas; these balances were subject to large errors and omissions (see Chapter 3, Section D).

[b] Using Appendix Table C-1 and allocating unallocated petroleum sales of U.K. and U.S. companies. This allocation altered over-all error totals; all U.K. unallocated petroleum was taken as sold to U.K. military and charged to error in the U.K. account; all except $42 million of U.S. company unallocated was taken as sold to U.S. military and charged to over-all error; the $42 million was charged to Canada and Latin America.

need not be considered in detail here. We conclude that the accounting limitations of the record do not destroy its usefulness, although the deficiencies in recording unilateral transfers and capital discussed above in Chapters 2 and 3 should be borne in mind.[1] The largest relative divergence between paired unilateral transfers in panel ii of the chart was between the U.S. and other Western Hemisphere countries and International Organizations located in the U.S.; the most striking divergence in the capital account was between the U.S. and the U.K., although several other interarea flows (the U.K. with the Rest of the Sterling Area; Other Western Hemisphere countries and International Organizations with Continental OEEC countries) also showed large absolute and relative divergences (more than $100 million and more than 50 per cent).

In contrast to net payments for services, which generally flowed from peripheral areas to the centers, unilateral transfers and capital flowed the other way on balance with few and relatively small exceptions.[2] Transfers from the U.S. consisted predominantly of government aid and flowed to every partner. There were also net transfers from the U.K. to every partner except the U.S. and Canada. They went to the Continent from every partner except Other Countries (we lack full reports on transfers between the Continent and the Overseas Territories).

Because of the large size of foreign grants by the U.S., adding them to goods and services reversed its surplus before aid with three of the five partners in Chart 5 according to paired records and also with a fourth (Rest of the Sterling Area) in the U.S. record (it was greatly reduced on the partner record). The direction of the U.S. balance with Other Western Hemisphere countries was not altered by the inclusion of transfers with trade, nor were any of the relations shown in Chart 5 other than those with the U.S.

The capital matrix shows the Continental OEEC countries sending a large amount of capital to the U.S. which, in turn, sent capital to every other partner but mainly to the rest of the Western Hemisphere (including International Organizations in the U.S.). The U.K. sent substantial amounts of capital to each of the peripheral areas and drew capital from the Continent and the U.S. (the U.S. record, however, shows little capital flowing to the U.K.).[3] The Continent sent capital to every area except Other Countries (Table A-4).[4] The Rest of the Sterling

---

[1] Notably the omission of unilateral transfers and capital from the accounts of Soviet Bloc and oil-source countries and from the bilateral accounts of France and Portugal and their Overseas Territories. In addition, deficiencies in recording goods and services are reflected in the residual matrix of balances met by multilateral settlements. Omissions of transactions from both sides of paired records, while not affecting the over-all total of net transactions of that type (the over-all discrepancy), do alter the observed pattern of interarea flows. Thus, the over-all discrepancy in the net capital matrix is not affected by the omission of French financial transactions with the rest of the franc area but the flows shown in Chart 5 between Continental OEEC countries and their Overseas Territories would be changed if these transactions could be included.

[2] Small transfers appear to have gone from the Rest of the Sterling Area and Other Countries to the Continent, and a small capital flow from Other Countries went to the Continent. In the more detailed table Canada shows sizable private transfers to the U.S. and some to other countries. Other smaller exceptions can be observed: the U.K. had tiny transfers from Canada, and Latin America shows private transfers to the U.K., the Continent, and the U.S. Both the U.K. and Latin America show capital receipts from each other.

[3] The official U.K. account does not distinguish the U.S. as a partner. To estimate its transactions with the U.S. we have deducted from transactions reported with the dollar area transactions between the U.K. and the other countries which the official British accounting includes in the dollar area, using figures drawn from our accounts of those partners.

[4] The close agreement between paired entries of capital flow between Continental OEEC countries and Continental Overseas Territories and Other Countries reflects the common accounting for capital transactions between Belgium and the Belgian Congo (almost the whole of the capital flow shown in Tables A–4 and B–26 between Continental OEEC countries and Continental Overseas Territories) and the use of partner records to allocate unallocated capital transactions of Continental OEEC countries. The latter results in one value being shown in Table A–4 for the flow of capital between Continental OEEC countries and Other Countries. It will be seen from Table B–26 that the unadjusted records agree three years out of five on the direction of the flow of capital between OEEC countries and Other Countries and that the two years when the direction was not agreed the amount shown by Continental OEEC countries was less than $10 million. The unadjusted records do not agree on the direction or magnitude of the flow over the five years (both showing an outflow), and in view of the large unallocated inflow in the account of Continental OEEC countries, we have used the partner area record in Table A–4.

The movement of capital between the Continent and its Overseas Territories is uncertain as to direction and may have been sizable (see footnote 1 in this chapter and footnote 17 in Chapter 3). Also see the U.S. Department of Commerce's *World Trade Information Service* reports on various of the Continental Overseas Territories and the United Nations studies of *The International Flow of Private Capital, 1946–52* (New York, 1954, pp. 23 ff.) and "Financing of Economic Development: The International Flow of Private Capital, 1953–55" (report by the U.N. Secretary

Area appears to have drawn capital from each of the five partner areas, and Other Western Hemisphere countries and International Organizations drew capital from the three centers and sent it to the other two peripheral areas. The outflow actually reflects the role of International Organizations, which channeled capital from each of the centers and Canada to the Rest of the Sterling area, Latin America, Overseas Territories, and Other Countries.

The capital flows in panel iv of Chart 5 modified the pattern of interarea balances for goods, services, and transfers in panel iii to the pattern shown in panel v. Capital flows made the balance between the U.S. and the Rest of the Sterling Area clearly in favor of the latter and reversed the balance of the latter with Other Western Hemisphere countries and International Organizations. Otherwise, net capital flows were not large enough to offset interarea balances for trade and transfers.

Comparing panel v with panel i, however, reveals that taking both capital and transfers into account results in balances opposite to trade balances in five out of fifteen interarea relations, i.e., the trading surpluses of the U.S. with four of its five partners (all except Other Western Hemisphere countries and International Organizations) and the trading deficit of the Rest of the Sterling Area with Other Western Hemisphere countries and International Organizations.

Panel v, which gives the balances covered by gold, multilateral settlements, and residual error, displays a nice symmetry. Each center ran a surplus with the peripheral area placed under it and a deficit with the other peripheral areas placed diagonally. Other Western Hemisphere countries and International Organizations ran a deficit with the Rest of the Sterling Area, which was in deficit with Overseas Territories and Other Countries, and in turn the last was in deficit with Other Western Hemisphere countries and International Organizations, thereby completing a circle. The U.S. was in deficit with the U.K., which was in deficit with the Continent; but here the symmetrical pattern of interarea balances is marred by an imperfection—the Continent was in surplus with the U.S. When gold transactions are taken into ac-

count, however, this departure from circularity disappears.

The conjectural nature of the gold account has been explained earlier.[5] The pattern of net gold trading in panel vi of Chart 5 is necessarily the result of our guesswork; it shows, first, net sales by the Rest of the Sterling Area to every partner and by the U.S. to every partner except the Rest of the Sterling Area; second, it shows net purchases by the Continent from every partner except Other Countries and by Other Countries from every partner.

2. Multilateral Settlements and Error

When the gold matrix is combined with the previously considered transactions, we arrive (panel vii) at the balance to be covered by multilateral settlements and error.[6] After taking account of gold purchases, we find that the Continental balance before gold (panel v) has been more than reversed by gold purchases from the U.S., and the Continent made settlements payments to the U.S. to cover gold payments in excess of its bilateral balance before gold. More will be said about this relationship in the next section where consideration will be given to evidence on reserve movements. No other interarea balances in panel v of Chart 5 were reversed by gold transactions.

With the Continent in deficit with the U.S. after gold transactions, we find the final circular flow of multilateral settlements between the six areas in Chart 5 perfectly symmetrical. It flows around the cylinder with paired entries agreeing in every instance on the direction of the balance, almost always on the order of magnitude of the balance (taking a 50 per cent divergence from the mean of paired entries as a criterion of agreement), and twice as often as not on the size of the balance to within 25 per cent of the mean.

The circularity of the flow of net multilateral set-

General, June 21, 1956, mimeographed, pp. 34 ff). *Economic Development in Africa, 1955–56* (supplement to the United Nation's *World Economic Survey, 1956*), gives some data on public investment in several African territories (Tables 24, 25, and 26, pp. 81–83).

[5] See Chapter 2, Section A–1, p. 12.
[6] Multilateral settlements given on line 8 of Table A–4 are equal in magnitude but opposite in sign to the sum of entries for other types of transactions, the balances to be settled. The latter are plotted in Chart 5, panel vii (and subsequent charts in this book), since the position before settlement is analogous to the position one usually thinks of as the financial result of trading. A surplus position is shown by an arrow pointing (opposite the goods flow) toward the area in surplus. One thinks of money flowing in that direction and of a pattern of money flows from deficit to surplus areas.

CHART 6
The Circular Flow of Multilateral Settlements over the Five Years 1950–54

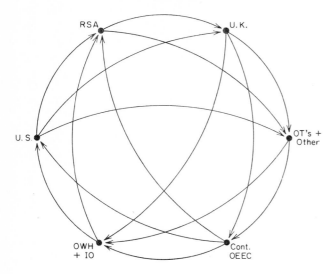

tlements in the six-area consolidation of the two-valued matrix is emphasized by diagraming the flow in a fashion similar to that used by Hilgerdt and the League of Nations in the *Network* study.[7] If centers and peripheral areas are placed alternatively around a circle, as in Chart 6, then multilateral

settlements flow from any area to the next two or three ahead and are received from the three or two areas earlier in the sequence.

After allowing for the different convention employed in Chart 6 for the direction of arrows (see footnote 6 above), the reader acquainted with Hilgerdt's *Network* study will observe a formal similarity in pattern between the *Network* diagram of trade balances between areas in the interwar years and the flow of multilateral settlements over the years 1950–54 (with Hilgerdt's Regions of Recent Settlement standing in place of Other Western Hemisphere countries and International Organizations, with Non-Continental Europe standing in place of the U.K., with Tropics standing in place of the Rest of the Sterling Area, with Continental Europe standing in place of Continental OEEC countries, and with Hilgerdt's Other standing in place of Continental Overseas Territories and Other Countries.)[8]

To investigate the reasons for this similarity, we have regrouped peripheral countries according to Hilgerdt's criterion and examined interarea balances over the five years 1950–54 for a grouping approximating that of the *Network* study. With both imports and exports valued f.o.b., the pattern of merchandise balances over the five years was found to conform in every respect but one with Hilgerdt's 1938 pattern

[7] *The Network of World Trade*, Geneva, 1942.

[8] Hilgerdt shows the following pattern of plus and minus balances between merchandise exports valued f.o.b. and imports valued c.i.f. in 1928 and 1938:

Balance of	U.S.		R.R.S.		Continental Europe		Non-Cont. Europe		Rest of World	
	1928	1938	1928	1938	1928	1938	1928	1938	1928	1938
Tropics										
Own record	+	+	+	+	+	+	−	+	+	−
Partner record	+	+	+	+	+	+	−	+	+	+
U.S.										
Own record			+	+	+	+	+	+	−	+
Partner record			+	+	+	+	+	+	+	+
Regions of Recent Settlement										
Own record					+	+	+	+	+	−
Partner record					+	+	+	+	+	+
Continental Europe										
Own record							+	+	−	−
Partner record							+	+	+	+
Non-Continental Europe										
Own record									−	−
Partner record									−	−

(*Network of World Trade*, Tables 44 and 48, pp. 77 and 90.)
The last two columns of this table reminds us that the direction of balances of areas with the Rest of the World was frequently ambiguous in Hilgerdt's data. Doubtless this ambiguity explains why he only charted relations between five areas. Note that the pattern of balances among the first five areas was the same in 1938 as in 1928, except that the balance of the Tropics with Non-Continental Europe was reversed.

(we do not have a clear-cut measure of the balance between the U.K. and the Continent). The Tropics ran merchandise surpluses with all three centers, a departure from Hilgerdt's 1928 pattern for the U.K. but like 1938.

Taking account of services, transfers, capital, and gold transactions, we found that among countries grouped in a way approximating Hilgerdt's pattern the flow of multilateral settlements over the five years 1950–54 conformed in almost all respects to the prewar pattern for net trade (as it was then measured) and also in almost all respects to Chart 6. The latter similarity was studied in some detail and we can say that it is to be explained by three circumstances:

First, if peripheral areas are grouped as in Chart 6 or according to Hilgerdt's criterion, the pattern of multilateral settlements of these groups with the three centers (U.S., U.K., and Continental OEEC countries) is not usually typical of individual countries in each group but represents only a small minority.

Second, groupings do, however, include a majority of countries with balances directed, as the group's balance is directed, toward each center taken separately, irrespective of the direction of the balances with other centers.

Third, certain large countries (Canada in Regions of Recent Settlement and in Other Western Hemisphere countries, British Colonies in the Tropics and in the Rest of the Sterling Area, and Soviet Bloc in Other Countries in both groupings) exhibit the group pattern of settlements with the centers and tend to set it.[9]

The adjustments to allocate unallocated transactions in arriving at Table A-4 are, of course, reflected in the flow of multilateral settlements depicted in Chart 5. They had the effect of improving the extent of agreement between paired entries in the matrix of multilateral settlements in contrast to the effect of widening divergence in the net goods and services matrix (see Chapter 4, Section A-3). In no case was the direction of settlements between the six areas in panel vii of Chart 5 altered by the adjustment.

The largest net settlements appear to run from a peripheral area to the economic center with which most of the countries in the group traded principally. The large net receipts of the Continent from Overseas Territories and Other Countries include, however, the $3,542 million surplus in Continental OEEC accounts with own Overseas Territories (and $3,996 million deficit in the accounts of Overseas Territories with their Own Currency Area). It will be recalled (Chapter 3, Section D, especially footnote 17) that this margin is balanced largely by error representing the omission of investment income, government and miscellaneous services, transfers, and capital movements between France and her Overseas Territories. If we were able to introduce the omitted transactions into the account, in combination they probably would eliminate or greatly reduce the surplus favoring the Continent.

B. BILATERAL BALANCES, LIQUID ASSETS, AND MULTILATERAL SETTLEMENTS

The residual matrix of multilateral settlements of panel vii of Chart 5 has never before been constructed. Its meaning and significance must be explained. First, it should be related to the financial flows which are usually thought of as "settlements."

1. Problem of Measuring Surpluses and Deficits

Since in any payments account the total credit and debit entries of all types of transactions should be equal, apart from error, the concept of a "payments balance" implies a division of transactions into two types: those thought of as being in some sense "basic" and the remaining transactions financing them. The same kind of distinction is drawn when one speaks of placing certain transactions "above

the line" and others "below the line." The latter are usually thought of as liquid assets—foreign exchange reserves and gold. Settlement of a country's payments balance is then thought of as an accumulation or loss of liquid assets. Multilateral settlements of the kind given in panel vii of Chart 5 should, conceptually, compensate, and are usually taken for granted

---

[9] The same explanation was found to account for a similarity which could be observed between the circular flow of multilateral settlements in Chart 6 and the flow between countries grouped by trading orientation (with U.S.-oriented countries standing in place of Other Western Hemisphere countries and International Organizations, with sterling-oriented countries standing in place of the Rest of the Sterling Area, and with Continental-oriented countries standing in place of Continental Overseas Territories and Other Countries).

or ignored. Concern usually is with a country's over-all gain or loss of reserves.

Actually, of course, the basic payments balance in a country's account with any individual partner may be offset both by changes in the liquid asset position with the partner and by the use of multi-lateral settlements. If it is able to meet its payments balance with every partner solely through multilateral settlement transactions and with no change in liquid asset position, the country would be in over-all balance. Otherwise it will use some combination of liquid asset transactions and multilateral settlements.

To prepare a table showing the basic payments balances between areas would require a definition distinguishing transactions to be considered part of the basic balance of each country from those to be considered liquid reserve assets. It would require, further, that this definition be the same in partner accounts. Identification of transactions according to the definition would also be required. In this book we have been able to present a gold matrix which treats gold (monetary or nonmonetary) alike in all accounts (see Chapter 2, Section A-2, and footnote 15), but we have not been able to surmount the problems of presenting a matrix of liquid capital assets and liabilities. For reasons given in Chapter 2, a special study of capital transactions was found necessary to make it possible to distinguish changes in assets and liabilities of different types—long- and short-term, official and private, etc. With further progress in the identification of different types of capital transactions, it may be possible to construct a matrix of liquid reserves. But, at best, such a matrix must be constructed according to an arbitrary standard defining the particular types of capital flows which are counted as reserves. Such an arbitrary standard cannot help but violate some country's own view as to changes in its reserve position since the treatment of liquid reserves is not symmetrical in all country accounts.

We have seen that gold transactions, for example, are not the same to South Africa (nonmonetary) and the U.K. (monetary). Similarly, private short-term capital flows may create liquid liabilities to one country without providing liquid reserve assets for another.[10] Countries cast up their balance of payments accounts in ways designed to reveal the finan-

cial problems they may meet under different circumstances. A country with an exchange control, formal or otherwise, may count private short-term assets abroad as reserve assets; another without controls may consider them unavailable at times of crisis and exclude them from consideration. Holdings of different types of marketable securities may be treated differently by different countries, some including them in reserves, some not. The task of producing a usable and defensible matrix of capital reserves is formidable.[11] We have not attempted such a task, but we can indicate from the accounts of the two main currency reserve countries, the U.S. and the U.K., how the official treatment by those countries of liquid liabilities to foreigners relates to the corresponding "payments balance" each had with partner areas and how these balances were offset by combinations of changes in liquid assets and multilateral settlements.

2. Over-All Deficits of the U.S. and the U.K.

Table 8 (column 5) shows the change in liquid U.S. and U.K. liabilities to partner areas over the five years, according to official U.S. and U.K. publications, in comparison with their other capital transactions (column 3) derived from the records of liquid capital transactions and the net capital matrix on line 6 of Table A-4. A "payments balance" is also calculated in Table 8 by combining other (i.e., non-liquid) capital with the net goods, services, and transfers balances of the U.S. and the U.K. with partner areas from Table A-4. The resulting balance (column 4) equals the negative of the sum of the offsetting financing transactions—changes in liquid capital (column 5) and gold transactions (column 6) and multilateral settlements (column 8), the last two items also being drawn from Table A-4.

Both the U.S. and U.K. experienced over-all payments deficits (column 4), the U.S. to the huge amount of $10 billion, the U.K. about $800 million. Thus, both the U.S. and the U.K. on balance sold liquid assets to the rest of the world, and every other area gained liquid assets. The U.S. deficit was offset by increased dollar liabilities to other countries, gold sales, and over-all net error in the ratios 4:2:1. The U.K. deficit was not as large as the increased sterling liabilities since some of these were offset by increased

[10] See Poul Høst-Madsen "Asymmetries Between Balance of Payments Surpluses and Deficits," *Staff Papers of International Monetary Fund,* July 1962, p. 182, and Walter S. Salant, *et al., The United States Balance of Payments in 1968,* Washington, 1963, p. 4.

[11] For a discussion of these problems, see Walther Michael, "International Capital Movements: The Experience of the Early Fifties, 1950–54," unpublished Ph.D. dissertation, Columbia University, 1965.

TABLE 8

Balance of Payments of the United States and the United Kingdom,
by Partner Areas over the Five Years 1950–54

(million U.S. dollars)

Balance with	Goods and Services[a] (1)	Unilateral Transfers[a] (2)	Capital Other Than Liquid Assets[b] (3)	Balance on Preceding Items (Cols. 1 + 2 + 3)[c] (4)	Liquid Capital[d] (5)	Gold Transactions[a] (6)	Balance on Liquid Assets (Cols. 5+6) (7)	Multilateral Settlements and Error[a] (8)
A. BALANCES OF THE UNITED STATES								
All areas	12,557	−14,183	−8,438	−10,064	5,863	2,779	8,642	1,422
United Kingdom	404	−1,891	−14	−1,501	1	646	647	854
Rest of Sterling Area	401	−468	−986	−1,053	133	−69	64	989
Continental OEEC countries (incl. EPU)	3,080	−7,513	−104	−4,537	3,237	1,534	4,771	−234
Continental Overseas Territories	−470	−18	−56	−544	25	26	51	493
Canada	4,316	−25	−2,977	1,314	742	92	834	−2,148
International Organizations	140	−355	−512	−727	306	—	306	421
Latin America	3,152	−315	−2,470	367	603	293	896	−1,263
Other Countries	1,534	−3,598	−1,319	−3,383	816	257	1,073	2,310
B. BALANCES OF THE UNITED KINGDOM								
All areas	180	748	−1,740	−812	1,780	−1,200	580	232
Rest of Sterling Area	4,598	−413	−2,509	1,676	2,140	−1,312	828	−2,504
Continental OEEC countries (incl. EPU and Overseas Territories)	−2,953	−307	533	−2,727	60	785	845	1,882
United States	−601	1,615	466	1,480	250	−646	−396	−1,084
Canada	−1,133	2	−312	−1,443	60	—	60	1,383
International Organizations	−3	−118	−31	−152	−280	1	−279	431
Latin America	101	−6	258	353	−200	−32	−232	−121
Other Countries	171	−25	−145	1	−250	4	−246	245

[a] From Table A-4.
[b] Calculated from net capital shown in Table A-4 and liquid capital shown in col. 5.
[c] Col. 4 also equals, with signs reversed, the sum of cols. 5, 6, and 8.
[d] Increase in foreign liquid assets in the U.S. (or U.K.) or decrease in U.S. (or U.K.) foreign liquid liabilities. For the U.S. from lines so designated in the official payments statement, Survey of Current Business, Balance of Payments Supplement (1963); in this source "Western Europe" (including Finland, Spain, and Yugoslavia, 1952–54) approximates our Continental OEEC countries and "all other countries excluding sterling area" approximates our Continental Overseas Territories and Other Countries. To distinguish U.S. liquid capital transactions with Continental Overseas Territories, we have used the IMF Yearbook account of U.S. short-term liabilities and assets to and with foreign official agencies and banks (for 1951–52, Vol. 5, U.S., pp. 2–3; for 1953–54, Vol. 6, U.S., pp. 5–6). For 1950, we have taken the short-term liabilities to foreigners reported by banks in the 1963 Supplement cited above (Tables 78 and 79).

For the U.K., figures for liquid capital are monetary movements (U.K. Balance of Payments, 1946–57, Table 9, lines 13–16) after deducting $1,200 million of gold purchased; monetary movements with the dollar area have been attributed to the U.S. after deducting the amount shown for Canadian liquid capital accumulations with the Sterling Area as a whole. The latter are the short-term liability and asset changes shown in the IMF Yearbook accounts for Canada (Vol. 5, p. 15; Vol. 6, p. 1; and Vol. 7, p. 4). Since the dollar area also includes some Latin American and Other Countries, some of the monetary movements attributed to the U.S. may have been with them.

gold purchases which the U.K. made as trustee for the Sterling Area gold pool. Over-all net error in the U.K. account also provided a comparatively sizable offset to the U.K.'s payments deficit.

The incidence of over-all error in the two accounts is, of course, uncertain, but it is less likely to affect the U.S. and the U.K. records of liquid capital and gold transactions than their over-all payments balances. It is likely, therefore, that the latter are overstated by the amount of error. The way in which we have allocated U.K. gold sales may have introduced error into their regional distribution, and the residual regional distribution of multilateral settlements reflects both that error and error in the regional distribution of payments balances. In the following discussion we disregard the incidence of error and write as though the regional figures were precise, knowing full well that they are not and that it is only possible to make a general qualification for the incidence of error in the table.

At the same time as they accumulated liquid liabilities to other countries, both the U.S. and the U.K. invested heavily abroad: the U.S. to 85 per cent of its total payments balance; the U.K. to twice its total payments balance. The outflow of nonliquid capital (column 3 of Table 8) from the U.S. was considerably greater than its increased liquid capital liabilities and the outflow from the U.K. was about equal to the inflow of liquid capital. Thus, both the U.S. and the U.K. were in the position of borrowing short while lending or investing long.

The over-all payments deficits of both the U.S. and the U.K. were associated with net unilateral transfer debits which were large in comparison. The U.S. deficit was considerably exceeded by the total of its unilateral transfer debits (mainly foreign aid); the U.K. deficit was exceeded by the net unilateral transfers ($869 million) it made to countries outside the dollar area from which it received aid. Both the U.S. and the U.K. thus "gave away" their payments deficits and the corresponding accumulation of liquid assets by other countries. The U.K. giving, however, was associated with even larger aid received from the U.S. and could be said to have been made possible by U.S. giving.

Altogether, the U.S. and the U.K. accounts show net sales of liquid assets (column 7) to other countries totaling $9.2 billion, and in addition other countries and international institutions accumulated the gold that was newly mined during the five years and that did not go into the arts or hoarding. Total

(non-Soviet) world gold reserves increased $1.9 billion over the period.[12]

3. Continental European Surpluses

Of the liquid assets sold by the U.S. and the U.K., Continental OEEC countries (and the European Payments Union) acquired $5.6 billion, an amount about equal to the published increase in the gold and foreign exchange reserves by the area ($5.9 billion).[13] They bought gold from both the U.S. and the U.K., but their main accumulation of liquid capital was in dollar assets ($3.2 billion); their net increase in sterling assets was less than $100 million. Continental purchases of liquid assets from the U.S. and the U.K. were part of the offset in each case to the large payments surplus the Continent and associated territories ran with the two financial centers. Indeed, the deficits of the U.S. and the U.K. with the Continent and associated Overseas Territories represented half the total U.S. payments deficit and considerably exceeded the U.K. over-all deficit. The Continent not only invested all of its bilateral payments surplus with the U.S. in liquid assets, but its purchases of such assets (column 7) exceeded the surplus (column 4) by more than $200 million, an excess met by Continental earnings from other areas and easily covered, in particular, by the U.S. deficit and multilateral settlements payments to Continental Overseas Territories.

The relationship between the U.S. and Continental OEEC countries was the only one among those shown in Table 8 in which a partner area both ran a surplus with the U.S. (or the U.K.) and used earnings from other areas, as well as the surplus, to increase its purchases of liquid assets from the U.S. (or the U.K.). Since the U.S. and U.K. were the only financial centers of the non-Soviet world where other countries held significant reserves, a complete record of payments balances and liquid asset flows between world areas would be unlikely to show another such situation.

4. Main Multilateral Links

Except for the U.S.-Continental relationship, the payments balances of the U.S. and the U.K. with in-

---

[12] *International Financial Statistics, Supplement to 1963 /64 Issues,* p. iv. The total includes Russian gold sold to non-Soviet Bloc countries.

[13] *Ibid.,* pp. iii and iv, including gold held by the European Payments Union and the Bank for International Settlements.

dividual areas were mostly offset by multilateral settlements. A large part of what each area earned from or paid to the U.S. or the U.K. (including U.K. earnings from the U.S.) was linked to its payments position with third areas. Peripheral areas trading principally with the U.S. (Canada and Latin America) and with the U.K. (the Rest of the Sterling Area) transferred multilateral settlements earnings from third partners in excess of their need to meet their payments deficits with the associated center, and with the excess they accumulated liquid assets in the associated center (column 7). The accumulations of assets by the Rest of the Sterling Area in the U.K. and by Canada and Latin America in the U.S., each in the range of $800 to $900 million, accounted for a good part of the total accumulation of liquid assets outside the two centers.

Canada was almost equally in payments surplus with the U.K. and in deficit with the U.S., and its multilateral settlements receipts from the U.K. unquestionably went to meet its payments deficit with the U.S. At the same time the U.K. surplus with the U.S. was only a little more than its deficit with Canada, and it is plain that, through multilateral settlements, the U.K. used its payments surplus with the U.S. mainly to meet its payments deficit with Canada. (Indeed, a good part of U.S. official aid to the U.K. during these years was directly used to finance U.K. purchases of Canadian wheat.) Part of the U.K. surplus with the U.S. was also used to buy gold from the U.S.[14] The payments surpluses and deficits among the U.S., the U.K., and Canada were thus interrelated via multilateral settlements.

Whereas the U.K.'s payments surplus with the U.S. enabled it to meet a deficit with Canada, its payments surplus and liquid asset transactions with the Rest of the Sterling Area enabled it to cover a deficit with the Continent. At the same time the Continental surplus with the U.K. was used to meet its deficit with the Rest of the Sterling Area. Transactions between the Continental currency areas and the Sterling Area during these years were, in fact,

settled through the European Payments Union. The U.K. payments balance with the Rest of the Sterling Area was not a great deal larger than its gold purchases there (mainly newly mined and mostly from South Africa), and its multilateral settlements receipts from the Rest of the Sterling Area were not much more than the latter's accumulations of liquid claims in the U.K. Considering that the accumulation of the sterling balances over the period was in good part by British Colonies, the surpluses of the latter with third areas (notably the U.S. and primarily in the trade account) were a great help to the U.K. in financing its deficit with the Continent.[15] The Continent, looked at from its side, ran a deficit on the order of $3 billion with the Rest of the Sterling Area (Chart 5) and a surplus of some $2.5 billion with the U.K. (Table 8, column 4). Its purchases of gold from the U.K. amounted to about 30 per cent of its basic surplus with the U.K., but most of its surplus was available to meet its deficit with the Rest of the Sterling Area. Thus, the payments surpluses and deficits among the U.K., the Rest of the Sterling Area, and the Continent were related to each other through multilateral settlements, a vital fact underlying the European Payments Union.

Next to the Continental OEEC countries, Other Countries (including the war-damaged Asian countries) received the most U.S. aid in the period, enough to give the group a large payments surplus with the U.S. It used about a third of the surplus to accumulate liquid dollar claims and gold (column 7) and the remaining $2.3 billion to make multilateral settlements. In addition, although it was about in balance bilaterally with the U.K., it drew down sterling balances by $250 million to make multilateral settlements. These multilateral payments by Other Countries contributed some $1.3 billion to the multilateral receipts of the Continent over the period (Table A-4).

---

[14] The U.K. record appears to imply a sale of liquid capital to the U.S. although this does not appear to have occurred from the U.S. account. The U.K. is separately specified as a partner in the U.S. account, but the U.S. is not distinguished from the other dollar countries in the official U.K. account. It is possible that the $250 million of liquid capital shown in Table 8 as sold to the U.S. was sold rather to dollar countries in Latin America or the Eastern Hemisphere (see note d to Table 8).

[15] The account for British Colonies (which excludes British Arabian Gulf oil-source countries), shows the Colonies' deficit to be settled with the U.K. amounting to $0.8 billion and its surplus to be settled with the U.S. amounting to $1.8 billion. The group also had a surplus with the Continent but large deficits with Other Countries. The accumulation of sterling balances by the British Colonies has been studied by Ida Greaves (*The Colonial Sterling Balances*, Essays in International Finance, No. 20, Princeton, 1954) and by A. Hazelwood ("Colonial External Finance Since the War," *Review of Economic Studies*, 1953–54, Vol. XXI (1), No. 54 p. 31).

Latin America, like Other Countries, accumulated reserves in the U.S. while drawing down sterling balances, but, unlike Other Countries, its gain in dollar reserves came from multilateral receipts from countries other than the U.S. and the U.K. Table A-4 shows that these sources were largely Continental Overseas Territories—i.e., the Netherlands Antilles.[16]

Table 8 gives us only a partial view of the way in which payments balances between areas, movements in reserves, and multilateral settlements were interrelated. But since the U.S. and U.K. were the principal reserve centers, we can judge that payments balances in the other interarea relationships in Table A-4 (i.e., between Continental OEEC countries and peripheral areas and among the latter) are approximately measured by the balances for goods, services, transfers, and capital (panel v of Chart 5) and that liquid asset flows were not much more important than the gold flows alone. In these other relationships it is most likely, therefore, that the bilateral surpluses and deficits were predominantly offset by multilateral settlements rather than by the creation or extinction of liquid claims.

Another important feature of the record is that peripheral areas made up of countries oriented toward one or the other of the two reserve centers, the U.S. and U.K., accumulated exchange reserves in, or bought gold from, the center with which they traded principally, apparently "banking" earnings realized from other areas. One can readily see that at other times these peripheral areas would have to reverse the process and liquidate reserves in the associated center to settle payments deficits with third areas.

From this review of the additional information given in Table 8 it can be concluded that the multilateral settlements flows in Table A-4 were a reflection primarily of interarea payments balances but also of transfers of funds into and out of liquid assets in the two main reserve centers, and that, moreover, the U.K. served in this capacity mainly for the Rest of the Sterling Area and the U.S. for the world at large.

If one wishes to explore causal connections among payments balances, liquid asset flows, and multilateral settlements, one must look beyond the record of payments transactions to the private and public practices and policies affecting them. While multilateral settlements are necessarily calculated as a residual, they cannot be explained merely as the net effect of all other transactions. For example, one could scarcely assign a main causal role to the additions to the dollar and gold holdings of Canada and Latin America or to the sterling balances of the Rest of the Sterling Area during the period. These additions as well as the multilateral transfers accompanying them reflect rather these countries' payments surpluses with third countries. Multilateral settlements were an intermediate step in the accumulation of asset holdings, and more fundamental causes lay behind the emergent payments surpluses and the regime of financial practices which permitted such multilateral settlements to occur or even provided for financing them (e.g., by U.S. official aid).

C. MULTILATERALISM AND THE MEASUREMENT OF MULTILATERAL SETTLEMENTS

1. The Concept of Multilateralism

The concept of multilateralism in world trade is widely and loosely used to describe a trading system among countries by which they achieve a greater measure of specialization and greater gains from trade through selling and buying in the most favorable markets, irrespective of whether trade with any particular partner country or area is balanced. A multilateral system of trading contrasts with a bilateral system in which partners balance their trade with each other. Under a bilateral system, the necessity for limiting trade to exchanges which will just balance poses the same kind of difficulty to countries that barter does to individuals: it is difficult to find the trading partners with a set of demands exactly complementing one's own. Economic efficiency is served by a money economy in which specialization can develop, where output is sold for money, and money spent where supplies are cheapest. Multi-

[16] The Venezuelan account shows multilateral settlements earnings by Venezuela from Continental Overseas Territories of $3,244 million over the five years; the Netherlands Antilles account shows multilateral settlements payments to Latin America of $2,184 million for the same period. Venezuelan exports (mostly of petroleum) to the Netherlands Antilles were $3,049 million in the period. Petroleum product trade was evidently of major significance, and sales were heavily to the Continent.

lateralism in international trade is an extension of the fundamental freedom of choice provided by a market economy. The abandonment of bilateralism and the restoration of a multilateral system of trade and payments relations among nations have been two faces of a cornerstone of Western international economic policy in the postwar era.

Under a multilateral trading system, deficits which a country runs with some partners are offset by surpluses with other partners. Country *A* balances its deficits with partner *C* through a surplus on country *B*; *B* covers its deficit with *A* by its surplus on *C*; *C* meets its obligation to *B* by drawing on its surplus with *A*, closing the circuit.

This simplified view of multilateralism is generally expounded in terms of merchandise trade only. The textbook usually assumes that there are no capital flows, unilateral transfers, or gold payments; net merchandise trade patterns are equated with final multilateral settlements. Payments flows are thought of as running opposite to trade flows. In fact, of course, capital flows may offset some or all of the bilateral trade balances. Indeed, given the variability and dynamic character of world trade, such a system requires that its members be able and willing to take a long view and to finance temporary disparities by the use of reserves or borrowing rights—by liquid asset flows such as we studied in Table 8 above.

Textbooks do not usually treat this complexity, but in theory it is easily handled. International assets represent claims on future production. Capital flows represent intertemporal exchanges, trades of current for future production. So we then think of the balances after allowing for such exchanges. Unilateral transfers are of a different nature; they represent current production provided without giving rise to future claims. They, too, must be taken into account. The interarea balances then remaining must balance off in each country's account. While the over-all balance of each country account should be zero (apart from error), surpluses or deficits may exist with individual partners, and these offsetting balances constitute the element of multilateralism in world trade and payments.[17]

[17] Michael Michaely finds that this approach offers conceptual difficulties. Focusing on the bilateral or multilateral character of trade (including services), he is troubled by situations in which bilateral surpluses or deficits are offset by the accumulation or use of short-term assets: "One cannot, therefore, term these transactions as either 'bilateral' or 'multilateral' " ("Multilateral Balancing in International Trade," *American Economic Review*, Septem-

The multilateral character of international transactions was largely ignored in the textbooks until the pre-1913 gold standard system of international payments with multilateral clearing of transactions through London and New York was interrupted by World War I and by the mismanagement of domestic and international economic relations in the interwar period. The system of trading between countries became in the 1930's increasingly subject to government intervention. Quantitative restrictions, exchange controls, bilateral trade agreements, and clearing accounts proliferated. In these circumstances, efforts of each country to improve or to safeguard its position worked to shift burdens to other countries. World trade dwindled as each country in self-defense bought less from the others.

In an effort to show what had happened, the League of Nations published *The Network of World Trade* in 1942, describing how the whole world made up a trading system in which each country offset balances with partners in a multilateral network.[18]

ber 1962, p. 686). Situations in which bilateral trading balances are offset by long-term capital transfers he finds equally troublesome. Here he recognizes the possibility of taking the exchange of goods for financial assets into account and calls it bilateral between *A* and *B* if *B*'s loan to *A* finances *B*'s exports to *A* and calls it multilateral if the proceeds of *B*'s loan finances *A*'s imports of goods from *C* (*ibid.*, p. 687). He also finds conceptual difficulties where goods and services are offset by unilateral transfers.

One suspects that, if Michaely had had a more complete record, he would not have been so troubled by these "conceptual difficulties," nor would he have limited his analysis to country situations where the over-all (merchandise) trade account was close to balance (he is unable, in practice, to include services and so relies on merchandise figures). I see no conceptual difficulty in extending the notion of a trade to include exchanges of current production for claims on future production and consider that Michaely's arguments do not justify relying upon an inadequate record for his analysis. It will be plain from the matrixes in this book and in the underlying country accounts that services must not be ignored and that enough can be known about financial transactions between world areas to take them also into account. However, for an analysis of multilateralism between countries such as Michaely has attempted, the only available record distinguishing country partners is the merchandise (customs) record.

[18] "When the [League's] work started, . . . it was thought possible that the chief balances of trade might be accounted for by triangular or multilateral settlement within smaller groups of countries and that only minor balances might have served settlement among the groups. The fact that all but a few countries partook directly in a world-wide system of settlement naturally stresses the importance of international interdependence so frequently overlooked in the past." (Folke Hilgerdt, "The Case for Multilateral Trade," *American Economic Review*, March 1943, p. 394). The League's regional grouping of countries differs from that employed in our two-valued matrixes.

While the *Network* examined only the pattern of merchandise trade, the existence of other types of transactions was recognized. The merchandise figures were used because of their overwhelming importance and because "they give a clue to the manner in which payments on account of other transactions are settled."[19] However, not until now, when we have a record of transactions not only for merchandise trade but also for services and for the accompanying financial flows, has it been possible to develop quantitative data on the extent to which areas engaged in the multilateral compensation of surpluses and deficits.

2. Components of the Final Matrix of Multilateral Settlements

The multilateral settlements matrix emerges after we take account of all other types of transactions including offsetting flows of liquid assets. The close interplay between these flows of liquid assets and multilateral settlements has been observed a few pages above in connection with Table 8. It may seem, as it has to some, that one should try to produce a record of multilateral settlements before entering asset flows, especially flows of monetary reserves and other liquid capital, or that one should try in other ways to measure the particular contribution of, say, merchandise trade or merchandise trade and services to multilateral settlements. I believe that such an approach is based on a misconception and that the attempt to measure multilateral settlements, or the contribution to multilateral settlements, on a less aggregative basis than that employed here does not accord with reality and does not yield concepts susceptible of statistical measurement, at least in the present state of knowledge.

To examine the issue, let us first suppose that international transactions are limited to merchandise trade and that each country balances its over-all trade account, offsetting deficits with some partners by surpluses with others. Next, assume that this situation is changed by flows of capital accompanied by increased trade between each pair of countries. In each bilateral relation the flow of capital may be either greater or smaller than the change in merchandise trade. Bilateral balances (and multilateral settlements) are, therefore, changed from the initial situation but continue to offset each other, so that each country is in over-all balance.

The outcome, then, is a matrix of multilateral settlements combining (a) the initial multilateralism in merchandise trade when there were no capital flows and (b) the additional element of multilateralism introduced by capital flows and the associated changes in merchandise trade. To extend this hypothetical example, we could also distinguish a multilateral element in unilateral transfers as the sum (having regard for sign) of such transfers and the associated changes in trade between paired countries. And we could similarly distinguish services from merchandise, and liquid claims and gold from other assets. Then we could say that the final matrix of multilateral settlements was the sum of the initial multilateralism in trade alone and the additional elements of multilateralism introduced by each new component.

Note, however, that in the example given the inter-area pattern of merchandise trade balances with capital flows differs from that prevailing before capital flows were introduced. And so it is as each new component alters the previous pattern of settlements not only by the new component itself but also by its effect on other components. In the real world, therefore, we cannot determine the contribution of any one component to multilateral settlements without knowing how it has been affected by other components of the final matrix.

A similar statement can be made about attempts to measure the element of multilateralism in a matrix combining all types of transactions down to a line which excludes certain balancing items. Some writers have been interested in the pattern of multilateral payments on such a basis. Frisch, for example, was concerned with a multilateral balance of payments on all transactions except the transfer of liquid means of payment; Ekker was prepared to consider the equilibrium component within a system defined with reference to the European Payments Agreement of 1948 in which certain payments were left outside the clearing arrangement.[20] Both of these writers

[19] *Ibid.*, p. 393. Several writers on multilateral trade have used the term trade analytically in a sense broader than merchandise but, in the absence of a quantitative record for other transactions, they drew for illustration on Hilgerdt's work or other merchandise trade figures. Cf. Ragner Frisch, "On the Need for Forecasting a Multilateral Balance of Payments," *American Economic Review,* September 1947, pp. 535 ff.; M. H. Ekker, "Equilibrium of International Trade and International Monetary Compensations," *Weltwirtschaftliches Archiv,* Vol. 64, No. 2, 1950; Karl-Erik Hansson, "A General Theory of the System of Multilateral Trade," *American Economic Review,* March 1952 pp. 58 ff.

[20] See footnote 19 above.

worked with a record of merchandise trade only. If they had had a full accounting and had sought to set forth the multilateralism of the matrix of transactions down to the line they drew, they would have been confronted with the necessity of trying to infer it from a record which at most gave the final multilateral settlements after taking account of liquid assets and the other types of transactions they wanted to exclude. They would have had to ask how the system of payments flows would have looked if there had been no liquid asset flows, and this would have involved introducing a functional relationship between such financing and the other types of transactions.

This is equivalent to asking how different the matrix of multilateral settlements in panel vii of Chart 5 would have been *if* there had been no gold transactions or no liquid capital asset flows. The answer must depend on how the whole set of accounts would have been affected by a different historical set of conditions and decisions. Would Continental countries have spent the proceeds, which they used to buy assets from the U.S., for more goods and services in the U.S.? Or in other countries? Would such an effort have bid up world prices and effected trading balances between other areas? Would the U.S. have extended less aid? Would more European capital have been invested in the U.S. over the long term? Would exchange rates have been altered? And so on. To ask such questions emphasizes the theoretical character of "elements of multilateralism" for any part of the whole.

The only way we could hope to measure these elements in the system contributing to the multilateralism of the final matrix after all types of transactions—i.e., the only way we could resolve the final multilateral matrix into components attributable to multilateralism in merchandise, services, transfers, etc. —would be to know the functional relationships between changes in one type of transaction and changes in the others. We would need to be able to say what the trade matrix would look like in the absence of asset flows and how asset flows would alter it. This we cannot say in our present state of knowledge about international economic life.

Moreover, in my opinion the effort to resolve the final matrix of multilateralism into such components in order to isolate a basic element of multilateralism, say, in goods and services trade or in merchandise trade alone, is not a fruitful exercise. The theoretical justification for seeking such an element of multilateralism lies in the desire to observe how economic specialization in international economic life and the division of labor among countries is working out. Now the division of labor among countries and economic specialization relevant to the real world goes beyond specialization in the current production of goods and services. It includes specialization in the supply of savings for investment; it may include, in the case of the United States, the function of providing a currency capable of serving as a reserve medium for other countries; for the U.K., it would also include buying gold newly produced in South Africa and selling it to hoarders on the Continent; it even includes the function assumed in the postwar period by the better-off countries of subsidizing the purchasing power of poorer countries in the interest of creating a better world. In short, the character of specialization and the division of labor which is interesting is the one which encompasses all the transactions in the full set of payments accounts.

3. Amount of Multilateral Settlements

The matrix on line 8 of Table A-4 is a statistical expression of the element of multilateralism in payments relations among the eight world areas and supplementary accounts distinguished in the table. Except for error, credit and debit entries on that line for each area would be exactly offsetting. The amount of multilateral settlements in the eight-area system would then be given by the sum of all credit entries or, equally, by the sum of all debit entries.

The result of summing credits and debits for each area in the matrix is given in Table 9. Since the record is imperfect, the sums of credits and debits are not equal. Interarea credits in the consolidated five-year record totaled $37.2 billion and interarea debits $33.4 billion. The difference, $3.8 billion, is accounted for by $1.5 billion of intra-area balances (which should be zero) and $2.3 billion of over-all error. The last figure is larger than the $29 million given in the tables in Chapter 3 because of the adjustments made to allocate unallocated transactions and reconcile the gold account.

The biggest errors in the record affecting the settlements matrix are those noted in footnote 1 of this chapter. It seems likely that a more complete accounting of transactions between France and her Overseas Territories would result in a multilateral

TABLE 9
Offsetting of Credit and Debit Balances in
Interarea Settlements over the Five Years 1950–54
(*million U.S. dollars*)

Balance Reported by	Over-All Balance[a] (1)	Intra-Area Balance (2)	Balances with Partner Areas	
			Sum of Net Debits (3)	Sum of Net Credits (4)
United Kingdom	232		-3,967	4,199
Rest of Sterling Area	-15	-697	-4,251	4,933
Cont. OEEC countries	-2,644	-1,252	-6,798[b]	5,406
Overseas Territories	4,161	5	-2,397	6,553[b]
EPU	98		-290	388
United States	1,422		-3,645	5,067
Canada	-5		-3,357	3,352
Internat. Organiz.	0		-1,156	1,156
Latin America	-680	387	-4,139	3,072
Other Countries	-290	28	-3,390	3,072
Total	2,279	-1,529	-33,390	37,198

SOURCE: Table A-4, line 8.
[a] Sum of columns 2, 3, and 4.
[b] Balance with Own Currency Area counted separately.

settlements record closer to the smaller of the two sums in each account. It is not clear how correcting the error in the Continental OEEC account represented by the intra-area settlement debit (offsetting an over-all excess of credits in the account) would affect interarea balances, nor what the incidence of the other errors in the accounting would be.

The calculation in Table 9 has been made from the consolidated account for the whole five years. The same kind of calculation made for each of the five years (but using Table B-28 in which unallocated transactions remain unallocated) showed a total of interarea net debits of $37.7 billion and credits of $43.6 billion, indicating that intertemporal offsetting within area accounts was on the order of $5 billion over the period. Another calculation for peripheral area countries, grouped homogeneously according to their pattern of incurring surpluses or deficits to be settled with the U.S., the U.K., and Continental OEEC countries, over the whole five years gave totals for interarea credits and debits $10 billion larger than can be observed from Table A-4.[21]

[21] Total credits and debits with the three centers came to $25.5 billion and –$20.3 billion, respectively, compared with $14.6 billion and –$10.7 billion summed up from Table A-4. In both sums (and as well the sums in Table

Evidently, even larger totals for international balances to be settled multilaterally could be obtained if country accounts could be elaborated by partner country rather than by partner area.[22]

The total of multilateral settlements within the eight-area matrix over the five years, a figure on the order of $35 billion, can be compared to the total of interarea trade in goods and services (excluding intra-area trades) which amounted over the five years to $393 billion, taking the mean of lines A and B in Table A-1. Thus, multilateral settlements were about 9 per cent of gross trade in goods and services. This comparison has a limited meaning since the

9) the balances to be settled within their Own Currency Area by Continental OEEC countries and by Continental Overseas Territories have been distinguished and International Organizations have been included as a peripheral area (but the European Payments Union account has been excluded since it is essentially a mechanism for providing capital accomodation and for making settlements between economic centers).

[22] Another measure of multilateral settlements could be derived from Table A–4, line 8, by taking the mean of each set of paired entries in the two-valued matrix. Since one record is a credit entry in the matrix and the other a debit entry, and since each entry is entered in either column 3 or column 4 of Table 9, the result of such a calculation would necessarily be the mean of the totals of columns 3 and 4, or $35 billion.

flow of multilateral settlements is related to all types of interarea transactions, not just to trade.

Even so, a comparison over a period of years of the way the sum of credits or debits in the multilateral settlements matrix developed in relation to gross trade might help to show whether multilateralism was increasing or decreasing. As further discussed below, however, the more important use of data such as those developed here showing the pattern of multilateral settlements is in providing a better basis for judgments about economic and financial interrelationships and how they are affected by policy changes.

4. Significance of the Multilateral Settlements Network

Apart from limitations of measurement, to be discussed below, the record we have of multilateral settlements is of significance primarily for the light it sheds on the circular flow of purchasing power underlying international economic relations and for the

expression it gives to the existing economic interdependence of world areas. One such expression was observed above in Table 8 where the basic balances of the U.S. and U.K. with partner areas were shown to be offset by various combinations of liquid asset flows and multilateral settlements. This kind of examination indicates the extent to which particular bilateral relationships were dependent upon multilateralism in the system in the broadest sense. The existence of such a dependence and the pattern of interdependence to which it is related have often been overlooked. Few have appreciated the significance of offshore purchases by Europe in other parts of the world financed by Marshall Plan Aid in strengthening the ability of third areas to buy in the U.S. during the 1950–54 period. The multilateral settlements matrix, while not measuring this particular element of multilateralism in U.S. aid, does reflect it.

Not many observers and analysts of the negotiations between the U.K., the countries of the European Common Market, and other Continental countries are aware of the underlying circular flow of

TABLE 10

Distribution of Nonsterling EPU Countries by Pattern of Balances to Be Settled with Nonsterling EPU Area, U.S., and Sterling Area, over the Five Years 1950–54 [a]

With Nonsterling EPU Area [b]	With U.S.	With Sterling Area	
		Plus	Minus
Plus	Minus	Netherlands [c]	Belgium [c] W. Germany [c]
	Plus	Belgium Congo [d]	France [c] Surinam [d] Portug.OT's [d]
Minus	Minus	Denmark Switzerland Sweden French OT's [d]	Austria Portugal
	Plus	Norway Italy [c]	Greece Turkey

SOURCE: Country accounts, NBER files.

[a] Nonsterling EPU countries listed do not include the Netherlands Antilles.

[b] Balances with nonsterling EPU partner area exclude transactions within Continental currency areas (see Chapter 2, Section 2, A-1, for discussion of grouping countries).

[c] European Common Market countries.

[d] Overseas Territories of Common Market countries.

TABLE 11
Balances to Be Settled Multilaterally by Nonsterling
EPU Subgroups with the Sterling Area and Nonsterling
EPU Area, over the Five Years 1950–54
(*million U.S. dollars*)

	Sterling Area	Nonsterling EPU Area (Other's Currency Areas)
Six Common Market countries	−800	2,265[a]
Overseas Territories of Common Market countries (excl.Netherlands Antilles)	226	252[a]
Total Common Market countries	−574	2,517
Scandinavian countries and Switzerland	1,337	−2,189
Austria, Greece, Turkey, Portugal and its Overseas Territories	−475	−542

SOURCE: Country accounts, NBER files.
[a] Excludes balances within Continental currency areas (e.g., excludes balance of France with rest of franc area and of French Overseas Territories with France).

multilateral settlements linking them.[23] Examination of country accounts underlying the multilateral settlements matrix for 1950–54 shows that Continental OEEC countries and their Overseas Territories were distributed according to the direction of their balances to be settled with the U.S., the Sterling Area, and the non sterling EPU area, as in Table 10. Balances to be settled multilaterally by the several parts of the nonsterling EPU area over the five years with the Sterling Area and the nonsterling EPU area can be seen in Table 11.

A striking feature of the Common Market is the way in which it drew a line between Continental countries in surplus with the Continent and those in deficit. Except for Italy and French Overseas Territories, the Common Market group lies in the upper bank of countries in Table 10 and includes all countries in the nonsterling EPU area which ran surpluses with that area except Portuguese Overseas Territories. The Common Market group as a whole was heavily in surplus with the rest of the Continent and substantially in deficit with the Sterling Area. The sterling deficit reflected the preponderance of Belgian, French, and German positions—Italy, Netherlands, the Belgian Congo, and French Overseas Territories had sterling surpluses.

[23] The six Continental countries of the European Common Market are Belgium-Luxembourg, France, Italy, Netherlands, and West Germany.

In the years prior to the crystallization of the Common Market trading arrangement, the circular flow of multilateral settlements within the EPU was from the Sterling Area to Scandinavia and Switzerland, from there to the Common Market countries, and then back to the Sterling Area. Negotiations over the best way to organize economic relations were conducted against the backdrop of these relations. The countries that ultimately joined up with the U.K. in a free trade area were heavily in surplus with the Sterling Area. The Common Market country that most strongly supported British participation in the Common Market (the Netherlands) was also heavily in surplus with the Sterling Area (to the extent of $1,013 million over the five years; Italy's surplus was much less, $210 million). France, Belgium, and West Germany all ran sterling deficits.

The "paradoxical" apprehensions of the Swiss and Scandinavians over the "direct consequences" of the Common Market movement untempered by the broader arrangement for a free trade area become understandable.[24] Already in deficit to the Common

[24] "What Future for *EPU*," *London Economist*, May 24, 1958, p. 715. About these apprehensions, the *Economist* observed further:
"They have been quick to point out that they buy more from the six common market countries than they sell to them; therefore, they say, they provide the common market as a whole with currencies which its members can spend freely elsewhere. They are not keen on supporting a system

TABLE 12

*Balances of Sterling Area Subgroups to Be Settled Multilaterally with
Nonsterling EPU Area Subgroups, over the Five Years 1950–54*
(*million U.S. dollars*)

	Sterling Area Report	Partner's Report
U.K. balance with:		
Continent	-1,482	-1,579
Continental Overseas Territories	-658	-765
European Payments Union	258	262
Rest of Sterling Area balance with:		
Continent	3,022	2,803
Continental Overseas Territories	-159	-213
European Payments Union	10	6
Sum of pluses	3,290	3,071
Sum of minuses	-2,298	-2,557
Balance of Sterling Area	991	514

SOURCE: Table A-4.

Market countries, the Continental countries of the European Free Trade Area saw in the Common Market development the prospect that the deficit would increase under the impact of discrimination.

Another eddy in the world-wide circular flow of multilateral settlements is helpful in understanding the British attitude toward trade with the Soviet Bloc. The pattern of multilateral settlements in the payments account of the Soviet Bloc with the free world shows a large Soviet deficit with the Rest of the Sterling Area met by net receipts from the U.K. The account about balanced with the whole Sterling Area. A mutuality of interest among parties to the triangular relationship is apparent (in spite of deficiencies in the account).[25]

of multilateral payments through EPU which would be conspicuously to the advantage of the common market countries, and even less keen on the tariff discrimination that the common market, they fear, will exert against them."

[25] The account also shows sizable net credits realized, apparently, from the U.S. and Canada covering deficits of the Soviet Bloc with the Continent, Latin America, and Other Countries. It is necessary to say "apparently" for some of the dollar earnings were actually realized in the first instance by middlemen. The U.S. account of trade with the Soviet Bloc shows imports of goods *originating* in the Bloc, and some of the goods in question came to the U.S. indirectly via middlemen mainly in Europe and the Far East. See *World-Wide Enforcement of Strategic Trade Controls,* Third Report to Congress on the Mutual Defense Assistance Control Act of 1951, Washington, 1953, p. 87.

A further interesting feature of the multilateral settlements flow and one of some practical importance is the way in which an economic center and its affiliated areas ran opposing balances with other centers and their affiliates so that the net amounts settled between currency areas were greatly reduced. The multilateral settlements matrix in Table A-4, line 8, shows settlements between components of the sterling and nonsterling EPU areas. Net earnings of the Sterling Area from the nonsterling EPU area of between $500 and $1,000 million over the 1950–54 period were the net of much larger gross balances to be settled, as can be seen from the details in Table 12.

It is more difficult to observe the similar offsetting of balances between European currency areas and the dollar area since we do not have countries grouped in a dollar area. But if we take the U.S., Canada, and International Organizations as a first approximation, then balances with partner areas to be settled can be seen in Table 13. The offsetting of balances with parts of the Sterling Area is particularly striking.

If the calculations had been made from the underlying country accounts, the offsetting of balances within currency areas would, of course, be seen to be considerably greater than appears from Tables 12 and 13.

TABLE 13
Balances of U.S., Canada, and International Organizations to
Be Settled Multilaterally with the Sterling Area and
Nonsterling EPU Area, over the Five Years 1950–54
(*million U.S. dollars*)

	Sterling Area		Nonsterling EPU Area (+EPU)	
	Own Report	Partner's Report	Own Report	Partner's Report
U.S. balance with center	−854	−1,084	114	−77
Canada's balance with center	1,260	1,383	1,461	933
Balance of International Organizations with center	582	431	253	243
U.S. balance with affiliates	−989	−781	−493	−286
Canada's balance with affiliates	146	159	−8	−27
Balance of International Organizations with affiliates	−377	−327	−40	−40
U.S. balance with EPU			120	120
Sum of pluses	1,988	1,973	1,948	1,296
Sum of minuses	−2,220	−2,192	−541	−430
Balance of U.S., Canada, and International Organizations	−232	−219	1,407	866

Source: Table A-4.

5. Statistical Limitations to the Multilateral Settlements Matrix

So far in the discussion of the meaning and significance of the matrix of multilateral settlements we have ignored a real and serious problem of measuring the flow of settlements while concentrating on conceptual matters which are, of course, to be distinguished from problems of measurement. The problem relates to the difficulty we have had of measuring the true direction of transactions. For example, if adjustments were made to channel petroleum through the U.S. and the U.K., the extent of offsetting of surpluses and deficits with parts of the Sterling Area would be considerably reduced.

It was stated in Chapter 2 that, conceptually, the record of transactions between world areas should show direction according to the assigned residence of transactors to each transaction. This implies that the fact of a transaction and the residence of parties to it are known. We discussed in Chapter 4 a major departure from this principle in the case of middlemen transactions, notably, those relating to world trade in petroleum. Accounting conventions were adopted to secure a consistent treatment of these and some other transactions (e.g., the direction of esti-

mated freight payments). The final matrix of multilateral settlements reflects such conventions. Although, conceptually, panel vii of Chart 5 should state the flow of multilateral settlements between areas, in fact it states what the flow would have been if the movement of petroleum from country of source to destination had been matched by a transaction between a resident in the source country and one in the destination country. Actually, petroleum drawn from wells, for example, in Saudi Arabia, was sold by the company resident there (which includes local government representatives on its board of directors) to American parent companies resident in the U.S. These in turn marketed the oil throughout the world. Our accounts in Appendixes A and B show the oil "sold" by Saudi Arabia to the country to which it was consigned. The pattern of transactions in this and most other instances of petroleum trade differs greatly from the physical flow of oil. Both sets of facts are of significance but of different meaning. It is relevant to international economic life that the oil going to Western Germany comes, say, from Saudi Arabia; it is also relevant that it is marketed by a company resident in the U.S. If the realities of the division of labor among countries are to be respected, both facts must be recognized. The same observation applies to the other kinds of middleman transactions discussed in Chapter 4, Section A-3.

Now countries do not particularly like to publicize the extent to which they conduct the trade of other countries. Some payments accounts obscure the extent and character of "offshore" merchandise trade. Such trade is simply netted out in the published accounts, for example, of the U.K. and the Netherlands, and the published account for British Colonies simply omits Hong Kong. Further study of the actual conduct of trade in the major bulk commodities subject to the intervention of middlemen would be needed to correct the multilateral settlements matrix to a purchase-sales basis. Unadjusted, it is conventional, giving an account to be understood in terms of: "It is as if payments flows followed the reverse direction of the recorded movements of trade."

I see no technical obstacle to doing the handful of studies of the conduct of bulk commodity trades required to account for most of the 15 per cent or so of world trade subject to middleman transactions. The special study made of petroleum transactions (Appendix C) illustrates the kind of study required. When sufficient recognition is given to the importance of measuring the international flow of multilateral settlements more accurately, I have no doubt that such studies will be undertaken and that it will then be possible to observe both the interarea flow of goods and the related (somewhat different) interarea flow of payments. Our knowledge of the role of the financial centers in the conduct of international economic relations will be more precise. For now we must recognize that the matrix of multilateral settlements arrived at from our account of all other transactions is limited and subject to uncertainty because the merchandise record and some other types of transactions have not been adjusted systematically for middleman activity.

From the work we have done on petroleum transactions we are able to show in panel viii of Chart 5 the extent to which the conventional treatment of petroleum affects the final matrix. Channeling petroleum transactions through the U.K. and the U.S. results in altering the size, but not the sign, of balances between centers and peripheral areas. It increases the surplus of Other Western Hemisphere countries with the U.K., the surplus of the Rest of the Sterling Area and Overseas Territories and Other Countries

with the U.S., and the deficit of Overseas Territories and Other Countries with the Continent. Deficits of the Continent with areas composed of countries trading principally with the U.S. and the Sterling Area and of the U.K. with Overseas Territories and Other Countries are reduced by the adjustment. The balance between the U.K. and the Continent swings around to favor the U.K., and the balance between the U.S. and the U.K. becomes ambiguous—either approximately zero in the adjusted U.S. record or favoring the U.K. in the U.K. account.

Our previous speculation (Chapter 4, Section A-2) on the likely effect of adjusting other merchandise items to reflect the extent to which they come under the control of middlemen, especially in the economic centers, can also be considered in relation to the pattern of balances to be settled multilaterally in panels vii and viii of Chart 5. From our previous analysis we may guess that the export trade of peripheral areas to partners other than the economic center with which they trade principally tended to be channeled through that center rather more heavily than their imports were so channeled. The deficits shown by peripheral areas with the center placed directly above them were likely, on a purchase-sales basis, to have been smaller than shown in the diagrams, and their surpluses with the other two economic centers were also likely to have been smaller. It is difficult to guess how the middleman activities of the U.S., the U.K., and the Continent affected the balances among these centers, but my guess is that on middleman account, apart from petroleum, the U.S. and the U.K. would earn from the Continent and the U.K. from the U.S.

If the record were adjusted for the extent to which intermediaries control the sale of products between country of origin and country of destination, there would probably be smaller balances between centers and between centers and peripheral areas than panel viii of Chart 5 shows and a smaller total of multilateral settlements.

In addition to the limitations placed on the multilateral settlements matrix by the accounting conventions used, as the final balancing matrix it reflects all other deficiencies in recording transactions of all types. Those mentioned in footnote 1 of this chapter are the most significant.

In view of all we know about the accounts, we must emphasize that the pattern of multilateral settlements given in panel vii of Chart 5 is subject to

TABLE 14

Three-Area, Four-Area, and Five-Area Consolidations
of Two-Valued Matrixes over the Five Years 1950–54

(million U.S. dollars)

Balance of \ Balance with	All Areas (1)	United States (2)	Western Europe (3)	THIRD AREAS Total (4)	Other Western Hemisphere[a] (5)	Other Eastern Hemisphere[b] Total (6)	RSA & OT's (7)	Other Countries (8)
A. NET GOODS AND SERVICES								
All areas	-3,097	-15,913	-1,152	13,968	1,927	12,041	9,808	2,233
United States	12,557	—	3,484	9,073	7,608	1,465	-69	1,534
Western Europe	2,238	-2,990	1,322	3,906	-1,328	5,234	3,975	1,259
Third areas	-17,892	-12,923	-5,958	989	-4,353	5,342	5,902	-560
Other Western Hemisphere	-5,438	-10,293	1,083	3,772	-367	4,139	2,792	1,347
Other Eastern Hemisphere	-12,454	-2,630	-7,041	-2,783	-3,986	1,203	3,110	-1,907
Rest of Sterling Area and Overseas Territories	-9,074	-231	-5,185	-3,658	-2,502	-1,156	749	-1,905
Other Countries	-3,380	-2,399	-1,856	875	-1,484	2,359	2,361	-2
B. NET UNILATERAL TRANSFERS, CAPITAL, AND GOLD								
All areas	818	13,647	1,322	-14,151	-5,212	-8,939	-4,598	-4,341
United States	-13,979	—	-4,104	-9,875	-4,618	-5,257	-1,413	-3,844
Western Europe	76	4,031	23	-3,978	-1,214	-2,764	-2,533	-231
Third areas	14,721	9,616	5,403	-298	620	-918	-652	-266
Other Western Hemisphere	6,123	4,971	2,040	-888	-39	-849	-548	-301
Other Eastern Hemisphere	8,598	4,645	3,363	590	659	-69	-104	35
Rest of Sterling Area and Overseas Territories	4,928	1,298	3,055	575	517	58	-3	61
Other Countries	3,670	3,347	308	15	142	-127	-101	-26
C. NET MULTILATERAL SETTLEMENTS AND ERROR								
All areas	2,279	2,266	-170	183	3,285	-3,102	-5,210	2,108
United States	1,422	—	620	802	-2,990	3,792	1,482	2,310
Western Europe	-2,314	-1,041	-1,345	72	2,542	-2,470	-1,442	-1,028
Third areas	3,171	3,307	555	-691	3,733	-4,424	-5,250	826
Other Western Hemisphere	-685	5,322	-3,123	-2,884	406	-3,290	-2,244	-1,046
Other Eastern Hemisphere	3,856	-2,015	3,678	2,193	3,327	-1,134	-3,006	1,872
Rest of Sterling Area and Overseas Territories	4,146	-1,067	2,130	3,083	1,985	1,098	-746	1,844
Other Countries	-290	-948	1,548	-890	1,342	-2,232	-2,260	28

SOURCE: Table A-4 (all transactions allocated and the gold account reconciled).
a Canada, Latin America, and International Organizations.
b Rest of the Sterling Area, Overseas Territories, and Other Countries.

considerable error; at most only direction and order of magnitude can be relied upon and these may be suspect when the balances are close to zero.

6. Three-Area, Four-Area, and Five-Area Consolidations of the Two-Valued Matrix

Confronted with a set of consolidated accounts for countries grouped in one way, one wonders how the pattern observed depends on the way in which countries have been grouped. We can answer this question by considering three-area, four-area, and five-area consolidations of the two-valued matrixes in Appendix A.

A three-area consolidation of Appendix A accounts to show the triangular relations between the U.S., Western Europe, and the rest of the world (third areas) is ambiguous in the circular flow of final multilateral settlements (Table 14). The entries drawn from both sides for goods, transfers, and capital flows between the three areas agree on direction and broad order of magnitude (to within 50 per cent of the mean of paired entries), but the entries for the balance after gold agree only between the U.S. and Western Europe. All three areas show deficits between the two centers and third areas.

This ambiguity, however, does not appear in the four-area grouping in which third areas are elaborated to distinguish areas made up largely of countries oriented in trade with the U.S., on the one hand, and with Western Europe, on the other. When the rest of the world is divided along hemispheric lines, a clear and unambiguous circular flow of net multilateral settlements can be observed with paired entries agreeing on both direction and magnitude of the interarea balances. Both centers realized net credits from the rest of their hemisphere and incurred net debits with peripheral countries in the other hemisphere; the U.S. ran net debits with Western Europe; and Eastern Hemisphere peripheral areas ran net

debits with those of the Western Hemisphere. A contrast also now appears in Western Europe's trade balance between peripheral countries of the East and West.

The contrast in the patterns of balances for the three-area and four-area groupings argues strongly against using the three-area scheme in analyses of international trade and payments relations.[26] Four areas are needed to disclose the opposing relations between the two centers and the two sets of peripheral countries trading principally with them.

By distinguishing peripheral countries affiliated with Western Europe from Other Eastern Hemisphere countries we arrive at a five-area grouping intermediate between the four-area grouping previously considered and the six-area grouping of Chart 5. This five-area consolidation may usefully be compared with another five-area grouping in Table A-4, namely, that combining the U.K. with the Rest of the Sterling Area into the Sterling Area, combining Continental OEEC countries with their Overseas Territories into the nonsterling EPU area, combining U.S. with Canada and International Organizations, and distinguishing Latin America and Other Countries. Comparison of the two five-area groupings shows how the divergence between paired entries in the record is widened when peripheral countries are disassociated from the metropolitan area with which they trade principally. Total divergence in the matrix of multilateral settlements was larger by three-quarters in the five-area grouping with affiliated areas distinguished than in the five-area matrix employing the two European currency areas. Moreover, the magnitudes of multilateral settlements in the five-area system combining metropolitan centers with affiliates were considerably smaller than in the five-area grouping distinguishing affiliates, which reflects the tendency for centers and affiliates to run opposing balances with partner areas as discussed above.

D. STRUCTURE AND MOVEMENT OF FINANCIAL FLOWS: THE ANNUAL RECORD

The annual matrixes in Tables B-3 and B-25 through B-28 permit examination of (a) the extent to which yearly financial flows deviate from the patterns we have observed in charting the five years as a whole;

(b) the extent of agreement between paired entries on direction and order of magnitude of the interarea

[26] As, for example, was attempted in the Brookings study by Salant *et al.*, *United States Balance of Payments in 1968*.

financial flows each year and of their change from year to year; and (c) systematic variations from year to year in the pattern of multilateral settlements around the world.[27]

1. Stability of Direction in Trade Balances and in Financial Flows Between Areas

The annual pattern of goods and services balances between areas on the whole was stable over the five years, but exhibited reversals from year to year where balances were small or subject to strong growth tendencies. We thus can say that the pattern given by the five-year totals was the pattern occurring most frequently. This can also be seen in the more detailed eight-area tables of Appendix B.

Similar observations can be made about stability in the pattern presented by annual net financial transactions. Table 15 shows a count of balances agreeing and disagreeing with the direction of the balance for the whole five-year period.[28] We see that, for net goods and services, nearly 90 per cent of all annual balances and of annual balances of $10 million or more were in the same direction as the balance for the five years as a whole, and that all transfers of $10 million or more went in the direction of the five-year total.

Capital flows were less regular; about 30 per cent of the time the annual balance was opposite to the five-year direction, and among capital movements of $10 million or more such opposite flows occurred about one time in four.[29] Among the fifty-three in-

TABLE 15

Stability of Direction of Trade and Financial Balances in Annual Matrixes, over the Five Years 1950–54

(number of interarea balances not zero)

	Goods and Services	Transfers	Capital	Gold	Settle-ments
All balances not zero	356	267	263	166	405
Direction same as 5-year total	315	255	188	147	353
Direction opposite to 5-year total	41	12	75	19	52
Balances of $10 million and over	311	153	206	106	363
Direction same as 5-year total	277	153	153	93	322
Direction opposite to 5-year total	34	0	53	13	41
Balances of under $10 million	45	114	57	60	42
Direction same as 5-year total	38	102	35	54	31
Direction opposite to 5-year total	7	12	22	6	11

Source: Appendix B tables.

Note: This tabulation includes balances for bilateral relations as reported by both partners. Intra-area balances have been excluded since they should have been zero.

The number of entries for net settlements is greater than that for net goods and services because the EPU account does not figure in the net goods and services matrix. Settlements in the EPU account were, understandably, the most variable of any account (only eight cases of $10 million or more were in the direction of the five-year total while six were in the opposite direction).

[27] It will be recalled that, in contrast to the matrix tables of Appendix A for the five years, the annual tables in Appendix B have not been adjusted to allocate unallocated transactions or to reconcile the gold matrix. In comparing annual patterns with those previously considered based on Appendix A, allowance must be made for those adjustments.

[28] We have distinguished in the count balances of less than $10 million, which is certainly smaller than the element of error. The few zero balances were excluded altogether.

[29] Three flows of $10 million or more were opposite to the five-year direction three out of the five years—the U.K. with the EPU, the Continent with Latin America (according to the Continent), and Latin America with Other Countries (according to Latin America).

CHART 7
Annual Financial Balances Between World Areas, 1950–54: Six-Area
Consolidation of the Two-Valued Matrix
(arrow points from area debited to area credited; figures are placed adjacent to
area of report; entries in boxes are the area's over-all balances)
(million U.S. dollars)

A. Net Transfers

B. Net Capital

1950

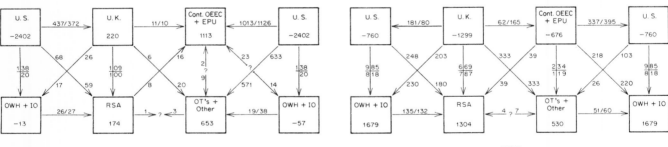

1951

1952

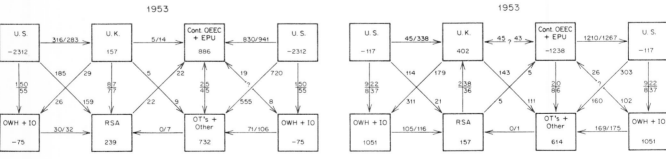

1953

1954

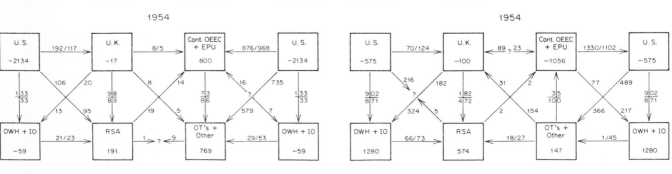

CHART 7 (concluded)

C. Net Gold

D. Balances to Be Settled Multilaterally

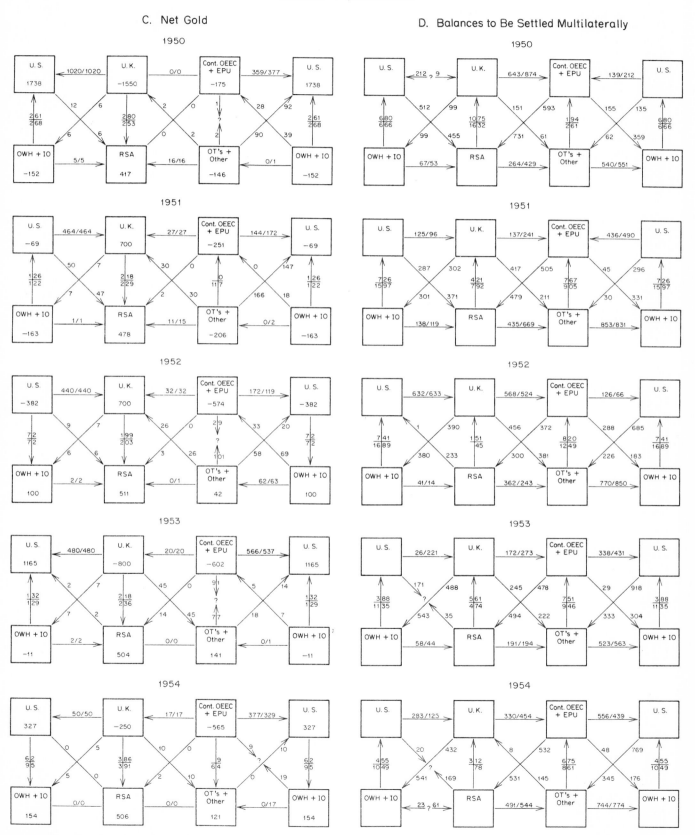

stances of capital flows of $10 million or more opposite to the five-year direction, twenty-two appear in accounts of centers with centers, and fourteen of these were balances with the EPU, which, of course, was intended to serve as a short-term capital lending agency. There were also frequent reversals of capital flows between peripheral areas and centers as the peripheral areas built up or drew down balances, or as balances under bilateral arrangements went one way and then the other. Even though capital flows between areas were less regular than net trade and net transfers, for most of the 263 reports of an interarea relationship they tended to persist year after year in the same direction.

Annual net multilateral settlements show a degree of year-to-year stability in direction about as high as that for net goods and services, in spite of the greater variability of capital flows. This also holds true for the country accounts underlying the net settlements matrix. A count of balances in fifty-eight individual country accounts with partner areas of significance indicated that, for balances of $10 million or more, only 110 out of 1,114 goods and services balances and only 111 out of 1,135 multilateral settlements balances were opposite to the five-year direction.

The stability of direction of annual financial flows and multilateral settlements is reflected in Chart 7 diagraming the annual flows of (A) net transfers, (B) net capital, (C) net gold, and (D) balances to be settled multilaterally.

2. Consistency of the Two-Valued Matrixes of Financial Flows

For the larger entries in the transfer matrix (Part A of Chart 7), agreement between paired entries is comparatively good in relation to agreement on goods and services balances, but for small transfers the paired records exhibit frequent ambiguities of direction and relatively wide divergence in magnitude. Every interarea transfer which was reported with a mean of paired entries of $250 million or more (thirteen out of seventy-five cases) was agreed as to direction and was also agreed as to magnitude to within approximately 25 per cent of the mean. This was also true of all but two interarea transfers with a mean of $100 million or more.[30] For smaller

[30] In the two exceptional cases (both transfers between the U.S. and Other Western Hemisphere countries), the U.S. record includes economic and technical assistance

transfers, entries agreed to within 25 per cent of the mean only about one-third of the time, to within 50 per cent only about half the time, and to within 100 per cent only about two-thirds of the time.[31] In nine of such small cases the direction of transfers was not agreed. The poor quality of the record for small transactions arises mostly because some private unilateral transfers are difficult to distinguish statistically from workers' remittances of earnings (a service transaction). When transfers are small, countries frequently include them with miscellaneous services.

A frequency distribution of the relative divergence between paired capital entries in the six-area matrix plotted in Part B of Chart 7 shows that in 37 per cent of the seventy-five cases the paired records agree to within 25 per cent of the mean, in half the cases to within 50 per cent, and in 71 per cent to within 100 per cent. In twenty-two of the seventy-five cases divergence was greater than 100 per cent and, of these, nine were instances of ambiguity of direction. As with transfers, smaller flows tended to be less well agreed. All of the ambiguities involved net flows of less than $100 million (largest mean value).[32] It is thus fair to say that, in spite of fairly large unallocated amounts, the direction and order of magnitude of interarea capital flows, especially the large flows, were agreed in paired records; however, the extent of agreement was not as good as that for

expenditures not entered in accounts of partners. Partly, this is explained by the extension of aid to the Organization of American States rather than directly to individual countries, but partly it reflects a difference of opinion on whether the services rendered (cost of administering aid programs) should be included in a balance-of-payments account (see Chapter 3, pp. 28–29).

[31] It will be recalled that where paired entries diverge by 100 per cent of their mean the two figures and their mean stand in proportions 3:2:1; where divergence is 50 per cent of the mean they are in proportions 5:4:3, and where divergence is 25 per cent of the mean they are in proportions 9:8:7.

[32] The frequency distribution is as follows:

Divergence from Mean of Paired Net Capital Flows (per cent)	Number of Interarea Relationships
0 – 2.5	8
2.6– 5.0	5
5.1– 10.0	3
10.1– 25.0	12
25.1– 50.0	9
50.1–100.0	16
Over 100.0	22
Total	75

The last group and the total include nine cases not agreed as to direction.

net goods and services, which can be observed in Table D-4.

It is not useful to tabulate divergences in the gold matrix (Part C of Chart 7) since many of the entries are drawn from one side of the record (notably the U.S. side) and entered in partner area accounts. The account itself provides sufficient indication of the extent of uncertainty attaching to the several inter-area figures: one need only look at the over-all excess of credits (for net gold sales) in the whole set of accounts and the sizable amounts of unallocated transactions (usually sales) in most accounts other than the U.S.

The direction of annual balances to be settled multilaterally between areas was generally indicated the same by both sides in the unadjusted two-value net settlements matrix charted in Part D of Chart 7, and the order of magnitude of the amount settled was agreed most of the time. A frequency distribution of the seventy-five interarea annual relationships in the six-area matrix according to the divergence between paired records (expressed as a percentage of the mean of the two observations) reveals that almost 60 per cent of the interarea balances show agreement within 50 per cent of the mean and 80 per cent show agreement within 100 per cent, but these are not as high proportions as for net goods and services.[33] If one were to allocate unallocated transactions and reconcile the gold account by the method followed in Table A-4, it would seem likely that the divergence between paired net settlements records could be reduced. Making such an adjustment for the five years as a whole did not alter the direction of net settlements.

The systematic character of divergence is expressed not only in the annual matrixes of net settlements but also in changes in the pattern from period

to period. Changes from the beginning to the end of the five-year period were measured about as well as annual flows. Changes from year to year within the period, however, were more poorly measured than the annual flows.[34] Even so, half of paired entries were agreed to within 50 per cent of the mean.

3. Systematic Variation in Multilateral Settlements

It is to be expected that, if one area's multilateral settlements with partner areas undergo a large shift during a period of time, the whole world-wide pattern will undergo related shifts. The record is good enough to show such a set of shifts over the five-year period. Between 1950 and 1954 the U.S., the U.K., and Continental OEEC countries (plus the European Payments Union) each experienced interrelated shifts of about $1 billion in balances settled multilaterally with partners distinguished in Chart 7. The Continental center increased its net receipts from peripheral areas by about $1 billion (according to partners) and its net payments to the U.S. and the U.K. In contrast, the U.K. experienced reduced settlements receipts from the Rest of the Sterling Area and increased payments due Other Western Hemisphere countries and International Organizations of more than $1 billion (partners put it at nearer $2 billion) matched by increased receipts from the U.S., the Continent, and to a lesser extent from Continental Overseas Territories and Other Countries, which partners placed at $1 billion. The U.S. record shows a complex shift: an increased outflow of $0.6 billion to areas associated with the Continent and Other Countries about matched the increased inflow from the Continent, and an increased inflow of $0.5 billion from the Rest of the Sterling Area about matched the increased outflow to the U.K. Partner records do not agree on the magnitudes of particular swings, but it is clear that a large change took place over the five

---

[33] The frequency distribution, which can be compared with Table D-4, is as follows:

Divergence from Mean of Paired Net Settlements (*per cent*)	*Number of Interarea Relationships*
0 – 2.5	6
2.6– 5.0	5
5.1– 10.0	5
10.1– 25.0	16
25.1– 50.0	12
50.1–100.0	17
Over 100.1	14
Total	75

The last group and the total include four cases not agreed as to direction.

[34] Relative frequency distributions for annual flows from footnote 33, for changes over the five years, and for year-to-year changes were as folows:

Divergence from Mean of Paired Measures (*per cent*)	*Annual Flows* (*75 cases*)	*Change from 1950 to 1954* (*15 cases*)	*Year-to-Year Change* (*60 cases*)
50.0 and under	59	60	50
50.1–100.00	23	13⅓	15
Over 100.0	13	13⅓	20
Direction not agreed	5	13⅓	15
Total	100	100	100

years in the world-wide pattern of interarea multilateral settlements. The largest of the shifts was the reversal of settlements between the U.S. and the Continent, and it went along with a reduction in the Continent's reliance on U.S. aid, a building up of short-term capital holdings in the U.S., and purchases of gold. In relation to the great expansion in gross Continental trade, this was a very small shift, but in relation to the "dollar shortage" of the time it was large.

6

CONCLUSION

A. SUMMARY

In setting out to construct a comprehensive record of the network of international transactions of all types for a number of years, we had in mind three objectives. The statistical objective was to show what was involved in constructing such a record from different national sources and to consider whether or not it was sufficiently reliable to be useful. Such a record had never been prepared before, and once we had it our second objective was to observe the nature of international economic relationships during the period —the size, composition, and geographic structure of trading, the pattern of financial interrelationships, and the character and extent of multilateralism. Our third objective was to employ the record to test hypotheses about the behavior of the world economy. This volume has dealt primarily with the first of these objectives, in a limited way with the second, and not at all with the third.

Our work on the 1950–54 period demonstrates that, with considerable adjustment and supplementation, it is possible to construct from available materials a usable annual record of current and financial transactions between world areas. Measures of interarea merchandise trade have long been available, but for the first time we have compiled a consistent set of measures for interarea services transactions of different types, net unilateral transfers, and capital and gold flows. And from these measures we have also derived the net multilateral settlements by which a particular country or area used surpluses from all transactions (including transactions in liquid capital and gold) with one group of partners to settle deficits from transactions with its other partners—the element of multilateralism in world trade and payments. These measures add to our knowledge of the nature and extent of specialization in international trade and finance.

A comprehensive, world-wide, double-entry rec-

ord is more than the sum of its parts. It is a record in which paired entries from both sides in principle should agree and can be compared to reveal deficiencies in the record. By auditing preliminary trial-run tabulations we have been led to make adjustments providing greater consistency between partner records and to prepare accounts for transactions of certain entities (e.g., International Organizations and some shipping fleets) which no reporting country included among its residents and for nonreporting countries (e.g., a number of oil-source countries). We have also used the two-valued record to elaborate certain consolidated area groupings and to derive estimates of transactions with partners which not all countries distinguished in official published accounts. By this means we have obtained world-wide totals for partner transactions with the U.S., the U.K., and Continental OEEC countries to compare with totals with the world carried in accounts constructed for those areas. The two-valued feature of the record also has been used to examine the possibility of improving accounts further: an effort to allocate unallocated transactions on the basis of internal evidence in the world-wide matrix indicated that divergence would very likely be reduced if all transactions were properly allocated by partner area. We have also studied divergences between paired entries in the record to provide one indication of the uncertainty attaching to the compilations.

Not all errors and omissions will be revealed by a comparison of the credit and debit entries for a given interarea transaction. We know that our record is deficient because it omits transactions between East and West Germany, between Spain and Spanish possessions, between the Soviet Bloc and non-Bloc countries except merchandise and gold, and between France and Portugal and their Own Currency Areas except merchandise and transportation. Because of such omissions from both sides of the record, it probably understates total world trade and particularly services.

Despite these and other weaknesses, paired entries in the matrix of gross goods and services transactions seem to agree well enough to reveal the basic structure of interarea trading. However, lack of information about trade conducted through middlemen (estimated at about 15 per cent of world trade) makes it difficult to adjust the record to a consistent purchase-sales basis, thereby understating the degree of concentration of trade between the economic centers (U.S., U.K., and Continental Western Europe) and the associated peripheral areas. Inadequacies in reporting which were of secondary importance in measuring the direction of gross trade were found to be of major importance in measuring trade balances and multilateral settlements between world areas. In general, only the order of magnitude of net transactions between world areas and year-to-year changes in balances could be measured; sometimes only the direction (sign) could be known.

The pattern of divergence between credit and debit measures of transactions has provided considerable insight into the nature of error in the accounts. Thus, unaccounted net capital and gold flows (transactions reported from the credit but not the debit side) equaled half the additions recorded to official reserves outside the U.S. in the period 1950–54. The pattern of error in the accounts indicated that, especially in times of political or currency crises, substantial foreign exchange earnings (apparently realized in good part on services account) moved into hidden capital and gold holdings. This result carries implications important for the interpretation of international financial crises in the postwar era. Moreover, it suggests not only that the financial problems of governments are made more difficult in times of stress by the flight of capital but also that recovery from financial difficulties may be eased by the cessation of these drains once confidence is restored. Corrective action may therefore sometimes overshoot the mark.

Net services transactions and financial flows between world areas were seen to be large in relation to net merchandise transactions, and measures of the pattern of multilateralism based on merchandise trade only were found to be seriously misleading. This study has thus aimed at going beyond the well-known *Network* study of the League of Nations,[1] which was largely concerned with merchandise trade balances. The pattern of net multilateral settlements —after allowing for all exchanges of currently produced goods, unilateral transfers, and assets (including large accumulations by Western Europe of liquid dollar assets and gold)— proved to be nicely symmetrical in the early 1950's. Each center—the U.S., the U.K., and Continental Western Europe— ran a surplus with the peripheral area composed of countries trading principally with it and a deficit with the other peripheral areas. Balances to be settled multilaterally among centers and among peripheral areas ran from the Western Hemisphere center (or peripheral area) to the sterling center (or peripheral area) on to the Continental center (or Other Eastern Hemisphere) and back to the Western Hemisphere center or peripheral area.[2]

Particular attention has been paid in this analysis to the matrix of multilateral settlements. As the residual account of bilateral balances, the matrix necessarily reflects all of the errors in accounting for transactions of other types between areas. Apart from error, it has the analytical meaning of representing the element of circularity in the trade and payments relations among areas.

The interarea balances offset by multilateral settlements are to be distinguished from the usual concept of bilateral payments balance in that the latter are met both by flows of reserve assets (liquid capital and gold) and by the residual multilateral settlements. The interrelations between payments balances, the flow of reserve assets, and multilateral settlements in transactions with the U.S. and the U.K. could be examined from the accounts of those reserve centers, and it was found that payments balances of the two centers with peripheral areas were predominantly met by multilateral settlements. A large part of what each peripheral area earned from or paid to the U.S. or the U.K. to meet its payments balance was linked, through multilateral settlements, to its payments position with other areas. Peripheral areas trading principally with the U.S. or the U.K. transferred receipts from other areas to the reserve centers in excess of their need to meet their payments deficits with these centers, banking reserves with them in 1950–54.

[1] *The Network of World Trade,* Geneva, 1942.
[2] See Chart 5 (panel vii), Chart 7, Part D, and Tables A–4 and B–28.

Two groups, Other Countries and the Continent, had payments surpluses with the U.S., attributable largely to unilateral transfers from the U.S., and in each case used the surplus to accumulate reserve assets from the U.S. The group Other Countries also used part of the surplus to meet payments deficits with areas other than the U.S. and the U.K., whereas the Continent used earnings from other areas to accumulate reserve assets in the U.S. in excess of its payments surplus. Every other area accumulated reserves from the two centers, altogether in an amount less than the aid extended by the two centers to the rest of the world. The U.S. and the U.K. thus "gave away" their payments deficit and the corresponding accumulation of liquid assets by the other areas. The U.K.'s ability to do this was made possible by U.S. aid received.

In the period the U.S. and the U.K. were both in the position of lending and investing at long term while incurring short-term liabilities.

Payments balances among the U.S., the U.K., and Canada and among the U.K., Continental OEEC countries, and the Rest of the Sterling Area were clearly interrelated through multilateral settlements. These eddies in the circular flow of multilateral settlements linking bilateral payments balances contribute to an understanding of a number of policies and practices of governments at the time. The first triangular flow involving Canada was directly related to the way in which U.S. aid to the U.K. was administered. The second involving the Rest of the Sterling Area was a feature of international economic life which affected the structure of the clearing arrangement established under the European Payments Union.

In other ways, too, the record of multilateral settlements sheds light on the nature of existing economic interdependence of world areas. The Continental countries which later formed the Common Market, those which later joined the U.K. in the European Free Trade Area, and the Sterling Area were linked in the period just prior to the crystallization of the Common Market and the European Free Trade Area arrangements in a circular flow of multilateral settlements in which the Sterling Area earned from the Common Market countries, the latter from the Continental European Free Trade Area members, and they in turn from the Sterling Area. Another significant eddy in the circular flow was the triangular relationship observable in the Soviet Bloc account in which earnings from the U.K. covered payments to the Rest of the Sterling Area. A considerable offsetting of balances to be settled with partner areas by economic centers and the peripheral areas with which they were affiliated economically was observable; amounts to be settled between currency areas were thus greatly reduced.

The multilateral settlements matrix in Appendix B provides an indication of the amount of such settlements between areas in the early 1950's. Over the five years they came to about $35 billion, about 9 per cent of gross interarea trade in goods and services and would have been $5 billion larger if measured so as to exclude intertemporal offsetting. They would have been larger still if country-to-country setttlements could be measured.

B. THE U.S. DEFICIT AND MULTILATERAL PAYMENTS

In the years following World War II problems of imbalance in international payments were widespread and exchange control was rampant and discriminatory. Imbalances in one country's accounts provoked imbalances in those of others. Thus, some Latin American countries experienced payments difficulties not because their over-all accounts were in deficit but because their deficits were with the U.S. and needed to be met in dollars, and their surpluses were in currencies which the debtor country would not convert.

Government policy-makers in the early postwar years would have been helped greatly in grappling with these problems if they had been able to assess alternative policies in the light of the kind of record of transactions between world areas presented in this book. As it was, decisions had to be taken in the light of the partial information supplied for particular situations—for example, the balance-of-payments position of a single country seeking financial assistance.

For a time in the mid-1950's the prospect of realizing the convertibility of European currencies led to the belief that the problem of payments imbalance, as a general phenomenon, was on its way out. Once convertibility was established, it no longer seemed necessary to be concerned with regional elaborations of payments accounts. To the extent that imbalance was created by the discrimination in previous exchange controls and was relieved by the removal of discrimination after the introduction of a wider measure of currency convertibility, this has been the case. Interregional payments relations remain significant, however, for a wider, seemingly chronic, and ever-changing problem of maintaining international financial balance. Trade and payments relations between world areas are asymmetrical, and therapeutic measures bear differently on different areas as they ramify out through a world-wide network of interarea relationships.

The concern of the Western world in the early 1960's has been largely focused on the dollar. The postwar dollar shortage has been succeeded by the U.S. balance-of-payments deficit as the subject absorbing the interest of policy-makers, economists, bankers, and others. Yet, with all that has been written on this problem, there is still inadequate attention given to the world-wide pattern of trade and payments relationships within which the U.S. position has deteriorated. It is important to assess the differential impact on the several parts of the world of different measures to rectify the imbalance. For this reason the effort of the Brookings Institution to evaluate the future prospects of the U.S. balance of payments in the context of a three-area trading model of the world economy is to be welcomed.[3]

Even now the United States may not give due regard to the interregional aspects of international payments relations. Shortly after requesting in 1963 legislative approval of an interest equalization tax on foreign security sales in the United States, the Treasury was led by the adverse impact of its proposal upon Canada to make provision for exceptions, and the impact on Japan threatened for a time to be equally alarming. Without debating the merits of the tax as a means of easing the U.S. payments position, we can say that the incident points to the necessity of recognizing the differential impact of measures to influence the flow of international transactions on different areas and hence back on the U.S. itself.[4]

It may be that the payments problem of the United States as it appears in the early 1960's will be solved or eased by actions on the part of Western European countries to liberalize restrictive arrangements affecting trade and capital movements and to assume a greater share of the common burdens of mutual security and world development. If, however, the United States has to rely more on unilateral measures to strengthen its balance of payments, these will most likely curb the flow of dollars to the rest of the world, since expenditures can be more easily reduced unilaterally than earnings increased. In that event, it would be desirable to minimize the adverse impact of such an action, both on the world economy in general and back on the United States itself. In principle, this objective could be sought either (1) by selecting measures which, by their nature, impinge more on Western European countries accumulating reserves than on other countries or (2) by applying measures in a discriminatory manner so as to produce this result. Opportunities for action of the first type are obviously limited and could conflict with other policy objectives—for example, the withdrawal of U.S. troops from Europe but not from other areas. There may also be little scope for action of the second type, since measures discriminating against Western Europe could easily invite, and be nullified by, retaliatory action. This would almost certainly be true of any action, and especially any discriminatory action, impeding imports by the United States from Western Europe. It is interesting to note, at the same time, that the interest equalization tax mentioned above, even though discriminating in favor of less-developed countries and Canada, did not arouse opposition from official circles in Western Europe.

The need to develop analyses and to frame policies with an eye to the evolving pattern of transactions between areas is suggested by the changes in the pattern which are evident in the regional distribution of U.S. balance-of-payments statistics. Chart 8

[3] Walter S. Salant, *et al.*, *The United States Balance of Payments in 1968*, Washington, 1963. For reasons noted in Chapter 5, Section C–6, the three-area model of the U.S., Western Europe, and third areas is inadequate.

[4] Interregional aspects of the balance-of-payments problem have been given some recognition by the U. S.

foreign aid agency. As it has sought to assess the impact of assistance on the U. S. payments position, it has found it necessary to recognize different "feedback ratios" expressing the proportions of U.S. aid to foreign countries which will ultimately be spent in the U.S. (*ibid.*, appendix to Chapter 4, based on a memorandum by Whitney Hicks). This particular approach seems too conservative in assuming that Western Europe would spend no incremental exchange earnings, but the effort to analyze the effect within the context of a world-wide trading system is a long step forward.

CHART 8

Multilateral Settlements of the U.S. with Partner Areas, 1950–62

(million U.S. dollars; balances to be settled)

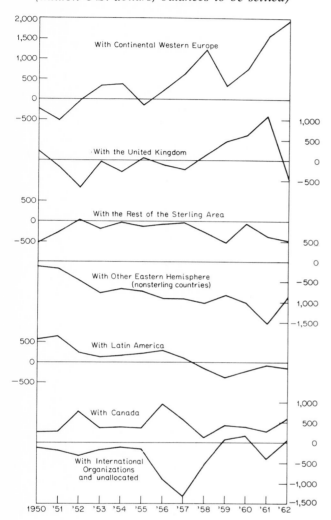

SOURCE: *Balance of Payments, Statistical Supplement* (1963); *Survey of Current Business,* March 1963; and correspondence with Office of Business Economics.

eralization, the U.S. has tended in recent years to receive increasingly large net settlements from Continental Western Europe and (except in 1962) from the U.K., and to make increasingly large net settlements to non-European areas. The main exceptions to this generalization are Canada and (perhaps) the Rest of the Sterling Area which, as far as these data permit conclusions, show little change over the period in their position in international settlements.

Some of the factors underlying these shifts emerge from the more detailed figures in Table 16 on U.S. transactions with Western Europe (combining Continental Western Europe and the U.K.) and with all other countries taken as an entity. It will be noted that in 1950–55 the U.S. paid out enough funds, including government aid, to Western Europe to permit that area to add $1 billion annually, on the average, to its gold and liquid dollar holdings [5] and still leave a small remainder for other uses. By 1958–59 economic aid extended by the United States to Western Europe was sharply reduced, but its direct balance with that area became even more adverse with the shrinkage of the U.S. surplus on goods and services and the rise in its military expenditures. At the same time, Western Europe's acquisitions of gold and dollar balances from the U.S. became so large as to point to additional dollar receipts of something like $1 billion annually from other sources. By 1961–62 the U.S. had greatly strengthened its trade position once more and achieved a surplus on goods and services transactions with Western Europe much larger than in 1950–55. In addition, the U.S. government obtained large special receipts, chiefly advance debt repayments, from Western Europe. These gains were offset in considerable part by a rise in the flow of private capital to that area, but not enough to prevent the emergence of a substantial surplus for the United States. Despite this shift in the balance, Western Europe continued to add, though less rapidly than in 1958–59, to its gold and dollar holdings, but now with dollar receipts from other sources on the order of $2 billion annually.

These developments in U.S. payments relations with Western European countries were related to

shows net multilateral settlements of the U.S. with six foreign areas over the period 1950–62. These are net receipts from, or net payments to, each area by the U.S. after allowing for all bilateral transactions, including transfers of gold and liquid dollar balances, with the area concerned. (The figures plotted are balances to be settled and are opposite in sign to the entries for multilateral settlements in the official U.S. payments statement.) As a broad gen-

[5] This analysis is based entirely on what can be observed from U.S. balance-of-payments statistics and does not take account of changes in other countries' gold holdings out of new gold production, Soviet gold sales, or private hoarding or dishoarding. It should also be noted that the division of items between I–A and I–B, or II–A and II–B, in Table 16 corresponds to official U.S. balance-of-payments practice.

TABLE 16

Bilateral Balances and Multilateral Settlements in the U.S.
Balance of Payments, 1950–62
(annual averages, million U.S. dollars)

		1950–55	1958–59	1961–62
I.	Western Europe			
A.	U.S. gold sales and increase in liquid liabilities to the area, net	1,029	2,546	1,134
B.	U.S. bilateral balance on other recorded transactions with the area	−1,202	−1,500	946
	Goods and services, excl. military, net	1,475	573	2,538
	Military expenditures, net	−917	−1,590	−1,158
	Remittances and pensions, net	−239	−343	−258
	Private capital, net	20	−79	−981
	U.S. govt. capital and grants, excl. special receipts, net	−1,542	−278	−228
	U.S. govt. special receipts, net[a]	—	217	1,033
C.	Area's dollar receipts from other sources (A + B)[b]	173	1,046	2,080
II.	Other Countries			
A.	U.S. gold sales and increase in liquid liabilities to the area, net	601	1,090	1,152
B.	U.S. bilateral balance on other recorded transactions with the area	−773	−2,585	−2,177
	Goods and services, excl. military, net	2,326	3,567	5,257
	Military expenditures, net	−901	−1,379	−1,312
	Remittances and pensions, net	−318	−413	−463
	Private capital, net	−916	−2,133	−2,432
	U.S. govt. capital and grants, excl. special receipts, net	−964	−2,227	−3,357
	U.S. govt. special receipts, net[a]	—	—	130
C.	Area's dollar receipts from other sources (A + B)[b]	172	−1,495	−1,025
III.	Unrecorded receipts or payments in U.S. global balance of payments (IC + IIC with signs reversed)[c]	345	449	−1,055

SOURCE: *Balance of Payments, Statistical Supplement* to the *Survey of Current Business*, rev. ed., Washington, 1963; *Survey of Current Business*, June 1964.

[a] Special receipts are somewhat more comprehensive here than in *Survey of Current Business*, June 1964, p. 10, Table 1, due to lack of geographic detail for items on latter basis.

[b] This is the U.S. total bilateral balance to be settled with the area and equals the entry in the U.S. payments statement for multilateral settlements and error with the partner area but is opposite in sign; it corresponds to the plotting in Chart 8.

[c] This is the entry in the column for all areas in the U.S. payments statement for multilateral settlements and error with the sign given in the official account.

the growing deficit in its transactions with non-European countries. This deficit reached its maximum in 1958–59, when the U.S. position vis-à-vis Western Europe was also most unfavorable, but remained almost as large in 1961–62 and was then almost three times as large as it had been in 1950–55. On goods and services only, the U.S. showed a large and growing surplus in transactions with non-European countries. But this result was outweighed by, and partly attributable to, the great increase since the early 1950's in net payments by the U.S. to these countries on other recorded transactions—government economic aid, private investment, and military expenditures. Only part of the estimated balance in favor of non-European countries in recent years has been settled by additions to their gold and dollar holdings. Half of the balance in 1961–62, and considerably more than half in 1958–59, was used for multilateral settlements, presumably in a triangular flow from the U.S. to third areas to Western Europe and then back for the European purchase of reserve assets from the U.S.

The data reproduced in Table 16 do not permit a precise estimate of the amount of dollar settlements received by Western Europe from other areas. On the basis of recorded transactions with Western European countries, these settlements appear to have averaged $450 million less in 1958–59, but close to $1 billion more in 1961–62, than would appear from recorded transactions with non-European countries (compare lines I-C and II-C of Table 16).[6] On either basis, however, it is clear that, in contrast to 1950–55, by 1961–62 Western Europe's gains of gold and liquid dollars from the U.S. were no longer attributable to its direct bilateral balance with this country, but rather to the settlements which it received from other areas and which were made possible by the rise in the U.S. deficit with these other areas.[7]

[6] These differences, it will be noted, relate to the residual entry for unreported transactions in the U.S. global balance of payments (line III) and to the switch in this residual from a positive item in 1958–59, indicative of net unexplained receipts, to a negative item in 1961–62, indicative of net unexplained payments. This shift was a progressive swing of $2 billion over the years 1957–62, with the change in direction coming in 1960. It seems to have reflected a decline in the preference previously enjoyed by the dollar over other currencies.

[7] Events in 1963 and 1964 do not alter this conclusion. The regionally elaborated payments accounts of the U.S. for these years, given in the June 1964 and March 1965 issues of the *Survey of Current Business,* show that Western Europe continued to accumulate gold and liquid dollar

The data presented in Table 16 can be further broken down to show U.S. transactions with each of the areas distinguished in Chart 8. What is seriously lacking at present, however, is information on the nature of the shifts which have occurred in transactions between these areas, particularly between the various non-European areas, on the one hand, and Continental Western Europe and the U.K., on the other. One can, of course, construct the merchandise account fairly well from published trade statistics and can examine, for instance, the extent to which Western Europe's net settlements from other areas may be attributable to a superior performance in merchandise export competition with the U.S. But one would also need to be able to construct for each area the whole current account in its regional dimensions and to measure the net flow of resources between areas; to obtain regionally elaborated data on the flows of government grants and credits for both donor and recipient countries; to build up similar two-valued records of private capital movements and develop them in appropriate detail by types of transaction; to integrate these various components of the accounts into a full matrix of international settlements; to consider the mutual consistency of the estimates and examine them, as we have tried to do here, for evidences of the drain of resources into flight capital and gold hoards; and to study the records year by year to see what changes have occurred in the pattern of transactions and in the ways countries react to each other.

As matters stand, we have to study international economic and monetary problems and address ourselves to major policy issues without these tools of analysis. The main elements concerning the United States are available, thanks to the full regional detail in which its balance-of-payments estimates are presented. But matching detail for other countries, even the most important ones, is frequently not available or not even compiled.

This book testifies that it is not necessary to remain in such ignorance. With sufficient effort, it is possible to measure the changing trade and payments relations among all world areas with tolerable accuracy.

assets in large amounts primarily through multilateral settlements rather than on bilateral account with the U.S. U.S. multilateral settlements with Western Europe continued in 1963 and 1964 at about the 1962 level and were associated with mixed developments in U.S. multilateral settlements with peripheral areas and International Organizations.

Appendixes

Figures in parentheses are estimates described in the text.

The term Own Currency Area refers to partner area for transactions between Belgium, France, the Netherlands, and Portugal and their own Overseas Territories. These transactions are not included in transactions of the nonsterling EPU area in the matrix tables.

For definition of other terms, see glossary.

A

TWO-VALUED MATRIXES FOR THE WHOLE FIVE YEARS 1950–54

TABLE A-1

Two-Valued Matrix of Gross Goods and Services Transactions
Between World Areas, 1950–54
(million U.S. dollars)

Exports of Area at Left and Imports of Area at Top:
Line A: As reported by area at left
Line B: As reported by area at top

Area		All Areas	Unallocated	Sterling Area — All	Sterling Area — U.K.	Sterling Area — RSA	Nonsterling EPU Area — All	Nonsterling EPU Area — Cont. OEEC	Nonsterling EPU Area — Cont. OT's	Own Currency Area	U.S., Canada, and IO — All	U.S., Canada, and IO — U.S.	U.S., Canada, and IO — Canada	U.S., Canada, and IO — IO	Latin America	Other Countries
All areas	A	460,672	5,489	123,012	57,383	65,629	139,853	121,285	18,568		98,360	72,762	25,182	416	43,439	50,519
	B	464,040		123,734	57,098	66,636	138,788	119,474	19,314		104,396	76,670	27,376	350	46,746	50,376
Unallocated	A	5,963		281	135	146	1,918	1,837	81						1,817	1,947
	B															
Sterling Area	A	119,416	515	60,185	21,938	38,247	25,021	(23,738)	(1,283)		16,655	(12,767)	(3,858)	30	4,272	12,768
	B	118,954		60,352	22,019	38,333	24,679	23,415	1,264		17,629	13,586	4,040	3	4,531	11,763
United Kingdom	A	57,726	508	26,622		26,622	13,610	(12,911)	(699)		8,295	5,534	2,731	30	3,430	5,261
	B	58,918		27,432		27,432	(13,423)	(12,733)	(690)		9,078	6,184	2,891	3	3,575	5,410
Rest of Sterling Area	A	61,690	7	33,563	21,938	11,625	11,411	(10,827)	(584)		8,360	(7,233)	(1,127)		842	7,507
	B	60,036		32,920	22,019	10,901	11,256	(10,682)	(574)		8,551	7,402	1,149		956	6,353
Nonsterling EPU area	A	135,847	2,251	25,203	(16,252)	(8,951)	54,919	53,209	(1,710)	15,833	16,095	(15,154)	906	(35)	8,540	13,006
	B	135,221		25,576	16,490	9,086	54,038	52,357	1,681	16,246	17,133	15,918	1,180	35	9,083	13,145
Cont. OEEC countries	A	120,661	1,750	23,149	(14,923)	(8,226)	52,212	(50,586)	(1,626)	9,506	14,128	(13,276)	817	(35)	7,465	12,451
	B	120,604		(23,491)	(15,143)	(8,348)	(51,208)	(49,616)	(1,592)	10,260	14,811	13,692	1,084	35	8,189	12,645
Cont. Overseas Territ.	A	15,186	501	2,054	(1,329)	(725)	2,707	(2,623)	(84)	6,327	1,967	1,878	89		1,075	555
	B	14,617		(2,085)	(1,347)	(738)	(2,830)	(2,741)	(89)	5,968	2,322	2,226	96		894	500
Own Currency Area	A						15,833	6,327	9,506	15,833						
	B						16,246	5,986	10,260	16,246						
U.S., Canada, and IO	A	114,380		19,756	10,508	9,248	20,723	18,879	1,844		34,706	(15,382)	18,983	(341)	24,897	14,298
	B	111,920		19,228	10,032	9,196	19,398	17,559	1,839		35,518	14,862	20,354	302	24,767	13,009
United States	A	89,227		14,391	6,588	7,803	18,528	16,772	1,756		19,318		18,978	340	23,699	13,291
	B	88,444		(13,891)	6,135	(7,756)	(17,757)	(15,980)	1,777		20,650		(20,349)	301	(23,918)	(12,228)
Canada	A	24,671		5,286	3,895	1,391	2,042	1,954	88		15,233	(15,232)		(1)	1,149	961
	B	22,936		(5,250)	3,864	(1,386)	1,488	1,426	62		14,663	14,662		1	800	735
Internat. Organiz.	A	482		79	25	54	153	153			155	150	5		49	46
	B	540		(87)	33	(54)	(153)	(153)			(205)	200	(5)		(49)	(46)
Latin America	A	44,033	1,153	4,319	3,477	842	11,274	7,687	3,587		20,335	(19,232)	1,098	(5)	4,340	2,612
	B	43,492		4,069	3,346	723	10,430	7,024	3,406		21,952	20,547	1,400	5	4,701	2,340
Other Countries	A	46,996	1,570	13,549	5,208	8,341	12,083	11,445	638		10,569	(10,227)	377	(5)	1,390	7,835
	B	48,490		14,228	5,076	9,152	12,079	11,296	783		12,164	11,757	402	5	1,847	8,172

TABLE A-2

Two-Valued Matrix of Net Goods and Services Transactions
Between World Areas, 1950–54

(million U.S. dollars)

Balance of Area at Left with Area at Top:
Line A: As reported by area at left
Line B: As reported by area at top

Area at Left		All Areas	Unallocated	Sterling Area: All	U.K.	RSA	Nonsterling EPU Area: All	Cont. OEEC	Cont. OT's	Own Currency Area	U.S., Canada, and IO: All	U.S.	Canada	IO	Latin America	Other Countries
All areas	A	-3,368	-474	4,058	-1,535	5,593	4,632	681	3,951		-13,560	-15,682	2,246	-124	-53	2,029
	B	3,368		4,318	-628	4,946	2,941	-1,187	4,128		-9,984	-12,557	2,705	-132	2,713	3,380
Unallocated	A	474		-234	-373	139	-333	87	-420						664	377
	B															
Sterling Area	A	-4,318	234	-167	-5,494	5,327	-555	(247)	(-802)		-2,573	(-1,124)	(-1,392)	(-57)	203	-1,460
	B	-4,058		167	-4,603	4,770	-524	266	-790		-2,127	-805	-1,246	-76	212	-1,786
United Kingdom	A	628	373	4,603		4,603	-2,880	(-2,232)	(-648)		-1,737	-601	-1,133	-3	84	185
	B	1,535		5,494		5,494	(-2,829)	-2,190	(-639)		-1,430	-404	-1,004	-22	98	202
Rest of Sterling Area	A	-4,946	-139	-4,770	-5,494	724	2,325	(2,479)	(-154)		-836	(-523)(	-259)	-54	119	-1,645
	B	-5,593		-5,327	-4,603	-724	(2,305)	(2,456)	(-151)		-697	-401	-242	-54	114	-1,988
Nonsterling EPU area	A	-2,941	333	524	(2,829)	(-2,305)	881	2,001	(-1,120)	-413	-3,303	-2,603	-582	(-118)	-1,890	927
	B	-4,632		555	2,880	-2,325	-881	145	-1,026	413	-3,590	-2,610	-862	-118	-2,191	1,062
Cont. OEEC countries	A	1,187	-87	-266	(2,190)	(-2,456)	-145	970	(-1,115)	3,520	-3,431	-2,704	-609	(-118)	441	1,155
	B	-681		(-247)	(2,232)	(-2,479)	(-2,001)	-970	(-1,031)	3,933	-4,068	-3,080	-870	-118	502	1,200
Cont. Overseas Territ.	A	-4,128	420	790	(639)	151	1,026	(1,031)	(-5)	-3,933	128	101	27		-2,331	-228
	B	-3,951		(802)	(648)	(154)	(1,120)	(1,115)	(-5)	-3,520	478	470	8		-2,693	-138
Own Currency Area	A						-413	-3,933	3,520	-413						
	B						413	-3,520	3,933	413						
U.S., Canada, and IO	A	9,984		2,127	1,430	697	3,590	4,068	-478		-812	(-5,268)	4,320	(136)	2,945	2,134
	B	13,560		2,573	1,737	836	3,303	3,431	-128		812	-4,456	5,121	147	4,432	2,440
United States	A	12,557		805	404	401	2,610	3,080	470		4,456		4,316	140	3,152	1,534
	B	15,682		(1,124)	601	(523)	1,603	2,704	101		(5,268)		(5,117)	151	(4,686)	2,042
Canada	A	-2,705		1,246	1,004	242	862	870	-8		-5,121	-5,117		(-4)	-251	559
	B	-2,246		(1,392)	1,133	(259)	582	609	-27		-4,320	-4,316		-4	-298	398
Internat. Organiz.	A	132		76	22	54	118	118			-147	-151	4		44	41
	B	124		(57)	3	(54)	(118)	(118)			(-136)	-140	4		(44)	(41)
Latin America	A	-2,713	-664	-212	-98	-114	2,191	-502	2,693		-4,432	-4,686	298	(-44)	-361	765
	B	53		-203	-84	-119	1,890	-441	2,331		-2,945	-3,152	251	-44	361	950
Other Countries	A	-3,380	-377	1,786	-202	1,988	-1,062	-1,200	138		-2,440	-2,001	-398	(-41)	-950	-337
	B	-2,029		1,460	-185	1,645	-927	-1,155	228		-2,134	-1,534	-559	-41	-765	337

TABLE A-3

Percentage Distribution of Gross Goods and Services Transactions Between World Areas, 1950–54
(million U.S. dollars)

Part I. Distribution of Imports of Area at Top:
Line A: As reported by area at left
Line B: As reported by area at top

Area	Line	All Areas	Unallocated	Sterling Area All	U.K.	RSA	Nonsterling EPU Area All	Cont. OEEC	Cont. OT's	Own Currency Area	U.S., Canada, and IO All	U.S.	Canada	IO	Latin America	Other Countries
All areas	A	100.00		100.00	100.00	100.00	100.00	100.00	100.01		99.99	100.01	100.00	99.99	99.99	99.99
	B	100.00		100.01	100.00	100.00	100.01	100.00	99.98		100.00	99.99	100.00	100.01	100.00	99.99
Unallocated	A	1.29		.23	.24	.22	1.38	1.54	.42						3.89	3.86
Sterling Area	A	25.92	9.38	48.93	38.23	58.28	17.89	19.57	6.91		16.93	17.55	15.32	7.21	9.83	25.27
	B	25.63		48.78	38.56	57.53	17.78	19.60	6.54		16.89	17.72	14.76	.86	9.69	23.35
United Kingdom	A	12.53	9.25	21.64		40.56	9.73	10.65	3.76		8.43	7.61	10.85	7.21	7.90	10.41
	B	12.69		22.14		41.11	9.67	10.66	3.57		8.70	8.07	10.56	.86	7.65	10.74
Rest of Sterling Area	A	13.39	0.13	27.28	38.23	17.71	8.16	8.93	3.15		8.50	9.94	4.48		1.94	14.86
	B	12.94		26.63	38.56	16.41	8.11	8.94	2.97		8.19	9.65	4.20		2.05	12.61
Nonsterling EPU area	A	29.49	41.01	20.49	28.32	13.64	39.27	43.87	9.21		16.36	20.83	3.60	8.41	19.66	25.74
	B	29.14		20.67	28.88	13.64	38.94	43.82	8.70		16.41	20.76	4.31	10.00	19.43	26.09
Cont. OEEC countries	A	26.19	31.88	18.82	26.01	12.53	37.33	41.71	8.76		14.36	18.25	3.24	8.41	17.19	24.65
	B	25.99		18.99	26.52	12.53	36.90	41.53	8.24		14.19	17.86	3.96	10.00	17.52	25.10
Cont. Overseas Territ.	A	3.30	9.13	1.67	2.32	1.10	1.94	2.16	.45		2.00	2.58	.36		2.47	1.10
	B	3.15		1.69	2.36	1.11	2.04	2.29	.46		2.22	2.90	.35		1.91	.99
Own Currency Area	A						11.32	5.22	51.20							
	B						11.71	5.01	53.12							
U.S., Canada, and IO	A	24.83	21.01	16.06	18.31	14.09	14.82	15.57	9.93		35.28	21.14	75.38	81.97	57.32	28.30
	B	24.12		15.54	17.57	13.80	13.98	14.70	9.52		34.02	19.38	74.35	86.29	52.98	25.82
United States	A	19.37		11.70	11.48	11.89	13.25	13.83	9.46		19.64		75.30	81.73	54.56	26.31
	B	19.06		11.23	10.74	11.64	12.79	13.38	9.20		19.78		74.33	86.00	51.17	24.27
Canada	A	5.36		4.30	6.79	2.12	1.46	1.61	.47		15.49	20.93		.24	2.65	1.90
	B	4.94		4.24	6.77	2.08	1.07	1.19	.32		14.05	19.12		.29	1.71	1.46
Internat. Organiz.	A	.10		.06	.04	.08	.11	.13			.16	.21	.02		.11	.09
	B	.12		.07	.06	.08	.11	.13			.20	.26	.02		.10	.09
Latin America	A	9.56		3.51	6.06	1.28	8.06	6.34	19.32		20.67	26.43	4.36	1.20	9.98	5.17
	B	9.37		3.29	5.86	1.08	7.52	5.88	17.63		21.03	26.80	5.11	1.43	10.06	4.65
Other Countries	A	10.20	28.60	11.01	9.08	12.71	8.64	9.44	3.44		10.75	14.06	1.34	1.20	3.20	15.51
	B	10.45		11.50	8.89	13.73	8.70	9.45	4.05		11.65	15.33	1.47	1.43	3.95	16.22

(continued)

TABLE A-3 (concluded)

Part II. Distribution of Exports of Area at Left:
Line A: As reported by area at left
Line B: As reported by area at top

		All Areas	Unallocated	Sterling Area			Nonsterling EPU Area			Own Currency Area	U.S., Canada, and IO				Latin America	Other Countries
				All	U.K.	RSA	All	Cont. OEEC	Cont. OT's		All	U.S.	Canada	IO		
All areas	A	100.00	1.19	26.70	12.46	14.25	30.36	26.33	4.03		21.35	15.79	5.47	.09	9.43	10.97
	B	100.00		26.66	12.30	14.36	29.91	25.75	4.16		22.50	16.52	5.90	.08	10.07	10.86
Unallocated	A	99.99		4.71	2.26	2.45	32.16	30.81	1.35						30.47	32.65
	B															
Sterling Area	A	100.00	.43	50.40	18.37	32.03	20.95	19.88	1.07		13.95	10.69	3.23	.03	3.58	10.69
	B	100.00		50.73	18.51	32.22	20.75	19.68	1.07		14.82	11.42	3.40	—	3.81	9.89
United Kingdom	A	100.00	.88	4.12		46.12	23.58	22.37	1.21		14.37	9.59	4.73	.05	5.94	9.11
	B	100.00		4.53		46.53	22.79	21.62	1.17		15.42	10.50	4.91	.01	6.07	9.19
Rest of Sterling Area	A	100.00	.01	54.41	35.56	18.85	18.50	17.55	.95		13.55	11.72	1.83		1.36	12.17
	B	100.00		54.86	36.65	18.21	18.74	17.78	.96		14.23	12.32	1.91		1.59	10.58
Nonsterling EPU area	A	100.00	1.66	18.55	11.96	6.59	40.43	39.17	1.26	11.65	11.85	11.15	.67	.03	6.29	9.57
	B	99.99		18.91	12.19	6.72	39.96	38.72	1.24	12.01	12.67	11.77	.87	.03	6.72	9.72
Cont. OEEC countries	A	100.00	1.45	19.18	12.37	6.81	43.27	41.92	1.35	7.88	11.71	11.00	.68	.03	6.19	10.32
	B	100.00		19.48	12.56	6.92	42.46	41.14	1.32	8.51	12.28	11.35	.90	.03	6.79	10.48
Cont. Overseas Territ.	A	100.00	3.30	13.53	8.75	4.78	17.83	17.27	.56	41.66	12.95	12.37	.58		7.08	3.65
	B	100.00		14.26	9.22	5.04	19.36	18.75	.61	40.95	15.89	15.23	.66		6.12	3.42
Own Currency Area	A															
	B															
U.S., Canada, and IO	A	99.99		17.27	9.19	8.08	18.12	16.50	1.62		30.34	13.45	16.59	.30	21.76	12.50
	B	99.99		17.18	8.96	8.22	17.33	15.69	1.64		31.73	13.28	18.18	.27	22.13	11.62
United States	A	100.00		16.13	7.38	8.75	20.76	18.80	1.96		21.65		21.27	.38	26.56	14.90
	B	100.00		15.71	6.94	8.77	20.08	18.07	2.01		23.35		23.01	.34	27.04	13.82
Canada	A	100.00		21.43	15.79	5.64	8.28	7.92	.36		61.74	61.74			4.66	3.89
	B	100.00		22.89	16.85	6.04	6.49	6.22	.27		63.93	63.92		.01	3.49	3.20
Internat. Organiz.	A	100.00		16.39	5.19	11.20	31.74	31.74			32.16	31.12	1.04		10.17	9.54
	B	100.01		16.11	6.11	10.00	28.34	28.34			37.97	37.04	.93		9.07	8.52
Latin America	A	100.00	2.62	9.81	7.90	1.91	25.60	17.46	8.14		46.18	43.68	2.49	.01	9.86	5.93
	B	100.00		9.36	7.69	1.67	23.98	16.15	7.83		50.47	47.24	3.22	.01	10.81	5.38
Other Countries	A	100.00	3.34	28.83	11.08	17.75	25.71	24.35	1.36		22.49	21.76	.72	.01	2.96	16.67
	B	99.99		29.34	10.47	18.87	24.91	23.29	1.62		25.08	24.24	.83	.01	3.81	16.85

TABLE A-4

Net Transactions Between World Areas, 1950–54, by Type [a]

(balance of area at left with area at top)

(million U.S. dollars)

	All Areas	Sterling Area			Nonsterling EPU Area				Own Currency Area	U.S., Canada, and IO				Latin America	Other Countries
		All	U.K.	RSA	All	Cont. OEEC	Cont. OT's	EPU		All	U.S.	Canada	IO		
ALL AREAS															
1. Merchandise f.o.b.	5,112	3,448	4,231	-783	14,768	11,036	3,732			-11,157	-11,351	186	8	-4,793	2,846
2. Services	-8,209	1,131	-5,591	6,722	-10,691	-10,828	137			-2,691	-4,562	1,998	-127	4,655	-613
3. Goods & services	-3,097	4,579	-1,360	5,939	4,077	208	3,869			-13,848	-15,913	2,184	-119	-138	2,233
4. Private transfers	-664	-223	-162	-61	-828	-885	57			1,250	1,210	27	13	-38	-825
5. Official transfers	-937	-1,827	-955	-872	-6,770	-6,633	-30	-107		11,197	11,470	125	-398	-191	-3,346
6. Capital	2,419	-403	1,269	-1,672	4,696	4,940	-167	-77		1,194	3,746	-2,446	-106	-2,270	-798
7. Gold	0	-650	1,200	-1,850	2,729	2,450	-3	282		-2,655	-2,779	-168	292	-52	628
8. Settlements & error	2,279	-1,476	8	-1,484	-3,904	-80	-3,726	-98		2,862	2,266	278	318	2,689	2,108
STERLING AREA															
1. Merchandise f.o.b.	-1,318	-43	-937	894	3,140	3,938	-798			-1,764	-289	-1,482	7	-785	-1,866
2. Services	-3,448	-177	-4,579	4,402	-3,778	-3,759	-19			-847	-873	90	-64	998	356
3. Goods & services	-4,766	-220	-5,516	5,296	-638	179	-817			-2,611	-1,162	-1,392	-57	213	-1,510
4. Private transfers	-7	5	-40	45	-109	-109				131	135	-4		-6	-28
5. Official transfers	1,579	-48	411	-459	-256	-110		-146		1,887	1,900	47	-60		-4
6. Capital	2,327	467	836	-369	782	441		341		1,378	1,569	-193	2	57	-357
7. Gold	650	0	1,312	-1,312	1,212	1,139		73		-566	-577		11	-32	36
8. Settlements & error	217	-204	2,997	-3,201	-991	-1,540	817	-268		-219	-1,865	1,542	104	-232	1,863
UNITED KINGDOM															
1. Merchandise f.o.b.	-3,907	119		119	-355	(225)	(-580)			-2,188	-874	-1,321	7	-978	-505
2. Services	4,087	4,479		4,479	-2,598	(-2,520)	(-78)			451	273	188	-10	1,079	676
3. Goods & services	180	4,598		4,598	-2,953	(-2,295)	(-658)			-1,737	-601	-1,133	-3	101	171
4. Private transfers	-100	45		45	-41	(-41)	(—)			-73	-69	-4		-6	-25
5. Official transfers	848	-458		-458	-266	(-116)		(-150)		1,572	1,684	6	-118		—
6. Capital	40	-369		-369	593	(258)		(335)		153	716	-252	-311	58	-395
7. Gold	-1,200	-1,312		-1,312	785	712		73		-645	-646		1	-32	4
8. Settlements & error	232	-2,504		-2,504	1,882	1,482	658	-258		730	-1,084	1,383	431	-121	245
REST OF STERLING AREA															
1. Merchandise f.o.b.	2,589	-162	-937	775	3,495	(3,713)	(-218)			424	585	-161		193	-1,361
2. Services	-7,535	-4,656	-4,579	-77	-1,180	(-1,239)	(59)			-1,298	-1,146	-98	-54	-81	-320
3. Goods & services	-4,946	-4,818	-5,516	698	2,315	(2,474)	(-159)			-874	-561	-259	-54	112	-1,681
4. Private transfers	93	-40	-40	-1	-68	(-68)	(—)			204	(204)	(—)			-3
5. Official transfers	731	410	411	-1	10	(6)		(4)		315	(216)	(41)	(58)		-4
6. Capital	2,287	836	836		189	(183)		(6)		1,225	(853)	(59)	(313)	-1	38
7. Gold	1,850	1,312	1,312	0	427	427				79	69		10		32
8. Settlements & error	-15	2,300	2,997	-697	-2,873	-3,022	159	-10		-949	-781	159	-327	-111	1,618

(continued)

TABLE A-4 (continued)

	All Areas	Sterling Area			Nonsterling EPU Area					U.S., Canada, and IO				Latin America	Other Countries
		All	U.K.	RSA	All	Cont. OEEC	Cont. OT's	EPU	Own Currency Area	All	U.S.	Canada	IO		
NONSTERLING EPU AREA															
1. Merchandise f.o.b.	-7,354	-1,733	1,158	-2,891	2,277	3,165	-888		-409	-5,694	-5,060	-634		-2,033	238
2. Services	5,284	2,914	2,170	744	-1,326	-1,086	-240		-4	2,941	3,001	53	-113	133	626
3. Goods & services	-2,070	1,181	3,328	-2,147	951	2,079	-1,128		-413	-2,753	-2,059	-581	-113	-1,900	864
4. Private transfers	899	112	43	69	106	91	15		7	484	480	4	0	142	48
5. Official transfers	6,438	187	187	0	58	-177	0	235	-23	6,434	6,434	-3	-6	-13	-196
6. Capital	-4,153	-782	-691	-91	61	586	0	-525	-25	-3,354	-3,052	-66	-236	-121	68
7. Gold	-2,729	-1,212	-785	-427	0	29	-29	0	0	-1,668	-1,560	-260	152	-112	263
8. Settlements & error	1,615	514	-2,082	2,596	-1,176	-2,608	1,142	290	454	866	-243	906	203	2,004	-1,047
CONT. OEEC COUNTRIES															
1. Merchandise f.o.b.	-3,748	-2,664	(498)	(-3,162)	1,202	2,094	-892	—	2,943	-5,989	-5,328	-661	—	324	436
2. Services	5,806	2,866	(2,066)	(800)	-1,272	-1,041	-231		577	2,879	2,939	53	-113	104	652
3. Goods & services	2,058	202	(2,564)	(-2,362)	-70	1,053	-1,123		3,520	-3,110	-2,389	-608	-113	428	1,088
4. Private transfers	967	116	(45)	(71)	121	(106)	(15)		60	480	476	4		142	48
5. Official transfers	6,324	41	(41)	(—)	293	(58)		235	-30	6,229	6,238	-3	-6	-13	-196
6. Capital	-4,255	-444	(-359)	(-85)	-490	35	—	-525	-8	-3,265	-2,923	-66	-276	-118	70
7. Gold	-2,450	-1,139	-712	-427	-29	29	-29			-1,433	-1,325	-260	152	-112	263
8. Settlements & error	-2,644	1,224	-1,579	2,803	175	-1,252	1,137	290	-3,542	1,099	-77	933	243	-327	-1,273
CONT. OVERSEAS TERRITT.															
1. Merchandise f.o.b.	-3,606	931	(660)	(271)	1,075	1,071	4		-3,352	295	268	27		-2,357	-198
2. Services	-522	48	(104)	(-56)	-54	-45	-9		-581	62	62	0		29	-26
3. Goods & services	-4,128	979	(764)	(215)	1,021	1,026	-5		-3,933	357	330	27		-2,328	-224
4. Private transfers	-68	-4	(-2)	(-2)	-15	(-15)	(—)		-53	4	4				
5. Official transfers	7								7						
6. Capital	25	3	(3)		26	(26)			-17	18	-22		40	-3	-2
7. Gold	3				29	29				-26	-26				
8. Settlements & error	4,161	-978	-765	-213	-1,061	-1,066	5		3,996	-353	-286	-27	-40	2,331	226
EPU															
5. Official transfers	107	146	146		-235	-235				196	196				
6. Capital	77	-341	-335		525	525				-107	-107				
7. Gold	-282	-73	-73	-6						-209	-209				
8. Settlements & error	98	268	262	6	-290	-290				120	120				
OWN CURRENCY AREA															
1. Merchandise f.o.b.					-409	-3,352	2,943		-409						
2. Services					-4	-581	577		-4						
3. Goods & services					-413	-3,933	3,520		-413						
4. Private transfers					7	-53	60		7						
5. Official transfers					-23	7	-30		-23						
6. Capital					-25	-17	-8		-25						
7. Gold															
8. Settlements & error					454	3,996	-3,542		454						

(continued)

93

TABLE A-4 (concluded)

	All Areas	Sterling Area All	U.K.	RSA	Nonsterling EPU Area All	Cont. OEEC	Cont. OT's	EPU	Own Currency Area	U.S., Canada, and IO All	U.S.	Canada	IO	Latin America	Other Countries
U.S., CANADA, & IO															
1. Merchandise f.o.b.	10,640	1,663	2,363	-700	6,626	6,901	-275			-45	-2,475	2,429	1	-1,133	3,529
2. Services	-656	464	-933	1,397	-3,036	-2,833	-203			-767	-2,793	1,891	135	4,078	-1,395
3. Goods & services	9,984	2,127	1,430	697	3,590	4,068	-478			-812	-5,268	4,320	136	2,945	2,134
4. Private transfers	-2,392	-375	-176	-199	-783	-765	-18			-184	-152	-25		-187	-863
5. Official transfers	-11,982	-2,007	-1,593	-414	-6,771	-6,575		-196		2	350		-348	-178	-3,028
6. Capital	318	-543	682	-1,225	3,703	3,667	-71	107		-61	2,374	-2,174	-261	-2,178	-603
7. Gold	2,655	566	645	-79	1,668	1,433	26	209			-92	92		248	173
8. Settlements & error	1,417	232	-988	1,220	-1,407	-1,828	541	-120		1,055	2,788	-2,213	480	-650	2,187
UNITED STATES															
1. Merchandise f.o.b.	10,409	216	1,102	-886	5,616	5,883	-257			2,430		2,429	1	-829	2,976
2. Services	2,148	589	-698	1,287	-3,006	-2,803	-203			2,026		1,887	139	3,981	-1,442
3. Goods & services	12,557	805	404	401	2,610	3,080	-470			4,456		4,316	140	3,152	1,534
4. Private transfers	-2,667	-383	-180	-203	-860	-842	-18			-32		-25	-7	-187	-805
5. Official transfers	-11,916	-1,976	-1,711	-265	-6,671	-6,475	-31	-196		-348			-348	-128	-2,793
6. Capital	-2,575	-866	-13	-853	3,102	3,026	26	107		-2,441		-2,235	-206	-1,867	-503
7. Gold	2,779	577	646	-69	1,560	1,325	92	209		92		92		293	257
8. Settlements & error	1,422	1,843	854	989	259	-114	493	-120		-1,727		-2,148	421	-1,263	2,310
CANADA															
1. Merchandise f.o.b.	231	1,447	1,261	186	1,010	1,018	-8			-2,475	-2,475			-304	553
2. Services	-2,936	-201	-257	56	-148	-148	0			-2,646	-2,642		-4	53	6
3. Goods & services	-2,705	1,246	1,004	242	862	870	-8			-5,121	-5,117		-4	-251	559
4. Private transfers	-125	8	4	4	77	77	—			-152	-152				-58
5. Official transfers	-66	-41		-41	-11	-11									-14
6. Capital	2,733	193	252	-59	265	265				2,262	2,317		-55	10	3
7. Gold	168				260	260				-92	-92				
8. Settlements & error	-5	-1,406	-1,260	-146	-1,453	-1,461	8			3,103	3,044		59	241	-490
INTERNAT. ORGANIZATIONS															
2. Services	132	76	22	54	118	118				-147	-151	4		44	41
4. Private transfers	—	10	118	-108	-89	-89									
5. Official transfers	160	130	443	-313	336	376	-40			350	350			-50	-221
6. Capital	-292	-11	-1	-10	-152	-152				118	57	61		-321	-103
7. Gold														-45	-84
8. Settlements & error	—	-205	-582	377	-213	-253	40			-321	-256	-65		372	367
LATIN AMERICA															
1. Merchandise f.o.b.	4,753	834	1,027	-193	2,924	319	2,605			303	8	295		-52	744
2. Services	-7,618	-1,194	-1,263	69	-991	-1,014	23			-5,096	-5,033	-19	-44	-340	3
3. Goods & services	-2,865	-360	-236	-124	1,933	-695	2,628			-4,793	-5,025	276	-44	-392	747
4. Private transfers	-159	-31	-29	-2	-67	-67				-58	-58			5	-8
5. Official transfers	93									93	93			0	
6. Capital	3,559	138	117	21	333	333				3,060	2,749	-10	321	0	28
7. Gold	52	32	32	—	112	112				-248	-293		45		156
8. Settlements & error	-680	221	116	105	-2,311	317	-2,628			1,946	2,534	-266	-322	387	-923
OTHER COUNTRIES															
1. Merchandise f.o.b.	-1,609	2,727	620	2,107	210	65	145			-3,957	-3,535	-422		-790	201
2. Services	-1,771	-876	-986	110	-1,556	-1,555	-1			1,078	1,136	-17	-41	-214	-203
3. Goods & services	-3,380	1,851	-366	2,217	-1,346	-1,490	144			-2,879	-2,399	-439	-41	-1,004	-2
4. Private transfers	995	66	40	26	18	18				877	805	52	20	8	26
5. Official transfers	2,935	41	40	1	222	222				2,790	2,693	81	16		-118
6. Capital	368	317	325	-8	-158	-70	-88			171	106	-3	68	-28	66
7. Gold	-628	-36	-4	-32	-263	-263				-173	-257		84	-156	0
8. Settlements & error	-290	-2,239	-35	-2,204	1,587	1,583	-56			-786	-948	309	-147	1,180	28

a All transactions allocated and gold account balanced.

B

TWO-VALUED MATRIXES ANNUALLY, 1950—54

Gross Goods and Services Transactions Between World Areas, Annually, 1950–54,
as Reported by Area Credited (million U.S. dollars)

	Year	All Areas	Unallocated	Sterling Area			Nonsterling EPU Area			Own Currency Area	U.S.	Canada	IO	Latin America	Other Countries
				All	U.K.	RSA	All	Cont. OEEC	Cont. OT's						
All areas	1950	72,980	803	19,558	9,015	10,543	21,678	18,938	2,740		11,992	3,964	114	7,009	7,862
	1951	97,001	1,083	27,474	12,849	14,625	28,510	24,811	3,699		14,524	4,967	79	9,692	10,667
	1952	95,083	1,141	25,468	11,650	13,818	28,719	24,628	4,091		14,947	5,241	77	9,109	10,381
	1953	94,706	1,125	24,479	11,675	12,804	28,636	24,798	3,838		15,748	5,656	70	8,381	10,611
	1954	100,902	1,332	26,033	12,194	13,839	32,310	28,110	4,200		15,551	5,354	76	9,248	10,998
Unallocated	1950														
	1951														
	1952														
	1953														
	1954														
Sterling Area	1950	20,262	62	9,820	3,362	6,458	4,019	(3,818)	(201)		(2,351)	(735)	17	857	2,401
	1951	25,674	42	12,549	4,401	8,148	5,190	(4,947)	(243)		(2,914)	(845)	6	1,008	3,120
	1952	24,428	113	12,583	4,580	8,003	5,041	(4,747)	(294)		(2,513)	(717)		884	2,577
	1953	24,005	53	12,346	4,808	7,538	5,193	(4,936)	(257)		(2,479)	(801)		742	2,391
	1954	25,047	245	12,887	4,787	8,100	5,578	(5,290)	(288)		(2,510)	(760)	7	781	2,279
United Kingdom	1950	9,859	63	4,367		4,367	2,221	(2,110)	(111)		893	489	17	701	1,108
	1951	11,891	40	5,483		5,483	2,711	(2,584)	(127)		1,074	543	6	775	1,259
	1952	12,005	113	5,652		5,652	2,809	(2,645)	(164)		1,133	529		736	1,033
	1953	11,552	51	5,340		5,340	2,867	(2,725)	(142)		1,191	620		591	892
	1954	12,419	241	5,780		5,780	3,002	(2,847)	(155)		1,243	550	7	627	969
Rest of Sterling Area	1950	10,403	-1	5,453	3,362	2,091	1,798	(1,708)	(90)		(1,458)	(246)		156	1,293
	1951	13,783	2	7,066	4,401	2,665	2,479	(2,363)	(116)		(1,840)	(302)		233	1,861
	1952	12,423		6,931	4,580	2,351	2,232	(2,102)	(130)		(1,380)	(188)		148	1,544
	1953	12,453	2	7,006	4,808	2,198	2,326	(2,211)	(115)		(1,288)	(181)		151	1,499
	1954	12,628	4	7,107	4,787	2,320	2,576	(2,443)	(133)		(1,267)	(210)		154	1,310
Nonsterling EPU area	1950	19,238	292	3,533	(2,414)	(1,119)	7,799	(7,625)	(174)	2,382	(1,939)	129	(5)	1,237	1,922
	1951	27,178	526	5,755	(3,750)	(2,005)	10,393	(10,092)	(301)	3,225	(2,588)	177	(7)	1,942	2,565
	1952	28,028	514	5,182	(3,282)	(1,900)	11,212	(10,807)	(405)	3,495	(3,036)	169	(7)	1,695	2,718
	1953	28,900	486	5,073	(3,219)	(1,854)	11,741	(11,367)	(374)	3,240	(3,685)	203	(8)	1,649	2,815
	1954	32,503	433	5,660	(3,587)	(2,073)	13,774	(13,318)	(456)	3,491	(3,906)	228	(8)	2,017	2,986
Cont. OEEC countries	1950	16,839	282	3,163	(2,161)	(1,002)	7,374	(7,209)	(165)	1,387	(1,621)	111	(5)	1,068	1,828
	1951	24,185	397	5,318	(3,465)	(1,853)	9,918	(9,631)	(287)	1,952	(2,222)	165	(7)	1,772	2,434
	1952	24,871	402	4,765	(3,018)	(1,747)	10,632	(10,248)	(384)	2,171	(2,661)	158	(7)	1,464	2,611
	1953	25,731	376	4,670	(2,963)	(1,707)	11,145	(10,790)	(355)	1,943	(3,291)	188	(8)	1,412	2,698
	1954	29,035	293	5,233	(3,316)	(1,917)	13,143	(12,708)	(435)	2,053	(3,481)	195	(8)	1,749	2,880
Cont. Overseas Territ.	1950	2,399	10	370	(253)	(117)	425	(416)	(9)	995	318	18		169	94
	1951	2,993	129	437	(285)	(152)	475	(461)	(14)	1,273	366	12		170	131
	1952	3,157	112	417	(264)	(153)	580	(559)	(21)	1,324	375	11		231	107
	1953	3,169	110	403	(256)	(147)	536	(577)	(19)	1,297	394	15		237	117
	1954	3,468	140	427	(271)	(156)	631	(610)	(21)	1,438	425	33		268	106
Own Currency Area	1950	—					2,382	995	1,387	2,382					
	1951						3,225	1,273	1,952	3,225					
	1952						3,495	1,324	2,171	3,495					
	1953						3,240	1,297	1,943	3,240					
	1954						3,491	1,438	2,053	3,491					
United States	1950	14,331		2,063	981	1,082	3,396	3,121	275			2,908	90	3,908	1,966
	1951	19,566		3,394	1,560	1,834	4,324	3,975	349			3,646	64	5,330	2,808
	1952	18,930		3,171	1,344	1,827	3,816	3,421	395			4,054	68	5,127	2,694
	1953	17,850		2,764	1,254	1,510	3,266	2,902	364			4,325	60	4,534	2,901
	1954	18,550		2,999	1,449	1,550	3,726	3,353	373			4,045	58	4,800	2,922
Canada	1950	3,795		754	540	214	230	218	12		2,554			156	101
	1951	4,769		1,050	767	283	408	390	18		2,918			225	168
	1952	5,579		1,261	923	338	553	524	29		3,190			314	261
	1953	5,369		1,124	826	298	434	421	13		3,338			232	241
	1954	5,159		1,097	839	258	417	401	16		(3,232)		(1)	222	190
Internat. Organizations	1950	71		9	5	4	28	28			25	1		4	4
	1951	86		11	5	6	31	31			30	1		8	5
	1952	96		16	6	10	30	30			31	1		9	9
	1953	114		22	5	17	32	32			33	1		12	14
	1954	115		21	4	17	32	32			31	1		16	14
Latin America	1950	7,640	150	878	745	133	1,909	1,256	653		(3,609)	121	(1)	644	328
	1951	9,239	233	1,125	930	195	2,369	1,616	753		(3,875)	214	(1)	895	527
	1952	8,552	225	658	487	171	2,215	1,497	718		(3,847)	251	(1)	864	491
	1953	9,058	238	836	692	144	2,233	1,558	675		(3,981)	259	(1)	967	543
	1954	9,544	307	822	623	199	2,548	1,760	788		(3,920)	253	(1)	970	723
Other Countries	1950	7,643	299	2,501	968	1,533	1,915	1,877	38		(1,514)	70	(1)	203	1,140
	1951	10,489	287	3,590	1,436	2,154	2,570	2,487	83		(2,199)	84	(1)	284	1,474
	1952	9,470	289	2,597	1,028	1,569	2,357	2,278	79		(2,330)	49	(1)	216	1,631
	1953	9,410	348	2,314	871	1,443	2,497	2,285	212		(2,232)	67	(1)	245	1,706
	1954	9,984	347	2,547	905	1,642	2,744	2,518	226		(1,952)	67	(1)	442	1,884

TABLE B-2
Gross Goods and Services Transactions Between World Areas, Annually, 1950–54,
as Reported by Area Debited (million U.S. dollars)

		All Areas	Unallocated	Sterling Area — All	U.K.	RSA	Nonsterling EPU Area — All	Cont. OEEC	Cont. OT's	Own Currency Area	U.S.	Canada	IO	Latin America	Other Countries
All areas	1950	72,775		19,712	9,043	10,669	21,325	18,431	2,894		12,262	4,240	58	7,445	7,733
	1951	98,210		27,983	13,074	14,909	28,521	24,684	3,837		15,285	5,463	63	10,226	10,669
	1952	96,727		25,882	11,695	14,187	28,654	24,317	4,337		15,895	5,639	72	10,091	10,494
	1953	95,518		24,463	11,356	13,107	28,289	24,305	3,984		16,882	6,167	77	9,082	10,558
	1954	100,810		25,694	11,930	13,764	31,999	27,737	4,262		16,346	5,867	80	9,902	10,922
Unallocated	1950	928		27	9	18	264	257	7					296	341
	1951	1,180		129	106	23	379	373	6					335	337
	1952	1,212		39	8	31	414	394	20					356	403
	1953	1,254		32	6	26	376	364	12					402	444
	1954	1,389		54	6	48	485	449	36					428	422
Sterling Area	1950	19,807		10,013	3,515	6,498	3,688	3,504	184		2,290	744		849	2,223
	1951	25,648		12,781	4,466	8,315	5,141	4,901	240		2,964	861		1,099	2,802
	1952	24,384		12,464	4,524	7,940	5,026	4,733	293		2,781	739	1	946	2,427
	1953	24,229		12,345	4,712	7,633	5,196	4,939	257		2,783	888	1	815	2,201
	1954	24,886		12,749	4,802	7,947	5,628	5,338	290		2,768	808	1	822	2,110
United Kingdom	1950	9,824		4,597		4,597	(2,038)	(1,936)	(102)		890	508		692	1,092
	1951	12,197		5,744		5,744	(2,687)	(2,560)	(127)		1,095	554		835	1,282
	1952	12,159		5,715		5,715	(2,800)	(2,637)	(163)		1,280	535	1	753	1,075
	1953	12,079		5,559		5,559	(2,869)	(2,727)	(142)		1,399	693	1	630	928
	1954	12,659		5,817		5,817	(3,029)	(2,873)	(156)		1,520	601	1	665	1,026
Rest of Sterling Area	1950	9,983		5,416	3,515	1,901	(1,650)	(1,568)	(82)		1,400	236		157	1,124
	1951	13,451		7,037	4,466	2,571	(2,454)	(2,341)	(113)		1,869	307		264	1,520
	1952	12,225		6,749	4,524	2,225	(2,226)	(2,096)	(130)		1,501	204		193	1,352
	1953	12,150		6,786	4,712	2,074	(2,327)	(2,212)	(115)		1,384	195		185	1,273
	1954	12,227		6,932	4,802	2,130	(2,599)	(2,465)	(134)		1,248	207		157	1,084
Nonsterling EPU area	1950	19,103		3,557	2,430	1,127	7,706	7,534	172	2,469	2,083	136	5	1,275	1,872
	1951	27,312		5,919	3,856	2,063	10,514	10,210	304	3,199	2,827	212	7	1,955	2,679
	1952	28,313		5,447	3,450	1,997	11,006	10,608	398	3,559	3,251	226	7	2,001	2,816
	1953	28,560		5,063	3,212	1,851	11,451	11,086	365	3,402	3,836	275	8	1,728	2,797
	1954	31,933		5,590	3,542	2,048	13,361	12,919	442	3,617	3,921	331	8	2,124	2,981
Cont. OEEC countries	1950	16,822		(3,185)	(2,176)	(1,009)	(7,286)	(7,123)	163	1,499	1,779	118	5	1,128	1,822
	1951	24,603		(5,469)	(3,563)	(1,906)	(10,033)	(9,743)	290	2,055	2,459	196	7	1,789	2,595
	1952	25,280		(5,008)	(3,172)	(1,836)	(10,436)	(10,059)	377	2,331	2,743	209	7	1,817	2,729
	1953	25,487		(4,661)	(2,957)	(1,704)	(10,869)	(10,523)	346	2,156	3,334	260	8	1,542	2,657
	1954	28,412		(5,168)	(3,275)	(1,893)	(12,584)	(12,168)	416	2,219	3,377	301	8	1,913	2,842
Cont. Overseas Territ.	1950	2,281		(372)	(254)	(118)	(420)	(411)	(9)	970	304	18		147	50
	1951	2,709		(450)	(293)	(157)	(481)	(467)	(14)	1,144	368	16		166	84
	1952	3,033		(439)	(278)	(161)	(570)	(549)	(21)	1,228	508	17		184	87
	1953	3,073		(402)	(255)	(147)	(582)	(563)	(19)	1,246	502	15		186	140
	1954	3,521		(422)	(267)	(155)	(777)	(751)	(26)	1,398	544	30		211	139
Own Currency Area	1950						2,469	970	1,499	2,469					
	1951						3,199	1,144	2,055	3,199					
	1952						3,559	1,228	2,331	3,559					
	1953						3,402	1,246	2,156	3,402					
	1954						3,617	1,398	2,219	3,617					
United States	1950	14,026		(2,009)	897	(1,112)	(3,246)	(2,958)	288			(3,087)	51	(3,894)	(1,739)
	1951	19,568		(3,345)	1,586	(1,759)	(4,184)	(3,842)	342			(4,025)	54	(5,309)	(2,651)
	1952	19,066		(3,090)	1,232	(1,858)	(3,713)	(3,291)	422			(4,291)	62	(5,314)	(2,596)
	1953	17,535		(2,612)	1,111	(1,501)	(3,045)	(2,683)	362			(4,615)	66	(4,569)	(2,628)
	1954	18,249		(2,835)	1,309	(1,526)	(3,569)	(3,206)	363			(4,331)	68	(4,832)	(2,614)
Canada	1950	3,612		(756)	536	(220)	170	160	10		2,506			113	67
	1951	4,468		(1,037)	765	(272)	316	304	12		2,843			144	128
	1952	5,060		(1,260)	916	(344)	411	391	20		3,022			197	170
	1953	5,000		(1,114)	818	(296)	314	304	10		3,192			180	200
	1954	4,796		(1,083)	829	(254)	277	267	10		3,099		1	166	170
Internat. Organizations	1950	87		(15)	11	(4)	(28)	(28)			35	(1)		(4)	(4)
	1951	95		(9)	3	(6)	(31)	(31)			41	(1)		(8)	(5)
	1952	101		(10)	—	(10)	(30)	(30)			42	(1)		(9)	(9)
	1953	129		(25)	8	(17)	(32)	(32)			45	(1)		(12)	(14)
	1954	128		(28)	11	(17)	(32)	(32)			37	(1)		(16)	(14)
Latin America	1950	7,509		868	718	150	1,800	1,171	629		3,590	199	1	751	300
	1951	9,246		1,089	898	191	2,248	1,537	711		4,139	266	1	1,001	502
	1952	8,574		632	503	129	2,024	1,334	690		4,249	301	1	948	419
	1953	8,918		783	658	125	1,982	1,351	631		4,354	317	1	1,008	473
	1954	9,245		697	569	128	2,376	1,631	745		4,215	317	1	993	646
Other Countries	1950	7,703		2,467	927	1,540	1,954	1,849	105		1,758	73	1	263	1,187
	1951	10,693		3,674	1,394	2,280	2,509	2,342	167		2,471	98	1	375	1,565
	1952	10,017		2,940	1,062	1,878	2,471	2,308	163		2,550	81	1	320	1,654
	1953	9,893		2,489	831	1,658	2,491	2,300	191		2,672	71	1	368	1,801
	1954	10,184		2,658	862	1,796	2,654	2,497	157		2,306	79	1	521	1,965

TABLE B-3
Net Goods and Services Transactions Between World Areas, Annually, 1950–54
(as reported by area at left, million U.S. dollars)

		All Areas	Unallocated	Sterling Area All	Sterling Area U.K.	Sterling Area RSA	Nonsterling EPU Area All	Nonsterling EPU Area Cont. OEEC	Nonsterling EPU Area Cont. OT's	Own Currency Area	U.S.	Canada	IO	Latin America	Other Countries
All areas	1950	205	-125	-249	-809	560	2,575	2,116	459		-2,034	352	27	-500	159
	1951	-1,209	-92	1,826	652	1,174	1,198	208	990		-5,044	499	-16	446	-26
	1952	-1,644	-71	1,084	-509	1,593	406	-652	1,058		-4,119	181	-24	535	364
	1953	-812	-129	250	-404	654	76	-689	765		-1,787	656	-59	-537	718
	1954	92	-57	1,147	-465	1,612	377	-302	679		-2,698	558	-52	3	814
Unallocated	1950														
	1951														
	1952														
	1953														
	1954														
Sterling Area	1950	550	35	-193	-1,235	1,042	462	(633)	(-171)		(342)	(-21)	(2)	-11	-66
	1951	-2,309	-87	-232	-1,343	1,111	-729	(-522)	(-207)		(-431)	(-192)	(-3)	-81	-554
	1952	-1,454	74	119	-1,135	1,254	-406	(-261)	(-145)		(-577)	(-543)	(-10)	252	-363
	1953	-458	21	1	-751	752	130	(275)	(-145)		(-133)	(-313)	(-25)	-41	-98
	1954	-647	191	138	-1,030	1,168	-12	(122)	(-134)		(-325)	(-323)	(-21)	84	-379
United Kingdom	1950	816	54	852		852	-209	(-66)	(-143)		-4	-47	6	-17	181
	1951	-1,183	-66	1,017		1,017	-1,145	(-979)	(-166)		-512	-222	3	-123	-135
	1952	310	105	1,128		1,128	-641	(-527)	(-114)		-99	-387		233	-29
	1953	196	45	628		628	-345	(-232)	(-113)		80	-198	-8	-67	61
	1954	489	235	978		978	-540	(-428)	(-112)		-66	-279	-4	58	107
Rest of Sterling Area	1950	-266	-19	-1,045	-1,235	190	671	(699)	(-28)		(-346)	(26)	(-4)	6	-247
	1951	-1,126	-21	-1,249	-1,343	94	416	(457)	(-41)		(-81)	(30)	(-6)	42	-419
	1952	-1,764	-31	-1,009	-1,135	126	235	(266)	(-31)		(-478)	(-156)	(-10)	19	-334
	1953	-654	-24	-627	-751	124	475	(507)	(-32)		(-213)	(-115)	(-17)	26	-159
	1954	-1,136	-44	-840	-1,030	190	528	(550)	(-22)		(-259)	(-44)	(-17)	26	-486
Nonsterling EPU area	1950	-2,087	28	-155	(376)	(-531)	93	(339)	(-246)	-87	-1,307	-41	(-23)	-563	-32
	1951	-1,343	147	614	(1,063)	(-449)	-121	(59)	(-180)	26	-1,596	-139	(-24)	-306	56
	1952	-626	100	156	(482)	(-326)	206	(371)	(-165)	-64	-677	-242	(-23)	-329	247
	1953	611	110	-123	(350)	(-473)	290	(498)	(-208)	-162	(640)	-111	(-24)	-333	324
	1954	504	-52	32	(558)	(-526)	413	(734)	(-321)	-126	(337)	-49	(-24)	-359	332
Cont. OEEC countries	1950	-1,592	25	-341	(225)	(-566)	-160	(86)	(-246)	417	-1,337	-49	(-23)	-103	-21
	1951	-499	24	417	(905)	(-488)	-292	(-112)	(-180)	808	-1,620	-139	(-24)	235	92
	1952	554	8	32	(381)	(-349)	24	(189)	(-165)	943	-630	-233	(-23)	130	303
	1953	1,426	12	-269	(236)	(-505)	59	(267)	(-208)	697	-608	-116	(-24)	61	398
	1954	1,298	-156	-105	(443)	(-548)	224	(540)	(-316)	655	-275	-72	(-24)	118	383
Cont. Overseas Territ.	1950	-495	3	186	(151)	(35)	253	(253)		-504	30	8		-460	-11
	1951	-844	123	197	(158)	(39)	171	(171)		-782	24			-541	-36
	1952	-1,180	92	124	(101)	(23)	182	(182)		-1,007	-47	-9		-459	-56
	1953	-815	98	146	(114)	(32)	231	(231)		-859	32	5		-394	-74
	1954	-794	104	137	(115)	(22)	189	(194)	(-5)	-781	62	23		-477	-51
Own Currency Area	1950						-87	-504	417	-87					
	1951						26	-782	808	26					
	1952						-64	-1,007	943	-64					
	1953						-162	-859	697	-162					
	1954						-126	-781	655	-126					
United States	1950	2,069		-227	91	-318	1,313	1,342	-29			402	55	318	208
	1951	4,281		430	465	-35	1,497	1,516	-19			803	23	1,191	337
	1952	3,035		390	64	326	565	678	-113			1,032	26	878	144
	1953	968		-19	-145	126	-570	-432	-138			1,133	15	180	229
	1954	2,204		231	-71	302	-195	-24	-171			946	21	585	616
Canada	1950	-445		10	32	-22	94	100	-6		(-533)		(-1)	-43	28
	1951	-694		189	213	-24	196	194	2		(-1,107)		(-1)	-41	70
	1952	-60		522	388	134	327	315	12		(-1,101)		(-1)	13	180
	1953	-798		236	133	103	159	161	-2		(-1,277)		(-1)	-85	170
	1954	-708		289	238	51	86	100	-14		(-1,099)		—	-95	111
Internat. Organizations	1950	13		9	5	4	23	23			-26	1		3	3
	1951	23		11	5	6	24	24			-24	1		7	4
	1952	24		15	5	10	23	23			-31	1		8	8
	1953	37		21	4	17	24	24			-33	1		11	13
	1954	35		20	3	17	24	24			-37	—		15	13
Latin America	1950	195	-146	29	53	-24	634	128	506		(-285)	8	(-3)	-107	65
	1951	-987	-102	26	95	-69	414	-173	587		(-1,434)	70	(-7)	-106	152
	1952	-1,539	-131	-288	-266	-22	214	-320	534		(-1,467)	54	(-8)	-84	171
	1953	-24	-164	21	62	-41	505	16	489		(-588)	79	(-11)	-41	175
	1954	-358	-121	—	-42	42	424	-153	577		(-912)	87	(-15)	-23	202
Other Countries	1950	-90	-42	278	-131	409	43	55	-12		(-225)	3	(-3)	-97	-47
	1951	-180	-50	788	154	634	-109	-108	-1		(-452)	-44	(-4)	-218	-91
	1952	-1,024	-114	-170	-47	217	-459	-451	-8		(-266)	-121	(-8)	-203	-23
	1953	-1,148	-96	113	-57	170	-300	-372	72		(-399)	-133	(-13)	-228	-95
	1954	-938	-75	437	-121	558	-237	-324	87		(-552)	-103	(-13)	-204	-81

TABLE B-4
Gross Merchandise Transactions Between World Areas, Annually, 1950–54, as Reported by Area Credited (million U.S. dollars)

		All Areas	Unallocated	Sterling Area: All	Sterling Area: U.K.	Sterling Area: RSA	Nonsterling EPU Area: All	Nonsterling EPU Area: Cont. OEEC	Nonsterling EPU Area: Cont. OT's	Own Currency Area	U.S.	Canada	IO	Latin America	Other Countries
All areas	1950	57,364	234	15,059	6,778	8,281	18,514	16,059	2,455		9,257	2,857		5,170	6,273
	1951	76,808	406	21,492	9,811	11,681	24,402	21,094	3,308		10,838	3,760	1	7,240	8,669
	1952	73,411	405	19,141	8,413	10,728	24,241	20,576	3,665		10,469	3,961		6,632	8,562
	1953	72,521	464	18,154	8,423	9,731	23,994	20,585	3,409		10,727	4,333		6,128	8,721
	1954	76,994	526	19,262	8,663	10,599	26,983	23,274	3,709		10,307	4,013	7	6,940	8,956
Unallocated	1950														
	1951														
	1952														
	1953														
	1954														
Sterling Area	1950	15,381	-3	7,312	2,543	4,769	3,376	(3,225)	(151)		1,713	555		578	1,850
	1951	19,860	-2	9,503	3,483	6,020	4,326	(4,149)	(177)		2,181	634		663	2,555
	1952	18,624	-6	9,402	3,546	5,856	4,126	(3,895)	(231)		1,720	552		567	2,263
	1953	18,181	-4	9,131	3,762	5,369	4,301	(4,097)	(204)		1,622	625		441	2,065
	1954	18,720	-7	9,539	3,700	5,839	4,638	(4,408)	(230)		1,588	565	7	465	1,925
United Kingdom	1950	6,300		2,831		2,831	1,679	(1,604)	(75)		409	359		432	590
	1951	7,694		3,573		3,573	1,979	(1,898)	(81)		543	392		451	756
	1952	7,915		3,710		3,710	2,058	(1,943)	(115)		562	371		440	774
	1953	7,482		3,385		3,385	2,135	(2,034)	(101)		564	451		312	635
	1954	7,896		3,731		3,731	2,234	(2,123)	(111)		538	380	7	333	673
Rest of Sterling Area	1950	9,081	-3	4,481	2,543	1,938	1,697	(1,621)	(76)		1,304	196		146	1,260
	1951	12,166	-2	5,930	3,483	2,447	2,347	(2,251)	(96)		1,638	242		212	1,799
	1952	10,709	-6	5,692	3,546	2,146	2,068	(1,952)	(116)		1,158	181		127	1,489
	1953	10,699	-4	5,746	3,762	1,984	2,166	(2,063)	(103)		1,058	174		129	1,430
	1954	10,824	-7	5,808	3,700	2,108	2,404	(2,285)	(119)		1,050	185		132	1,252
Nonsterling EPU area	1950	15,476	15	2,697	(1,780)	(917)	6,636	(6,497)	(139)	2,169	1,238	103		1,063	1,555
	1951	22,092	133	4,486	(2,723)	(1,763)	8,882	(8,646)	(236)	2,943	1,739	149		1,687	2,073
	1952	22,005	127	3,753	(2,155)	(1,598)	9,430	(9,098)	(332)	3,169	1,736	136		1,463	2,191
	1953	22,265	118	3,654	(2,085)	(1,569)	9,729	(9,423)	(306)	2,873	2,021	165		1,409	2,296
	1954	24,677	153	4,036	(2,296)	(1,740)	11,201	(10,835)	(366)	3,100	1,846	182		1,736	2,423
Cont. OEEC countries	1950	13,247	5	2,354	(1,554)	(800)	6,261	(6,130)	(131)	1,237	939	85		904	1,462
	1951	19,311	4	4,079	(2,476)	(1,603)	8,467	(8,242)	(225)	1,754	1,394	137		1,530	1,946
	1952	19,088	15	3,367	(1,933)	(1,434)	8,919	(8,605)	(314)	1,943	1,387	125		1,243	2,089
	1953	19,361	8	3,286	(1,875)	(1,411)	9,199	(8,910)	(289)	1,697	1,653	150		1,185	2,183
	1954	21,492	13	3,651	(2,077)	(1,574)	10,648	(10,300)	(348)	1,781	1,447	149		1,481	2,322
Cont. Overseas Territ.	1950	2,229	10	343	(226)	(117)	375	(367)	(8)	932	299	18		159	93
	1951	2,781	129	407	(247)	(160)	415	(404)	(11)	1,189	345	12		157	127
	1952	2,917	112	386	(222)	(164)	511	(493)	(18)	1,226	349	11		220	102
	1953	2,904	110	368	(210)	(158)	530	(513)	(17)	1,176	368	15		224	113
	1954	3,185	140	385	(219)	(166)	553	(535)	(18)	1,319	399	33		255	101
Own Currency Area	1950						2,169	932	1,237	2,169					
	1951						2,943	1,189	1,754	2,943					
	1952						3,169	1,226	1,943	3,169					
	1953						2,873	1,176	1,697	2,873					
	1954						3,100	1,319	1,781	3,100					
United States	1950	10,101		1,325	522	803	2,617	2,384	233			2,011		2,720	1,438
	1951	14,120		2,331	933	1,398	3,299	2,997	302			2,682	1	3,748	2,059
	1952	13,301		2,048	714	1,334	2,872	2,525	347			2,976		3,476	1,929
	1953	12,435		1,641	622	1,019	2,417	2,100	317			3,223		3,072	2,082
	1954	12,940		1,757	713	1,044	2,841	2,521	320			2,950		3,351	2,041
Canada	1950	3,040		652	458	194	190	178	12		1,976			136	86
	1951	3,938		897	635	262	369	351	18		2,316			205	151
	1952	4,659		1,097	782	315	512	483	29		2,514			291	245
	1953	4,407		960	694	266	392	379	13		2,617			213	225
	1954	4,230		926	705	221	376	360	16		2,549			204	175
Internat. Organizations	1950														
	1951														
	1952														
	1953														
	1954														
Latin America	1950	6,657	10	788	696	92	1,792	1,147	645		3,187	120		482	278
	1951	7,886	59	966	837	129	2,185	1,447	738		3,343	213		678	442
	1952	7,159	76	498	395	103	1,987	1,283	704		3,310	250		640	398
	1953	7,684	95	720	604	116	2,039	1,377	662		3,347	258		773	452
	1954	8,113	131	705	535	170	2,358	1,584	774		3,271	252		770	626
Other Countries	1950	6,709	212	2,285	779	1,506	1,734	1,696	38		1,143	68		191	1,076
	1951	8,912	216	3,309	1,200	2,109	2,398	2,315	83		1,259	82		259	1,389
	1952	7,663	208	2,343	821	1,522	2,145	2,066	79		1,189	47		195	1,536
	1953	7,549	255	2,048	656	1,392	2,243	2,033	210		1,120	62		220	1,601
	1954	8,314	249	2,299	714	1,585	2,469	2,247	222		1,053	64		414	1,766

TABLE B-5
Gross Merchandise Transactions Between World Areas, Annually, 1950–54,
as Reported by Area Debited (million U.S. dollars)

	Year	All Areas	Unallocated	Sterling Area			Nonsterling EPU Area			Own Currency Area	U.S.	Canada	IO	Latin America	Other Countries
				All	U.K.	RSA	All	Cont. OEEC	Cont. CT's						
All areas	1950	56,142		14,879	6,672	8,207	17,728	15,118	2,610		9,095	3,056		5,184	6,200
	1951	75,774		21,396	9,775	11,621	23,412	19,984	3,428		11,193	4,087		7,151	8,535
	1952	73,239		19,109	8,243	10,866	23,436	19,566	3,870		10,840	4,164		7,086	8,604
	1953	71,309		17,938	8,087	9,851	23,025	19,496	3,529		10,997	4,505		6,262	8,582
	1954	75,051		18,762	8,417	10,345	25,839	22,083	3,756		10,363	4,231		7,021	8,835
Unallocated	1950	397		11		11	67	66	1					84	235
	1951	371		9		9	105	104	1					37	220
	1952	504		14		14	158	147	11					54	278
	1953	519		9		9	133	121	11					88	289
	1954	518		22		22	158	122	36					107	231
Sterling Area	1950	14,951		7,424	2,660	4,764	3,067	2,930	137		1,606	595		543	1,716
	1951	19,658		9,628	3,540	6,088	4,209	4,036	173		2,182	694		682	2,263
	1952	18,411		9,241	3,473	5,768	4,038	3,812	226		1,864	552		595	2,121
	1953	18,140		9,192	3,707	5,485	4,233	4,032	201		1,708	650		510	1,847
	1954	18,282		9,412	3,731	5,681	4,533	4,308	225		1,526	594		496	1,721
United Kingdom	1950	6,275		3,021		3,021	(1,525)	(1,457)	(68)		337	370		419	603
	1951	7,808		3,779		3,779	(1,925)	(1,846)	(79)		470	399		462	773
	1952	7,951		3,774		3,774	(2,014)	(1,901)	(113)		550	363		451	799
	1953	7,693		3,621		3,621	(2,101)	(2,001)	(100)		544	476		347	604
	1954	7,894		3,769		3,769	(2,184)	(2,076)	(108)		501	405		361	674
Rest of Sterling Area	1950	8,676		4,403	2,660	1,743	(1,542)	(1,473)	(69)		1,269	225		124	1,113
	1951	11,850		5,849	3,540	2,309	(2,284)	(2,190)	(94)		1,712	295		220	1,490
	1952	10,460		5,467	3,473	1,994	(2,024)	(1,911)	(113)		1,314	189		144	1,322
	1953	10,447		5,571	3,707	1,864	(2,132)	(2,031)	(101)		1,164	174		163	1,243
	1954	10,388		5,643	3,731	1,912	(2,349)	(2,232)	(117)		1,025	189		135	1,047
Nonsterling EPU area	1950	14,963		2,500	1,650	850	6,346	6,213	133	2,250	1,216	107		1,020	1,524
	1951	21,376		4,336	2,632	1,704	8,463	8,238	225	2,918	1,772	172		1,584	2,131
	1952	21,490		3,638	2,088	1,550	8,858	8,546	312	3,236	1,696	160		1,609	2,293
	1953	21,389		3,372	1,924	1,448	9,226	8,936	290	3,036	1,925	186		1,386	2,258
	1954	23,906		3,772	2,146	1,626	10,676	10,327	349	3,223	1,821	204		1,738	2,472
Cont. OEEC countries	1950	12,901		(2,182)	(1,440)	(742)	(5,986)	(5,861)	(125)	1,354	936	89		879	1,475
	1951	18,975		(3,942)	(2,393)	(1,549)	(8,068)	(7,853)	(215)	1,870	1,465	156		1,426	2,048
	1952	18,847		(3,264)	(1,873)	(1,391)	(8,378)	(8,083)	(295)	2,110	1,310	143		1,434	2,208
	1953	18,713		(3,032)	(1,730)	(1,302)	(8,723)	(8,449)	(274)	1,912	1,546	171		1,209	2,120
	1954	20,940		(3,412)	(1,941)	(1,471)	(10,149)	(9,817)	(332)	1,948	1,387	174		1,536	2,334
Cont. Overseas Territ.	1950	2,062		(318)	(210)	(108)	(360)	(352)	(8)	896	280	18		141	49
	1951	2,401		(394)	(239)	(155)	(395)	(385)	(10)	1,048	307	16		158	83
	1952	2,643		(374)	(215)	(159)	(480)	(463)	(17)	1,126	386	17		175	85
	1953	2,676		(340)	(194)	(146)	(503)	(487)	(16)	1,124	379	15		177	138
	1954	2,966		(360)	(205)	(155)	(527)	(510)	(17)	1,275	434	30		202	138
Own Currency Area	1950						2,250	896	1,354	2,250					
	1951						2,918	1,048	1,870	2,918					
	1952						3,236	1,126	2,110	3,236					
	1953						3,036	1,124	1,912	3,036					
	1954						3,223	1,275	1,948	3,223					
United States	1950	9,984		1,337	507	830	2,553	2,303	250			2,095		2,697	1,302
	1951	14,080		2,330	1,037	1,293	3,235	2,949	286			2,882		3,706	1,927
	1952	13,663		2,098	678	1,420	2,876	2,518	358			3,095		3,722	1,872
	1953	12,251		1,608	576	1,032	2,302	2,007	295			3,306		3,096	1,939
	1954	12,748		1,736	692	1,044	2,677	2,374	303			3,069		3,393	1,873
Canada	1950	2,907		630	458	172	151	141	10		1,953			111	62
	1951	3,732		888	635	253	291	279	12		2,288			142	123
	1952	4,167		1,068	782	286	386	366	20		2,354			195	164
	1953	4,024		928	694	234	288	278	10		2,445			168	195
	1954	3,851		899	705	194	253	243	10		2,373			164	162
Internat. Organizations	1950														
	1951														
	1952														
	1953														
	1954														
Latin America	1950	6,474		779	663	116	1,628	1,004	624		3,091	195		521	260
	1951	7,862		941	800	141	2,021	1,319	702		3,510	259		698	433
	1952	7,180		495	410	85	1,794	1,110	684		3,569	290		671	361
	1953	7,484		683	581	102	1,765	1,139	626		3,581	306		740	409
	1954	7,754		596	492	104	2,129	1,390	739		3,445	303		710	571
Other Countries	1950	6,466		2,198	734	1,464	1,565	1,565	101		1,229	64		208	1,101
	1951	8,695		3,264	1,131	2,133	2,170	2,011	159		1,441	80		302	1,438
	1952	7,824		2,555	812	1,743	2,090	1,941	149		1,357	67		240	1,515
	1953	7,502		2,146	605	1,541	2,042	1,859	183		1,338	57		274	1,645
	1954	7,992		2,325	651	1,674	2,190	2,044	146		1,198	61		413	1,805

TABLE B-6
Net Merchandise Transactions Between World Areas, Annually, 1950–54
(as reported by area at left, million U.S. dollars)

Area	Year	All Areas	Unallocated	Sterling Area All	Sterling Area U.K.	Sterling Area RSA	Nonsterling EPU Area All	Nonsterling EPU Cont. OEEC	Nonsterling EPU Cont. OT's	Own Currency Area	U.S.	Canada	IO	Latin America	Other Countries
All areas	1950	1,222	-163	108	503	-395	3,551	3,158	393		-727	-50		-1,304	-193
	1951	1,034	35	1,834	2,003	-169	3,026	2,119	907		-3,242	28	1	-622	-26
	1952	172	-99	730	462	268	2,751	1,729	1,022		-3,194	-206		-548	738
	1953	1,212	-55	14	730	-716	2,605	1,872	733		-1,524	309		-1,356	1,219
	1954	1,943	8	980	769	211	3,077	2,334	743		-2,441	162	7	-814	964
Unallocated	1950														
	1951														
	1952														
	1953														
	1954														
Sterling Area	1950	502	-14	-112	-478	366	876	(1,043)	(-167)		376	-75		-201	-348
	1951	-1,536	-11	-125	-296	171	-10	(207)	(-217)		-149	-254		-278	-709
	1952	-485	-20	161	-228	389	488	(631)	(-143)		-378	-516		72	-292
	1953	243	-13	-61	141	-202	929	(1,065)	(-136)		14	-303		-242	-81
	1954	-42	-29	127	-69	196	866	(996)	(-130)		-148	-334	7	-131	-400
United Kingdom	1950	-372		171		171	29	(164)	(-135)		-98	-99		-231	-144
	1951	-2,081		33		33	-653	(-495)	(-158)		-494	-243		-349	-375
	1952	-328		237		237	-30	(70)	(-100)		-116	-411		30	-38
	1953	-605		-322		-322	211	(304)	(-93)		-12	-243		-269	30
	1954	-521		—		—	88	(182)	(-94)		-154	-325	7	-159	22
Rest of Sterling Area	1950	874	-14	-283	-478	195	847	(879)	(-32)		474	24		30	-204
	1951	545	-11	-158	-296	138	643	(702)	(-59)		345	-11		71	-334
	1952	-157	-20	-76	-228	152	518	(561)	(-43)		-262	-105		42	-254
	1953	848	-13	261	141	120	718	(761)	(-43)		26	-60		27	-111
	1954	479	-29	127	-69	196	778	(814)	(-36)		6	-9		28	-422
Nonsterling EPU area	1950	-2,252	-52	-370	(255)	(-625)	290	(511)	(-221)	-81	-1,315	-48		-565	-111
	1951	-1,320	28	277	(798)	(-521)	419	(578)	(-159)	25	-1,496	-142		-334	-97
	1952	-1,431	-31	-285	(141)	(-426)	572	(720)	(-148)	-67	-1,140	-250		-331	101
	1953	-760	-15	-579	(-16)	(-563)	503	(700)	(-197)	-163	-281	-123		-356	254
	1954	-1,162	-5	-497	(112)	(-609)	525	(686)	(-161)	-123	-831	-71		-393	233
Cont. OEEC countries	1950	-1,871	-61	-576	(97)	(-673)	48	(269)	(-221)	341	-1,364	-56		-100	-103
	1951	-673	-100	43	(630)	(-587)	229	(389)	(-160)	706	-1,555	-142		211	-65
	1952	-478	-132	-445	(32)	(-477)	373	(522)	(-149)	817	-1,131	-241		133	148
	1953	-135	-113	-746	(-126)	(-620)	263	(461)	(-198)	573	-354	-128		46	324
	1954	-591	-109	-657	(1)	(-658)	321	(483)	(-162)	506	-927	-94		91	278
Cont. Overseas Territ.	1950	-381	9	206	(158)	(48)	242	(242)		-422	49	8		-465	-8
	1951	-647	128	234	(168)	(66)	190	(189)	(1)	-681	59			-545	-32
	1952	-953	101	160	(109)	(51)	199	(198)	(1)	-884	-9	-9		-464	-47
	1953	-625	98	167	(110)	(57)	240	(239)	(1)	-736	73	5		-402	-70
	1954	-571	104	160	(111)	(49)	204	(203)	(1)	-629	96	23		-484	-45
Own Currency Area	1950						-81	-422	341	-81					
	1951						25	-681	708	25					
	1952						-67	-884	817	-67					
	1953						-163	-736	573	-163					
	1954						-123	-629	506	-123					
United States	1950	1,006		-281	185	-466	1,401	1,448	-47			58		-371	199
	1951	2,927		149	463	-314	1,527	1,532	-5			394	1	238	618
	1952	2,461		184	164	20	1,176	1,215	-39			622		-93	572
	1953	1,438		-67	78	-145	492	554	-62			778		-509	744
	1954	2,577		231	212	19	1,020	1,134	-114			577		-94	843
Canada	1950	-16		57	88	-31	83	89	-6		-119			-59	22
	1951	-149		203	236	-33	197	195	2		-566			-54	71
	1952	495		545	419	126	352	340	12		-581			1	178
	1953	-98		310	218	92	206	208	-2		-689			-93	168
	1954	-1		332	300	32	172	186	-14		-520			-99	114
Internat. Organizations	1950														
	1951														
	1952														
	1953														
	1954														
Latin America	1950	1,473	-74	245	277	-32	772	268	504		490	9		-39	70
	1951	735	22	284	375	-91	601	21	580		-363	71		-20	140
	1952	73	22	-97	-56	-41	378	-151	529		-412	55		-31	158
	1953	1,422	7	210	257	-47	653	168	485		251	90		33	178
	1954	1,092	24	209	174	35	620	48	572		-122	88		60	213
Other Countries	1950	509	-23	569	176	393	210	221	-11		-159	6		-69	-25
	1951	377	-4	1,046	427	619	267	267			-668	-41		-174	-49
	1952	-941	-70	222	22	200	-148	-142	-6		-683	-117		-166	21
	1953	-1,033	-34	201	52	149	-15	-87	72		-819	-133		-189	-44
	1954	-521	18	578	40	538	-3	-87	84		-820	-98		-157	-39

TABLE B-7
Gross Services Transactions Between World Areas, Annually, 1950–54, as Reported by Area Credited (million U.S. dollars)

		All Areas	Unallocated	Sterling Area All	U.K.	RSA	Nonsterling EPU All	Cont. OEEC	Cont. OT's	Own Currency Area	U.S.	Canada	IO	Latin America	Other Countries
All areas	1950	15,616	569	4,499	2,237	2,262	3,164	2,879	285		2,735	1,107	114	1,839	1,589
	1951	20,193	682	5,982	3,038	2,944	4,108	3,717	391		3,686	1,207	78	2,452	1,998
	1952	21,672	736	6,327	3,237	3,090	4,478	4,052	426		4,478	1,280	77	2,477	1,819
	1953	22,185	661	6,325	3,252	3,073	4,642	4,213	429		5,021	1,323	70	2,253	1,890
	1954	23,908	806	6,771	3,531	3,240	5,327	4,836	491		5,244	1,341	69	2,308	2,042
Unallocated	1950														
	1951														
	1952														
	1953														
	1954														
Sterling Area	1950	4,881	65	2,508	819	1,689	643	(593)	(50)		(638)	(180)	(17)	279	551
	1951	5,814	44	3,046	918	2,128	864	(798)	(66)		(733)	(211)	(6)	345	565
	1952	5,804	119	3,181	1,034	2,147	915	(852)	(63)		(793)	(165)		317	314
	1953	5,824	57	3,215	1,046	2,169	892	(839)	(53)		(857)	(176)		301	326
	1954	6,327	252	3,348	1,087	2,261	940	(882)	(58)		(922)	(195)		316	354
United Kingdom	1950	3,559	63	1,536		1,536	542	(506)	(36)		484	130	17	269	518
	1951	4,197	40	1,910		1,910	732	(686)	(46)		531	151	6	324	503
	1952	4,090	113	1,942		1,942	751	(702)	(49)		571	158		296	259
	1953	4,070	51	1,955		1,955	732	(691)	(41)		627	169		279	257
	1954	4,523	241	2,049		2,049	768	(724)	(44)		705	170		294	296
Rest of Sterling Area	1950	1,322	2	972	819	153	101	(87)	(14)		(154)	(50)		10	33
	1951	1,617	4	1,136	918	218	132	(112)	(20)		(202)	(60)		21	62
	1952	1,714	6	1,239	1,034	205	164	(150)	(14)		(222)	(7)		21	55
	1953	1,754	6	1,260	1,046	214	160	(148)	(12)		(230)	(7)		22	69
	1954	1,804	11	1,299	1,087	212	172	(158)	(14)		(217)	(25)		22	58
Nonsterling EPU area	1950	3,762	277	836	(634)	(202)	1,163	(1,128)	(35)	213	(701)	26	(5)	174	367
	1951	5,086	393	1,269	(1,027)	(242)	1,511	(1,446)	(65)	282	(849)	28	(7)	255	492
	1952	6,023	387	1,429	(1,127)	(302)	1,782	(1,709)	(73)	326	(1,300)	33	(7)	232	527
	1953	6,635	368	1,419	(1,134)	(285)	2,012	(1,944)	(68)	367	(1,664)	38	(8)	240	519
	1954	7,826	280	1,624	(1,291)	(333)	2,573	(2,483)	(90)	391	(2,060)	46	(8)	281	563
Cont. OEEC countries	1950	3,592	277	809	(607)	(202)	1,113	(1,079)	(34)	150	(682)	26	(5)	164	366
	1951	4,874	393	1,239	(989)	(250)	1,451	(1,389)	(62)	198	(828)	28	(7)	242	488
	1952	5,783	387	1,398	(1,085)	(313)	1,713	(1,643)	(70)	228	(1,274)	33	(7)	221	522
	1953	6,370	368	1,384	(1,088)	(296)	1,946	(1,880)	(66)	246	(1,638)	38	(8)	227	515
	1954	7,543	280	1,582	(1,239)	(343)	2,495	(2,408)	(87)	272	(2,034)	46	(8)	268	558
Cont. Overseas Territ.	1950	170		27	(27)		50	(49)	(1)	63	19			10	1
	1951	212		30	(38)	(-8)	60	(57)	(3)	84	21			13	4
	1952	240		31	(42)	(-11)	69	(66)	(3)	98	26			11	5
	1953	265		35	(46)	(-11)	66	(64)	(2)	121	26			13	4
	1954	283		42	(52)	(-10)	78	(75)	(3)	119	26			13	5
Own Currency Area	1950						213	63	150	213					
	1951						282	84	198	282					
	1952						326	98	228	326					
	1953						367	121	246	367					
	1954						391	119	272	391					
United States	1950	4,230		738	459	279	779	737	42			897	90	1,188	538
	1951	5,446		1,063	627	436	1,025	978	47			964	63	1,582	749
	1952	5,629		1,123	630	493	944	896	48			1,078	68	1,651	765
	1953	5,415		1,123	632	491	849	802	47			1,102	60	1,462	819
	1954	5,610		1,242	736	506	885	832	53			1,095	58	1,449	881
Canada	1950	755		102	82	20	40	40			578			20	15
	1951	831		153	132	21	39	39			602			20	17
	1952	920		164	141	23	41	41			676			23	16
	1953	962		164	132	32	42	42			721			19	16
	1954	929		171	134	37	41	41			(683)		(1)	18	15
Internat. Organizations	1950	71		9	5	4	28	28			25	1		4	4
	1951	86		11	5	6	31	31			30	1		8	5
	1952	96		16	6	10	30	30			31	1		9	9
	1953	114		22	5	17	32	32			33	1		12	14
	1954	115		21	4	17	32	32			31	1		16	14
Latin America	1950	983	140	90	49	41	117	109	8		(422)	1	(1)	162	50
	1951	1,353	174	159	93	66	184	169	15		(532)	1	(1)	217	85
	1952	1,393	149	160	92	68	228	214	14		(537)	1	(1)	224	93
	1953	1,374	143	116	88	28	194	181	13		(634)	1	(1)	194	91
	1954	1,431	176	117	88	29	190	176	14		(649)	1	(1)	200	97
Other Countries	1950	934	87	216	189	27	181	181			(371)	2	(1)	12	64
	1951	1,577	71	281	236	45	172	172			(940)	2	(1)	25	85
	1952	1,807	81	254	207	47	212	212			(1,141)	2	(1)	21	95
	1953	1,861	93	266	215	51	254	252	2		(1,112)	5	(1)	25	105
	1954	1,670	98	248	191	57	275	271	4		(899)	3	(1)	28	118

TABLE B-8

Gross Services Transactions Between World Areas, Annually, 1950–54,
as Reported by Area Debited (million U.S. dollars)

		All Areas	Unallocated	Sterling Area All	U.K.	RSA	Nonsterling EPU Area All	Cont. OEEC	Cont. OT's	Own Currency Area	U.S.	Canada	IO	Latin America	Other Countries
All areas	1950	16,633		4,833	2,371	2,462	3,597	3,313	284		3,167	1,184	58	2,261	1,533
	1951	22,436		6,587	3,299	3,288	5,109	4,700	409		4,092	1,376	63	3,075	2,134
	1952	23,488		6,773	3,452	3,321	5,218	4,751	467		5,055	1,475	72	3,005	1,890
	1953	24,209		6,525	3,269	3,256	5,264	4,809	455		5,885	1,662	77	2,820	1,976
	1954	25,759		6,932	3,513	3,419	6,160	5,654	506		5,983	1,636	80	2,881	2,087
Unallocated	1950	531		16	9	7	197	191	6					212	106
	1951	809		120	106	14	274	269	5					298	117
	1952	708		25	8	17	256	247	9					302	125
	1953	735		23	6	17	243	243	–					314	155
	1954	871		32	6	26	327	327	–					321	191
Sterling Area	1950	4,856		2,589	855	1,734	621	574	47		684	149		306	507
	1951	5,990		3,153	926	2,227	932	865	67		782	167		417	539
	1952	5,973		3,223	1,051	2,172	988	921	67		917	187	1	351	306
	1953	6,089		3,153	1,005	2,148	963	907	56		1,075	238	1	305	354
	1954	6,604		3,337	1,071	2,266	1,095	1,030	65		1,242	214	1	326	389
United Kingdom	1950	3,549		1,576		1,576	(513)	(479)	(34)		553	138		273	496
	1951	4,389		1,965		1,965	(762)	(714)	(48)		625	155		373	509
	1952	4,208		1,941		1,941	(786)	(736)	(50)		730	172	1	302	276
	1953	4,386		1,938		1,938	(768)	(726)	(42)		855	217	1	283	324
	1954	4,765		2,048		2,048	(845)	(797)	(48)		1,019	196	1	304	352
Rest of Sterling Area	1950	1,307		1,013	855	158	(108)	(95)	(13)		131	11		33	11
	1951	1,601		1,188	926	262	(170)	(151)	(19)		157	12		44	30
	1952	1,765		1,282	1,051	231	(202)	(185)	(17)		187	15		49	30
	1953	1,703		1,215	1,005	210	(195)	(181)	(14)		220	21		22	30
	1954	1,839		1,289	1,071	218	(250)	(233)	(17)		223	18		22	37
Nonsterling EPU area	1950	4,140		1,057	780	277	1,360	1,321	39	219	867	29	5	255	348
	1951	5,936		1,583	1,224	359	2,051	1,972	79	281	1,055	40	7	371	548
	1952	6,823		1,809	1,362	447	2,148	2,062	86	323	1,555	66	7	392	523
	1953	7,171		1,691	1,288	403	2,225	2,150	75	366	1,911	89	8	342	539
	1954	8,027		1,818	1,396	422	2,685	2,592	93	394	2,100	127	8	386	509
Cont. OEEC countries	1950	3,921		(1,003)	(736)	(267)	(1,300)	(1,262)	(38)	145	843	29	5	249	347
	1951	5,628		(1,527)	(1,170)	(357)	(1,965)	(1,890)	(75)	185	994	40	7	363	547
	1952	6,433		(1,744)	(1,299)	(445)	(2,058)	(1,976)	(82)	221	1,433	66	7	383	521
	1953	6,774		(1,629)	(1,227)	(402)	(2,146)	(2,074)	(72)	244	1,788	89	8	333	537
	1954	7,472		(1,756)	(1,334)	(422)	(2,435)	(2,351)	(84)	271	1,990	127	8	377	508
Cont. Overseas Territ.	1950	219		(54)	(44)	(10)	(60)	(59)	(1)	74	24			6	1
	1951	308		(56)	(54)	(2)	(86)	(82)	(4)	96	61			8	1
	1952	390		(65)	(63)	(2)	(90)	(86)	(4)	102	122			9	2
	1953	397		(62)	(61)	(1)	(79)	(76)	(3)	122	123			9	2
	1954	555		(62)	(62)	–	(250)	(241)	(9)	123	110			9	1
Own Currency Area	1950						219	74	145						
	1951						281	96	185						
	1952						323	102	221						
	1953						366	122	244						
	1954						394	123	271						
United States	1950	4,042		(672)	390	(282)	(693)	(655)	38			(992)	51	(1,197)	(437)
	1951	5,488		(1,015)	549	(466)	(949)	(893)	56			(1,143)	54	(1,603)	(724)
	1952	5,403		(992)	554	(438)	(837)	(773)	64			(1,196)	62	(1,592)	(724)
	1953	5,284		(1,004)	535	(469)	(743)	(676)	67			(1,309)	66	(1,473)	(689)
	1954	5,501		(1,099)	617	(482)	(892)	(832)	60			(1,262)	68	(1,439)	(741)
Canada	1950	705		(126)	78	(48)	19	19			553			2	5
	1951	736		(149)	130	(19)	25	25			555			2	5
	1952	893		(192)	134	(58)	25	25			668			2	6
	1953	976		(186)	124	(62)	26	26			747			12	5
	1954	945		(184)	124	(60)	24	24			726		1	2	8
Internat. Organizations	1950	87		(15)	11	(4)	(28)	(28)			35	(1)		(4)	(4)
	1951	95		(9)	3	(6)	(31)	(31)			41	(1)		(8)	(5)
	1952	101		(10)	–	(10)	(30)	(30)			42	(1)		(9)	(9)
	1953	129		(25)	8	(17)	(32)	(32)			45	(1)		(12)	(14)
	1954	128		(28)	11	(17)	(32)	(32)			37	(1)		(16)	(14)
Latin America	1950	1,035		89	55	34	172	167	5		499	4	1	230	40
	1951	1,384		148	98	50	227	218	9		629	7	1	303	69
	1952	1,394		137	93	44	230	224	6		680	11	1	277	58
	1953	1,434		100	77	23	217	212	5		773	11	1	268	64
	1954	1,491		101	77	24	247	241	6		770	14	1	283	75
Other Countries	1950	1,237		269	193	76	288	284	4		529	9	1	55	86
	1951	1,998		410	263	147	339	331	8		1,030	18	1	73	127
	1952	2,193		385	250	135	381	367	14		1,193	14	1	80	139
	1953	2,391		343	226	117	449	441	8		1,334	14	1	94	156
	1954	2,192		333	211	122	464	453	11		1,108	18	1	108	160

Net Services Transactions Between World Areas, Annually, 1950–54
(as reported by area at left, million U.S. dollars)

		All Areas	Unal-located	Sterling Area — All	U.K.	RSA	Nonsterling EPU Area — All	Cont. OEEC	Cont. OT's	Own Currency Area	U.S.	Canada	IO	Latin America	Other Countries
All areas	1950	-1,017	38	-357	-1,277	920	-976	-1,042	66		-1,307	402	27	804	352
	1951	-2,243	-127	-8	-1,351	1,343	-1,828	-1,911	83		-1,802	471	-17	1,068	
	1952	-1,816	28	354	-971	1,325	-2,345	-2,381	36		-925	387	-24	1,083	-374
	1953	-2,024	-74	236	-1,134	1,370	-2,529	-2,561	32		-263	347	-59	819	-501
	1954	-1,851	-65	167	-1,234	1,401	-2,700	-2,636	-64		-257	396	-59	817	-150
Unallocated	1950														
	1951														
	1952														
	1953														
	1954														
Sterling Area	1950	48	49	-81	-757	676	-414	(-410)	(-4)		(-34)	(54)	(2)	190	282
	1951	-773	-76	-107	-1,047	940	-719	(-729)	(10)		(-282)	(62)	(-3)	197	155
	1952	-969	94	-42	-907	865	-894	(-892)	(-2)		(-199)	(-27)	(-10)	180	-71
	1953	-701	34	62	-892	954	-799	(-790)	-9		(-147)	(-10)	(-25)	201	-17
	1954	-605	220	11	-961	972	-878	-874	-4		(-177)	(11)	(-28)	215	21
United Kingdom	1950	1,188	54	681		681	-238	(-230)	(-8)		94	52	6	214	325
	1951	898	-66	984		984	-492	(-484)	(-8)		-18	21	3	226	240
	1952	638	105	891		891	-611	(-597)	(-14)		17	24		203	9
	1953	801	45	950		950	-556	(-536)	(-20)		92	45	-8	202	31
	1954	1,010	235	978		978	-628	(-610)	(-18)		88	46	-11	217	85
Rest of Sterling Area	1950	-1,140	-5	-762	-5	-757	-176	(-180)	(4)		(-128)	(2)	(-4)	-24	-43
	1951	-1,671	-10	-1,091	-1,047	-44	-227	(-245)	(18)		(-264)	(41)	(-6)	-29	-85
	1952	-1,607	-11	-933	-907	-26	-283	(-295)	(12)		(-216)	(-51)	(-10)	-23	-80
	1953	-1,502	-11	-888	-892	4	-243	(-254)	(11)		(-239)	(-55)	(-17)	-1	-48
	1954	-1,615	-15	-967	-961	-6	-250	(-264)	(14)		(-265)	(-35)	(-17)	-2	-64
Nonsterling EPU area	1950	165	80	215	(121)	(94)	-197	(-172)	(-25)	-6	(8)	7	(-23)	2	79
	1951	-23	119	337	(265)	(72)	-540	(-519)	(-21)	1	(-100)	3	(-24)	28	153
	1952	805	131	441	(341)	(100)	-366	(-349)	(-17)	3	(-463)	8	(-23)	2	146
	1953	1,371	125	456	(366)	(90)	-213	(-202)	(-11)	1	(-921)	12	(-24)	23	70
	1954	1,666	-47	529	(446)	(83)	-112	(48)	(-160)	-3	(1,168)	22	(-24)	34	99
Cont. OEEC countries	1950	279	86	235	(128)	(107)	-208	(-183)	(-25)	76	(27)	7	(-23)	-3	82
	1951	174	124	374	(275)	(99)	-521	(-501)	(-20)	102	(-65)	3	(-24)	24	157
	1952	1,032	140	477	(349)	(128)	-349	(-333)	(-16)	126	(501)	8	(-23)	-3	155
	1953	1,561	125	477	(362)	(115)	-204	(-194)	(-10)	124	(962)	12	(-24)	15	74
	1954	1,889	-47	552	(442)	(110)	-97	(57)	(-154)	149	(1,202)	22	(-24)	27	105
Cont. Overseas Territ.	1950	-114	-6	-20	(-7)	(-13)	11	(11)		-82	-19			5	-3
	1951	-197	-5	-37	(-10)	(-27)	-19	(-18)	(-1)	-101	-35			4	-4
	1952	-227	-9	-36	(-8)	(-28)	-17	(-16)	(-1)	-123	-38			5	-9
	1953	-190		-21	(4)	(-25)	-9	(-8)	(-1)	-123	-41			8	-4
	1954	-223		-23	(4)	(-27)	-15	(-9)	(-6)	-152	-34			7	-6
Own Currency Area	1950						-6	-82	76	-6					
	1951						1	-101	102	1					
	1952						3	-123	126	3					
	1953						1	-123	124	1					
	1954						-3	-152	149	-3					
United States	1950	1,063		54	-94	148	-88	-106	18			344	55	689	9
	1951	1,354		281	2	279	-30	-16	-14			409	22	953	-281
	1952	574		206	-100	306	-611	-537	-74			410	26	971	-428
	1953	-470		48	-223	271	-1,062	-986	-76			355	15	689	-515
	1954	-373			-283	283	-1,215	-1,158	-57			369	21	679	-227
Canada	1950	-429		-47	-56	9	11	(11)			(-414)		(-1)	16	6
	1951	-545		-14	-23	9	-1	(-1)			(-541)		(-1)	13	-1
	1952	-555		-23	-31	8	-25	(-25)			(-520)		(-1)	12	2
	1953	-700		-74	-85	11	-47	(-47)			(-588)		(-1)	8	2
	1954	-707		-43	-62	19	-86	(-86)			-579			4	-3
Internat. Organizations	1950	13		9	5	4	23	23			-26	1		3	3
	1951	23		11	5	6	24	24			-24	1		7	4
	1952	24		15	5	10	23	23			-31	1		8	8
	1953	37		21	4	17	24	24			-33	1		11	13
	1954	35		20	3	17	24	24			-37			15	13
Latin America	1950	-1,278	-72	-216	-224	8	-138	-140	2		(-775)	-1	(-3)	-68	-5
	1951	-1,722	-124	-258	-280	22	-187	-194	7		(-1,071)	-1	(-7)	-86	12
	1952	-1,612	-153	-191	-210	19	-164	-169	5		(-1,055)	-1	(-8)	-53	13
	1953	-1,446	-171	-189	-195	6	-148	-152	4		(-839)	-11	(-11)	-74	-3
	1954	-1,450	-145	-209	-216	7	-196	-201	5		(-790)	-1	(-15)	-83	-11
Other Countries	1950	-599	-19	-291	-307	16	-167	-166	-1		(-66)	-3	(-3)	-28	-22
	1951	-557	-46	-258	-273	15	-376	-375	-1		(216)	-3	(-4)	-44	-42
	1952	-83	-44	-52	-69	17	-311	-309	-2		(417)	-4	(-8)	-37	-44
	1953	-115	-62	-88	-109	21	-285	-285			(423)		(-13)	-39	-51
	1954	-417	-93	-141	-161	20	-234	-237	3		(158)	-5	(-13)	-47	-42

TABLE B-10
Gross Transportation Transactions Between World Areas, Annually, 1950–54, as Reported by Area Credited (million U.S. dollars)

	Year	All Areas	Unallocated	Sterling Area All	U.K.	RSA	Nonsterling EPU Area All	Cont. OEEC	Cont. OT's	Own Currency Area	U.S., Canada, and IO All	U.S.	Canada	IO	Latin America	Other Countries
All areas	1950	5,195	23	1,532			1,704				821				604	511
	1951	7,428	40	2,349			2,453				1,008				882	696
	1952	7,915	41	2,494			2,622				1,126				862	770
	1953	7,155	28	2,196			2,404				1,025				774	728
	1954	7,492	18	2,279			2,533				1,099				804	759
Unallocated	1950															
	1951															
	1952															
	1953															
	1954															
Sterling Area	1950	1,531	23	701	172	529	409				198				80	120
	1951	2,069	40	973	221	752	570				237				116	133
	1952	2,177	40	1,038	223	815	621				247				104	127
	1953	1,927	27	916	232	684	541				227				93	123
	1954	1,972	17	935	233	702	549				240				93	138
United Kingdom	1950	1,176	23	491	—	491	322				164	114	33	17	70	106
	1951	1,608	40	710	—	710	450				200	153	41	6	96	112
	1952	1,697	39	771	—	771	482				208	165	43	—	85	112
	1953	1,432	26	632	—	632	410				193	150	43		71	100
	1954	1,466	16	650	—	650	414				206	166	40		71	109
Rest of Sterling Area	1950	355		210	172	38	87				34				10	14
	1951	461		263	221	42	120				37				20	21
	1952	480	1	267	223	44	139				39				19	15
	1953	495	1	284	232	52	131				34				22	23
	1954	506	1	285	233	52	135				34				22	29
Nonsterling EPU area	1950	1,704		438			566			106	303	288	15		121	170
	1951	2,491		701			826			170	376	360	16		184	234
	1952	2,821	1	821			934			195	409	396	13		168	293
	1953	2,733	1	768			935			212	392	379	13		167	258
	1954	3,039	1	848			1,044			220	463	450	13		197	266
Cont. OEEC countries	1950	1,572		413			520			70	287	272	15		113	169
	1951	2,323		674			770			117	359	343	16		173	230
	1952	2,633	1	794			869			133	389	376	13		159	288
	1953	2,534	1	736			872			144	371	358	13		156	254
	1954	2,815	1	811			972			145	440	427	13		185	261
Cont. Overseas Territ.	1950	132		25			46			36	16	16			8	1
	1951	168		27			56			53	17	17			11	4
	1952	188		27			65			62	20	20			9	5
	1953	199		32			63			68	21	21			11	4
	1954	224		37			72			75	23	23			12	5
Own Currency Area	1950						106	70	36	106						
	1951						170	117	53	170						
	1952						195	133	62	195						
	1953						212	144	68	212						
	1954						220	145	75	220						
United States	1950	1,033		174	109	65	377	360	17		85		68	17	261	136
	1951	1,556		336	162	174	565	540	25		91		90	1	368	196
	1952	1,488		287	156	131	501	471	30		124		119	5	375	201
	1953	1,198		220	124	96	363	341	22		92		92		320	203
	1954	1,171		211	130	81	360	334	26		86		86		312	202
Canada	1950	131		42	35	7	13				62	62			5	9
	1951	165		70	58	12	18				59	59			8	10
	1952	185		76	68	8	17				74	74			8	10
	1953	154		63	55	8	17				60	60			5	9
	1954	145		60	50	10	16				57	57			4	8
Internat. Organizations	1950															
	1951															
	1952															
	1953															
	1954															
Latin America	1950	474		84	43	41	105	97	8		112	112			125	48
	1951	759		147	81	66	170	155	15		179	179			182	81
	1952	800		145	77	68	199	185	14		179	179			186	91
	1953	681		99	71	28	157	144	13		172	172			165	88
	1954	702		99	70	29	161	147	14		180	180			171	91
Other Countries	1950	322		93	89	4	128	128			61	61			12	28
	1951	388		122	103	19	134	134			66	66			24	42
	1952	444		127	105	22	155	155			93	93			21	48
	1953	462		130	108	22	179	177	2		82	79	3		24	47
	1954	463		126	98	28	183	180	3		73	72	1		27	54

TABLE B-11
Gross Transportation Transactions Between World Areas, Annually, 1950–54, as Reported by Area Debited (million U.S. dollars)

		All Areas	Unallocated	Sterling Area			Nonsterling EPU Area			Own Currency Area	U.S.	Canada	IO	Latin America	Other Countries
				All	U.K.	RSA	All	Cont. OEEC	Cont. OT's						
All areas	1950	5,766		1,552	745	807	1,988	1,820	168		818	118		809	481
	1951	8,556		2,345	1,110	1,235	3,031	2,741	290		974	164		1,242	800
	1952	8,846		2,500	1,234	1,266	2,998	2,662	336		1,115	180		1,263	790
	1953	7,695		1,963	986	977	2,679	2,399	280		1,081	182		1,026	764
	1954	8,070		2,042	1,021	1,021	2,936	2,597	339		1,026	186		1,100	780
Unallocated	1950	43		13	9	4	12	12							18
	1951	38		14	9	5	6	6							18
	1952	38		12	8	4	7	7							19
	1953	41		12	6	6	8	8							21
	1954	56		13	6	7	6	6							37
Sterling Area	1950	1,576		708	201	507	443	412	31		161	36		121	107
	1951	2,251		971	230	741	690	641	49		194	46		188	162
	1952	2,325		962	234	728	737	683	54		243	48		163	172
	1953	1,999		763	194	569	667	631	36		217	49		107	196
	1954	2,132		826	218	608	749	696	53		206	43		118	190
United Kingdom	1950			476		476					131	33		90	103
	1951			666		666					157	41		152	145
	1952			672		672					205	43		120	155
	1953			530		530					179	43		88	185
	1954			557		557					168	40		99	179
Rest of Sterling Area	1950			232	201	31					30	3		31	4
	1951			305	230	75					37	5		36	17
	1952			290	234	56					38	5		43	17
	1953			233	194	39					38	6		19	11
	1954			269	218	51					38	3		19	11
Nonsterling EPU area	1950	1,990		465	289	176	707	574	33	108	304	13		214	179
	1951	3,075		787	509	278	1,137	1,066	71	167	344	20		314	306
	1952	3,294		947	617	330	1,135	1,061	74	191	368	19		341	293
	1953	2,947		757	496	261	1,053	991	62	209	347	23		277	281
	1954	3,138		785	514	271	1,143	1,067	76	226	339	43		317	285
Cont. OEEC countries	1950										297			208	178
	1951										335			306	305
	1952										355			332	292
	1953										338			268	279
	1954										329			308	284
Cont. Overseas Territ.	1950										7			6	1
	1951										9			8	1
	1952										13			9	1
	1953										9			9	2
	1954										10			9	1
Own Currency Area	1950						108	39	69	108					
	1951						167	57	110	167					
	1952						191	61	130	191					
	1953						209	67	142	209					
	1954						226	73	153	226					
U.S., Canada, & IO	1950	1,126		207	143	64	424	398	26		88	62		246	99
	1951	1,748		305	197	108	640	597	43		91	89		441	182
	1952	1,693		310	212	98	534	476	58		94	106		464	185
	1953	1,275		235	157	78	358	331	27		95	103		345	139
	1954	1,266		219	148	71	390	350	40		83	89		338	147
United States	1950				108		416	390	26			62		245	94
	1951				139		630	587	43			89		439	177
	1952				144		525	467	58			106		462	180
	1953				102		350	323	27			103		340	136
	1954				98		381	341	40			89		337	146
Canada	1950				35		8	8			88			1	5
	1951				58		10	10			91			2	5
	1952				68		9	9			94			2	5
	1953				55		8	8			95			5	3
	1954				50		9	9			83			1	1
Internat. Organizations	1950														
	1951														
	1952														
	1953														
	1954														
Latin America	1950	616		75	42	33	119	114	5		200	1		183	38
	1951	863		132	83	49	165	156	9		256	1		242	67
	1952	835		117	73	44	151	145	6		282	3		227	55
	1953	774		80	57	23	147	142	5		269	3		214	61
	1954	794		85	61	24	163	157	6		241	4		232	69
Other Countries	1950	415		84	61	23	175	171			65	6		45	40
	1951	581		136	82	54	226	218	8		89	8		57	65
	1952	661		152	90	62	243	229	14		128	4		68	66
	1953	659		116	76	40	237	229	8		153	4		83	66
	1954	684		114	74	40	259	248	11		157	7		95	58

TABLE B-12
Net Transportation Transactions Between World Areas, Annually, 1950–54
(as reported by area at left, million U.S. dollars)

Area / Year	All Areas	Unal-located	Sterling Area All	Sterling U.K.	Sterling RSA	Nonsterling EPU Area All	Cont. OEEC	Cont. OT's	Own Currency Area	U.S., Canada, and IO All	U.S.	Canada	IO	Latin America	Other Countries
All areas 1950	-571	-20	-44			-286				-305				-12	96
1951	-1,128	2	98			-622				-740				19	115
1952	-931	3	169			-672				-567				27	109
1953	-540	-13	197			-543				-250				–	69
1954	-578	-38	147			-605				-167				10	75
Unallocated 1950															
1951															
1952															
1953															
1954															
Sterling Area 1950	-21	10	-7	-304	297	-56				-9				5	36
1951	-276	26	2	-445	447	-217				-68				-16	-3
1952	-323	28	76	-449	525	-326				-63				-13	-25
1953	-36	15	153	-298	451	-216				-8				13	7
1954	-70	4	109	-324	433	-236				21				8	24
United Kingdom 1950	431	14	290		290	33				21	6	-2	17	28	45
1951	498	31	480		480	-59				3	14	-17	6	13	30
1952	463	31	537		537	-135				-4	21	-25	–	12	22
1953	446	20	438		438	-86				36	48	-12	–	14	24
1954	445	10	432		432	-100				58	68	-10	–	10	35
Rest of Sterling Area 1950	-452	-4	-297	-304	7	-89				-30				-23	-9
1951	-774	-5	-478	-445	-33	-158				-71				-29	-33
1952	-786	-3	-461	-449	-12	-191				-59				-25	-47
1953	-482	-5	-285	-298	13	-130				-44				-1	-17
1954	-515	-6	-323	-324	1	-136				-37				-2	-11
Nonsterling EPU area 1950	-284	-12	-5			-141			-2	-121	-128	7		2	-5
1951	-540	-6	11			-311			3	-264	-270	6		19	8
1952	-177	-6	84			-201			4	-125	-129	4		17	50
1953	54	-7	101			-118			3	34	29	5		20	21
1954	103	-5	99			-99			-6	73	69	4		34	7
Cont. OEEC countries 1950	-248	-12	1			-154			31	-111	-118	7		-1	-2
1951	-418	-6	33			-296			60	-238	-244	6		17	12
1952	-29	-6	111			-192			72	-87	-91	4		14	59
1953	135	-7	105			-119			77	40	35	5		14	25
1954	218	-5	115			-95			72	90	86	4		28	13
Cont. Overseas Territ. 1950	-36		-6			13			-33	-10	-10			3	-3
1951	-122		-22			-15			-57	-26	-26			2	-4
1952	-148		-27			-9			-68	-38	-38			3	-9
1953	-81		-4			1			-74	-6	-6			6	-4
1954	-115		-16			-4			-78	-17	-17			6	-6
Own Currency Area 1950						-2	-33	31	-2						
1951						3	-57	60	3						
1952						4	-68	72	4						
1953						3	-74	77	3						
1954						-6	-78	72	-6						
United States 1950	215		13	-22	35	73	63	10		-3		-20	17	61	71
1951	582		142	5	137	221	205	16		–		-1	1	112	107
1952	373		44	-49	93	133	116	17		30		25	5	93	73
1953	117		3	-55	58	16	3	13		-3		-3		51	50
1954	145		5	-38	43	21	5	16		3		3		71	45
Canada 1950	13		6	2	4	–				–	–			4	3
1951	1		24	17	7	-2				-30	-30			7	2
1952	5		28	25	3	-2				-32	-32			5	6
1953	-28		14	12	2	-6				-43	-43			2	5
1954	-41		17	10	7	-27				-32	-32			–	1
Internat. Organizations 1950															
1951															
1952															
1953															
1954															
Latin America 1950	-335		-37	-47	10	-109	-111	2		-134	-133	-1		-58	3
1951	-483		-41	-71	30	-144	-151	7		-262	-260	-2		-60	24
1952	-463		-18	-43	25	-142	-147	5		-285	-283	-2		-41	23
1953	-345		-8	-17	9	-120	-124	4		-173	-168	-5		-49	5
1954	-398		-19	-29	10	-156	-161	5		-158	-157	-1		-61	-4
Other Countries 1950	-159	-18	-14	-14	–	-51	-50	-1		-38	-33	-5		-26	-12
1951	-412	-18	-40	42	2	-172	-171	-1		-116	-111	-5		-43	-23
1952	-346	-19	-45	-50	5	-138	-137	-1		-92	-87	-5		-34	-18
1953	-302	-21	-66	-77	11	-102	-102	–		-57	-57	–		-37	-19
1954	-317	-37	-64	-81	17	-102	-104	2		-74	-74	–		-42	2

TABLE B-13
Gross Travel Transactions Between World Areas, Annually, 1950–54, as Reported by Area Credited (million U.S. dollars)

		All Areas	Unal-located	Sterling Area — All	U.K.	RSA	Nonsterling EPU Area — All	Cont. OEEC	Cont. OT's	Own Currency Area	U.S., Canada, and IO — All	U.S.	Canada	IO	Latin America	Other Countries
All areas	1950	1,938	109	359			296				920				183	71
	1951	2,188	129	443			381				958				164	113
	1952	2,328	115	406			432				1,090				189	96
	1953	2,635	94	418			532				1,254				229	108
	1954	2,970	124	466			662				1,365				244	109
Unallocated	1950															
	1951															
	1952															
	1953															
	1954															
Sterling Area	1950	339		180	98	82	38				100				6	15
	1951	415		222	113	109	46				114				6	27
	1952	434		227	111	116	45				134				6	22
	1953	466		234	109	125	51				147				5	29
	1954	494	2	241	105	136	62				165				6	18
United Kingdom	1950	171		67	–	67	34				56	38	18		6	8
	1951	210		90	–	90	42				64	42	22		6	8
	1952	224		95	–	95	39				76	45	31		6	8
	1953	246		101	–	101	45				87	56	31		5	8
	1954	266		107	–	107	50				95	62	33		6	8
Rest of Sterling Area	1950	168		113	98	15	4				44					7
	1951	205		132	113	19	4				50					19
	1952	210		132	111	21	6				58					14
	1953	220		133	109	24	6				60					21
	1954	228	2	134	105	29	12				70					10
Nonsterling EPU area	1950	573		128			218			5	164	159	5		22	36
	1951	685	1	176			291			6	133	130	3		18	60
	1952	683		121			333			6	154	152	2		21	48
	1953	838		126			421			12	214	211	3		20	45
	1954	1,080		161			526			18	285	281	4		29	61
Cont. OEEC countries	1950	568		128			218			2	163	158	5		21	36
	1951	680	1	176			291			3	132	129	3		17	60
	1952	678		121			333			4	152	150	2		20	48
	1953	833		125			421			10	213	210	3		19	45
	1954	1,075		160			526			15	284	280	4		29	61
Cont. Overseas Territ.	1950	5								3	1	1			1	
	1951	5								3	1	1			1	
	1952	5								2	2	2			1	
	1953	5		1						2	1	1			1	
	1954	5		1						3	1	1				
Own Currency Area	1950						5	2	3	5						
	1951						6	3	3	6						
	1952						6	4	2	6						
	1953						12	10	2	12						
	1954						18	15	3	18						
United States	1950	392		34	19	15	26	23	3		193		193		126	13
	1951	430		27	11	16	26	24	2		246		246		113	18
	1952	511		36	15	21	26	22	4		294		294		138	17
	1953	574		35	15	20	24	22	2		307		307		185	23
	1954	584		36	18	18	30	28	2		311		311		190	17
Canada	1950	254		9	6	3	4				240	240			1	
	1951	260		10	8	2	4				245	245			1	
	1952	281		13	10	3	4				263	263			1	
	1953	306		15	12	3	4				286	286			1	
	1954	310		16	13	3	4				288	288			1	1
Internat. Organizations	1950															
	1951															
	1952															
	1953															
	1954															
Latin America	1950	330	98	1	1		1	1			202	202			28	
	1951	349	115	1	1						208	208			25	
	1952	358	99	1	1		4	4			231	231			23	
	1953	383	78				3	3			284	284			18	
	1954	427	108				3	3			298	298			18	
Other Countries	1950	50	11	7	2	5	4	4			21	21				7
	1951	49	13	7	3	4	8	8			12	12			1	8
	1952	61	16	8	5	3	14	14			14	14				9
	1953	68	16	8	4	4	17	17			16	16				11
	1954	75	14	12	7	5	19	19			18	18				12

TABLE B-14
Gross Travel Transactions Between World Areas, Annually, 1950–54, as Reported by Area Debited (million U.S. dollars)

		All Areas	Unal- located	Sterling Area			Nonsterling EPU Area			Own Currency Area	U.S.	Canada	IO	Latin America	Other Countries
				All	U.K.	RSA	All	Cont. OEEC	Cont. OT's						
All areas	1950	1,991		412	238	174	335	326	9		727	208		225	84
	1951	2,383		519	291	228	484	475	9		722	266		269	123
	1952	2,489		434	232	202	521	511	10		811	348		261	114
	1953	2,784		471	249	222	592	573	19		929	371		303	118
	1954	3,068		517	283	234	699	674	25		1,009	392		330	121
Unallocated	1950	90		1		1								83	6
	1951	121		3		3								107	11
	1952	127		1		1								118	8
	1953	141		—										130	11
	1954	200		4		4								171	25
Sterling Area	1950	371		223	106	117	32	31	1		83	22		2	9
	1951	424		252	112	140	45	44	1		90	23		2	12
	1952	445		261	118	143	39	38	1		98	33		1	13
	1953	483		267	106	161	42	40	2		121	38		2	13
	1954	529		276	104	172	58	55	3		135	43		2	15
United Kingdom	1950			90		90					37	17		1	3
	1951			110		110					37	19		1	4
	1952			108		108					41	28		1	7
	1953			128		128					57	32		2	6
	1954			136		136					67	36		2	8
Rest of Sterling Area	1950			133	106	27					46	5		1	6
	1951			142	112	30					53	4		1	8
	1952			153	118	35					57	5			6
	1953			139	106	33					64	6			7
	1954			140	104	36					68	7			7
Nonsterling EPU area	1950	624		134	115	19	261	260	1	5	174	7		9	34
	1951	771		172	157	15	374	373	1	6	146	8		6	59
	1952	798		110	95	15	408	405	3	4	201	13		9	53
	1953	904		137	118	19	450	445	5	11	226	18		13	49
	1954	1,054		175	154	21	515	510	5	17	270	24		11	42
Cont. OEEC countries	1950										172			9	34
	1951										143			6	59
	1952										195			9	53
	1953										220			13	49
	1954										263			11	42
Cont. Overseas Territ.	1950										2				
	1951										3				
	1952										6				
	1953										6				
	1954										7				
Own Currency Area	1950						5	—	5	5					
	1951						6	1	5	6					
	1952						4	1	3	4					
	1953						11	2	9	11					
	1954						17	3	14	17					
U.S., Canada, & IO	1950	597		23	11	12	24	22	2		261	178		94	17
	1951	671		29	14	15	33	31	2		255	234		104	16
	1952	744		30	14	16	38	35	3		257	300		101	18
	1953	805		28	14	14	37	34	3		282	312		128	18
	1954	821		30	14	16	51	48	3		284	321		116	19
United States	1950				8		23	21	2			178		94	17
	1951				8		29	27	2			234		104	16
	1952				9		36	33	3			300		101	18
	1953				8		35	32	3			312		128	18
	1954				8		49	46	3			321		116	19
Canada	1950				3		1	1			261				
	1951				6		4	4			255				
	1952				5		2	2			257				
	1953				6		2	2			282				
	1954				6		2	2			284				
Internat. Organizations	1950														
	1951														
	1952														
	1953														
	1954														
Latin America	1950	227					1	1			194	1		31	
	1951	261					2	2			216	1		42	
	1952	262					1	1			235	1		25	
	1953	299					2	2			273	2		22	
	1954	320					7	7			288	2		23	
Other Countries	1950	82		31	6	25	12	12			15			6	18
	1951	135		63	8	55	24	24			15			8	25
	1952	113		32	5	27	31	31			20	1		7	22
	1953	152		39	11	28	50	50			27	1		8	27
	1954	144		32	11	21	51	51			32	2		7	30

TABLE B-15
Net Travel Transactions Between World Areas, Annually, 1950–54
(as reported by area at left, million U.S. dollars)

		All Areas	Unallocated	Sterling Area — All	Sterling Area — U.K.	Sterling Area — RSA	Nonsterling EPU Area — All	Nonsterling EPU Area — Cont. OEEC	Nonsterling EPU Area — Cont. OT's	Own Currency Area	U.S., Canada, and IO — All	U.S., Canada, and IO — U.S.	U.S., Canada, and IO — Canada	U.S., Canada, and IO — IO	Latin America	Other Countries
All areas	1950	-53	19	-12			-328				323				-44	-11
	1951	-195	8	19			-390				287				-97	-22
	1952	-161	-12	-39			-366				346				-73	-17
	1953	-149	-47	-65			-372				449				-70	-44
	1954	-98	-76	-63			-392				544				-76	-35
Unallocated	1950															
	1951															
	1952															
	1953															
	1954															
Sterling Area	1950	-73	-1	-43	8	-51	-96				77				6	-16
	1951	-104	-3	-30	3	-33	-126				85				6	-36
	1952	—	-1	-34	3	-37	-65				104				6	-10
	1953	-5	—	-33	-19	-14	-86				119				5	-10
	1954	-23	-2	-35	-31	-4	-113				135				6	-14
United Kingdom	1950	-67		-39		-39	-81				45	30	15		6	2
	1951	-81		-22		-22	-115				50	34	16		6	-
	1952	-8		-23		-23	-56				62	36	26		6	3
	1953	-3		-5		-5	-73				73	48	25		5	-3
	1954	-17		3		3	-104				81	54	27		6	-3
Rest of Sterling Area	1950	-6	-1	-4	8	-12	-15				32					-18
	1951	-23	-3	-8	3	-11	-11				35					-36
	1952	8	-1	-11	3	-14	-9				42					-13
	1953	-2	-	-28	-19	-9	-13				46					-7
	1954	-6	-2	-38	-31	-7	-9				54					-11
Nonsterling EPU area	1950	238	-	96			-43			—	140	136	4		21	24
	1951	201	1	131			-83			—	100	101	-1		16	36
	1952	162	—	82			-75			2	116	116	—		20	17
	1953	246	—	84			-29			1	177	176	1		18	-5
	1954	381	—	103			11			1	234	232	2		22	10
Cont. OEEC countries	1950	242		97			-42			2	141	137	4		20	24
	1951	205	1	132			-82			2	101	102	-1		15	36
	1952	167		83			-72			3	117	117	—		19	17
	1953	260		85			-24			8	179	178	1		17	-5
	1954	401		105			16			12	236	234	2		22	10
Cont. Overseas Territ.	1950	-4		-1			-1			-2	-1	-1			1	
	1951	-4		-1			-1			-2	-1	-1			1	
	1952	-5		-1			-3			-1	-1	-1			1	
	1953	-14		-1			-5			-7	-2	-2			1	
	1954	-20		-2			-5			-11	-2	-2			-	
Own Currency Area	1950						—	-2	2	—						
	1951						—	-2	2	—						
	1952						2	-1	3	2						
	1953						1	-7	8	1						
	1954						1	-7	12	1						
United States	1950	-335		-49	-18	-31	-148	-149	1		-68		-68		-68	-2
	1951	-292		-63	-26	-37	-120	-119	-1		-9		-9		-103	3
	1952	-300		-62	-26	-36	-175	-173	-2		37		37		-97	-3
	1953	-355		-86	-42	-44	-202	-198	-4		25		25		-88	-4
	1954	-425		-99	-49	-50	-240	-235	-5		27		27		-98	-15
Canada	1950	46		-13	-11	-2	-3				62	62			-	-
	1951	-6		-13	-11	-2	-4				11	11			-	-
	1952	-67		-20	-18	-2	-9				-37	-37			-	-1
	1953	-65		-23	-20	-3	-14				-26	-26			-1	-1
	1954	-82		-27	-23	-4	-20				-33	-33			-1	-1
Internat. Organizations	1950															
	1951															
	1952															
	1953															
	1954															
Latin America	1950	105	15	-1	—	-1	-8	-8			108	108			-3	-6
	1951	80	8	-1	—	-1	-6	-6			104	104			-17	-8
	1952	97	-19	—	—	—	-5	-5			130	130			-2	-7
	1953	80	-52	-2	-2	—	-10	-10			156	156			-4	-8
	1954	97	-63	-2	-2	—	-8	-8			182	182			-5	-7
Other Countries	1950	-34	5	-2	-1	-1	-30	-30			4	4			—	-11
	1951	-74	2	-5	-1	-4	-51	-51			-4	-4			1	-17
	1952	-53	8	-5	-2	-3	-39	-39			-4	-4			—	-13
	1953	-50	5	-5	-2	-3	-32	-32			-2	-2			—	-16
	1954	-46	-11	-3	-1	-2	-23	-23			-1	-1			—	-8

TABLE B-16
Gross Investment Income Transactions Between World Areas, Annually, 1950–54, as Reported by Area Credited (million U.S. dollars)

		All Areas	Unallocated	Sterling Area			Nonsterling EPU Area			Own Currency Area	U.S., Canada, and IO				Latin America	Other Countries
				All	U.K.	RSA	All	Cont. OEEC	Cont. OT's		All	U.S.	Canada	IO		
All areas	1950	4,464	129	1,354			449				993				838	701
	1951	5,304	154	1,706			493				994				1,132	825
	1952	5,262	136	1,875			485				1,030				1,147	589
	1953	5,473	143	2,045			566				1,134				956	629
	1954	5,944	82	2,240			723				1,178				979	742
Unallocated	1950															
	1951															
	1952															
	1953															
	1954															
Sterling Area	1950	1,717		895	137	758	88				207				157	370
	1951	1,876		1,075	157	918	93				212				174	322
	1952	1,686		1,114	221	893	81				210				178	103
	1953	1,801		1,189	246	943	106				232				168	106
	1954	1,950		1,258	263	995	126				243				184	139
United Kingdom	1950	1,556		738		738	88				203	152	51		157	370
	1951	1,691		894		894	93				208	154	54		174	322
	1952	1,425		868		868	74				202	145	57		178	103
	1953	1,514		916		916	99				225	167	58		168	106
	1954	1,635		959		959	121				232	168	64		184	139
Rest of Sterling Area	1950	161		157	137	20					4				—	
	1951	185		181	157	24					4					
	1952	261		246	221	25	7				8					
	1953	287		273	246	27	7				7					
	1954	315		299	263	36	5				11					
Nonsterling EPU area	1950	415	126	97			58			40	50	48	2		6	38
	1951	500	151	111			72			41	59	56	3		11	55
	1952	550	134	142			81			53	75	72	3		10	55
	1953	629	140	177			96			58	88	84	4		9	61
	1954	764	79	220			185			63	151	146	5		6	60
Cont. OEEC countries	1950	407	126	96			58			35	49	47	2		5	38
	1951	489	151	110			72			34	57	54	3		10	55
	1952	538	134	141			81			45	73	70	3		9	55
	1953	613	140	175			96			48	85	81	4		8	61
	1954	751	79	217			185			56	149	144	5		5	60
Cont. Overseas Territ.	1950	8		1						5	1	1			1	
	1951	11		1						7	2	2			1	
	1952	12		1						8	2	2			1	
	1953	16		2						10	3	3			1	
	1954	13		3						7	2	2			1	
Own Currency Area	1950						40	35	5	40						
	1951						41	34	7	41						
	1952						53	45	8	53						
	1953						58	48	10	58						
	1954						63	56	7	63						
United States	1950	2,068		332	171	161	226	206	20		562		556	6	663	285
	1951	2,634		469	272	197	246	228	18		544		537	7	934	441
	1952	2,704		553	286	267	228	214	14		559		548	11	941	423
	1953	2,686		604	304	300	261	241	20		608		595	13	763	450
	1954	2,868		676	342	334	297	276	21		600		586	14	766	529
Canada	1950	198		13	6	7	13				160	160			9	3
	1951	214		33	29	4	13				158	158			7	3
	1952	219		37	30	7	13				158	158			9	2
	1953	232		43	29	14	13				167	167			7	2
	1954	226		53	36	17	12				151	151			8	2
Internat. Organizations	1950	36		3	1	2	24	24			6	6			3	
	1951	42		3	—	3	26	26			7	7			6	
	1952	52		9	1	8	25	25			9	9			7	2
	1953	62		13	—	13	27	27			9	9			9	4
	1954	70		14	—	14	27	27			10	10			14	5
Latin America	1950	6	3								3	3				
	1951	9	3								6	6				
	1952	12	2	1	1		1	1			6	6			2	
	1953	12	2								10	10				
	1954	18	2	4	4						10	10			1	1
Other Countries	1950	24		14	14						5	5				5
	1951	29		15	15		2	2			8	8				4
	1952	39		19	19		3	3			13	13				4
	1953	51	1	19	19		5	5			20	20				6
	1954	48	1	15	15		13	12	1		13	13				6

TABLE B-17
Gross Investment Income Transactions Between World Areas, Annually, 1950–54, as Reported by Area Debited (million U.S. dollars)

		All Areas	Unallocated	Sterling Area All	U.K.	RSA	Nonsterling EPU Area All	Cont. OEEC	Cont. OT's	Own Currency Area	U.S.	Canada	IO	Latin America	Other Countries
All areas	1950	4,553		1,501	496	1,005	390	338	52		478	575	8	923	678
	1951	5,490		1,964	714	1,250	424	370	54		481	612	10	1,186	813
	1952	5,353		2,075	812	1,263	425	372	53		472	624	16	1,148	593
	1953	5,772		2,267	875	1,392	518	413	105		549	728	21	1,061	628
	1954	6,079		2,405	935	1,470	717	634	83		549	675	26	1,032	675
Unallocated	1950	130		1		1	72	72						55	2
	1951	186		2		2	77	77						103	4
	1952	171		9		9	68	68						92	2
	1953	156		6		6	59	59						89	2
	1954	144		7		7	76	76						59	2
Sterling Area	1950	1,662		895	137	758	38	29	9		179	51		146	353
	1951	1,836		1,075	157	918	42	33	9		183	54		176	306
	1952	1,608		1,114	221	893	38	33	5		175	57	1	159	64
	1953	1,745		1,189	246	943	54	37	17		205	58	1	158	80
	1954	1,902		1,258	263	995	72	64	8		220	64	1	171	116
United Kingdom	1950			738		738					176	51		145	353
	1951			894		894					179	54		169	306
	1952			868		868					172	57	1	153	64
	1953			916		916					200	58	1	155	80
	1954			959		959					214	64	1	168	115
Rest of Sterling Area	1950			157	137	20					3			1	
	1951			181	157	24					4			7	
	1952			246	221	25					3			6	
	1953			273	246	27					5			3	
	1954			299	263	36					6			3	1
Nonsterling EPU area	1950	538		242	212	30	73	73		41	113	6		13	50
	1951	677		314	287	27	90	89	1	42	125	8		25	73
	1952	713		342	292	50	84	83	1	54	126	11	1	21	74
	1953	827		394	320	74	111	105	6	58	146	11	2	19	86
	1954	960		411	333	78	225	217	8	59	153	14	2	20	76
Cont. OEEC countries	1950										112			13	50
	1951										124			25	73
	1952										124		1	21	74
	1953										142		2	19	86
	1954										152		2	20	76
Cont. Overseas Territ.	1950										1				
	1951										1				
	1952										2				
	1953										4				
	1954										1				
Own Currency Area	1950						41	8	33	41					
	1951						42	8	34	42					
	1952						54	9	45	54					
	1953						58	11	47	58					
	1954						59	7	52	59					
U.S., Canada, & IO	1950	2,149		335	124	211	152	142	10		167	516	8	704	267
	1951	2,709		545	248	297	151	141	10		151	548	10	876	428
	1952	2,761		573	262	311	158	156	2		148	554	14	867	447
	1953	2,950		640	272	368	223	188	35		173	657	18	785	454
	1954	2,969		696	306	390	255	240	15		152	595	23	774	474
United States	1950				115		144	134	10			516	8	703	267
	1951				219		143	133	10			548	10	876	428
	1952				232		150	148	2			554	14	867	447
	1953				243		217	182	35			657	18	784	452
	1954				270		248	233	15			595	22	773	470
Canada	1950				6		8	8			160			1	
	1951				29		8	8			142				
	1952				30		8	8			136				
	1953				29		6	6			157			1	2
	1954				36		7	7			143		1	1	4
Internat. Organizations	1950										7				
	1951										9				
	1952										12				
	1953										16				
	1954										9				
Latin America	1950	30		7	6	1	2	2			13	1		5	2
	1951	30		4	3	1	6	6			14	1		4	1
	1952	33		6	6		3	3			15	1		7	1
	1953	37		6	6		3	3			17	1		10	
	1954	38		5	5		5	5			18	1		8	1
Other Countries	1950	44		21	17	4	12	12			6	1			4
	1951	52		24	19	5	16	16			8	1		2	
	1952	67		31	31		20	20			8	1		2	5
	1953	57		32	31	1	10	10			8	1		2	6
	1954	66		28	28		25	25			6	1			6

TABLE B-18
Net Investment Income Transactions Between World Areas, Annually, 1950–54
(as reported by area at left, million U.S. dollars)

	Year	All Areas	Unallocated	Sterling Area — All	U.K.	RSA	Nonsterling EPU Area — All	Cont. OEEC	Cont. OT's	Own Currency Area	U.S., Canada, and IO — All	U.S.	Canada	IO	Latin America	Other Countries
All areas	1950	-89	-1	-308			-89				-1,156				808	657
	1951	-186	-32	-130			-184				-1,715				1,102	773
	1952	-91	-35	267			-228				-1,731				1,114	522
	1953	-299	-13	300			-261				-1,816				919	572
	1954	-135	-62	338			-237				-1,791				941	676
Unallocated	1950															
	1951															
	1952															
	1953															
	1954															
Sterling Area	1950	216	-1	—	-601	601	-154				-128				150	349
	1951	-88	-2	—	-737	737	-221				-333				170	298
	1952	-389	-9	—	-647	647	-261				-363				172	72
	1953	-466	-6	—	-670	670	-288				-408				162	74
	1954	-455	-7	—	-696	696	-285				-453				179	111
United Kingdom	1950	1,060		601		601	-124				79	34	45		151	353
	1951	977		737		737	-194				-40	-65	25		171	303
	1952	613		647		647	-218				-60	-87	27		172	72
	1953	639		670		670	-221				-47	-76	29		162	72
	1954	700		696		696	-212				-74	-102	28		179	111
Rest of Sterling Area	1950	-844	-1	-601	-604	—	-30				-207				-1	-4
	1951	-1,065	-2	-737	-737	—	-27				-293				-1	-5
	1952	-1,002	-9	-647	-647	—	-43				-303				—	—
	1953	-1,105	-6	-670	-670	—	-67				-361				—	-1
	1954	-1,155	-7	-696	-696	—	-73				-379				—	—
Nonsterling EPU area	1950	25	54	59			-15			-1	-102	-96	-6		4	26
	1951	76	74	69			-18			-1	-92	-87	-5		5	39
	1952	125	66	104			-3			-1	-83	-78	-5		7	35
	1953	111	81	123			-15			—	-135	-133	-2		6	51
	1954	47	3	148			-40			4	-104	-102	-2		1	35
Cont. OEEC countries	1950	69	54	67			-15			27	-93	-87	-6		3	26
	1951	119	74	77			-17			26	-84	-79	-5		4	39
	1952	166	66	108			-2			36	-83	-78	-5		6	35
	1953	200	81	138			-9			37	-103	-101	-2		5	51
	1954	117	3	153			-32			49	-91	-89	-2		—	35
Cont. Overseas Territ.	1950	-44		-8			—			-28	-9	-9			1	
	1951	-43		-8			-1			-27	-8	-8			1	
	1952	-41		-4			-1			-37	—	—			1	
	1953	-89		-15			-6			-37	-32	-32			1	
	1954	-70		-5			-8			-45	-13	-13			1	
Own Currency Area	1950						-1	-28	27	-1						
	1951						-1	-27	26	-1						
	1952						-1	-37	36	-1						
	1953						—	-37	37	—						
	1954						4	-45	48	4						
United States	1950	1,590		153	-5	158	113	94	19		395		396	-1	650	279
	1951	2,153		286	93	193	121	104	17		393		395	-2	920	433
	1952	2,232		378	114	264	102	90	12		411		412	-1	926	415
	1953	2,137		399	104	295	115	99	16		435		438	-3	746	442
	1954	2,319		456	128	328	144	124	20		448		443	5	748	523
Canada	1950	-377		-38	-45	7	7				-356	-356			8	2
	1951	-398		-21	-25	4	5				-390	-390			6	2
	1952	-405		-20	-27	7	2				-396	-396			8	1
	1953	-496		-15	-29	14	2				-490	-490			6	1
	1954	-449		-11	-28	17	-2				-444	-444			7	1
Internat. Organizations	1950	28		3	1	2	24	24			-2	-2	—		3	—
	1951	32		3	—	3	26	26			-3	-3	—		6	—
	1952	36		8	—	8	24	24			-5	-5	—		7	2
	1953	41		12	-1	13	25	25			-9	-9	—		9	4
	1954	44		13	-1	14	25	25			-13	-12	-1		14	5
Latin America	1950	-917	-52	-146	-145	-1	-13	-13			-701	-700	-1		-5	—
	1951	-1,177	-100	-176	-169	-7	-25	-25			-870	-870	—		-4	-2
	1952	-1,136	-90	-158	-152	-6	-20	-20			-861	-861	—		-5	-2
	1953	-1,049	-87	-158	-155	-3	-19	19			-775	-774	-1		-10	—
	1954	-1,014	-57	-167	-164	-3	-20	20			-764	-763	-1		-7	1
Other Countries	1950	-654	-2	-339	-339	—	-50	-50	—		-262	-262	—		-2	1
	1951	-784	-4	-291	-291	—	-71	-71	—		-420	-420	—		-1	3
	1952	-554	-2	-45	-45	—	-71	-71	—		-434	-434	—		-1	-1
	1953	-577	-1	-61	-61	—	-81	-81	—		-434	-432	-2		—	—
	1954	-627	-1	-101	-100	-1	-63	-64	1		-451	-457	-4		-1	—

TABLE B-19
Gross Government Transactions Between World Areas, Annually, 1950–54, as Reported by Area Credited (million U.S. dollars)

		All Areas	Unal-located	Sterling Area			Nonsterling EPU Area			Own Currency Area	U.S., Canada, and IO				Latin America	Other Countries
				All	U.K.	RSA	All	Cont. OEEC	Cont. OT's		All	U.S.	Canada	IO		
All areas	1950	1,278	42	377			139				594				43	83
	1951	2,028	39	441			167				1,227				53	101
	1952	2,818	98	516			193				1,842				60	109
	1953	3,292	82	586			224				2,197				58	145
	1954	3,193	78	588			261				2,069				59	138
Unallocated	1950															
	1951															
	1952															
	1953															
	1954															
Sterling Area	1950	410	2	273	214	59	12				111				1	11
	1951	479		295	252	43	16				145					23
	1952	513	2	363	289	74	12				128					8
	1953	602	3	409	280	129	18				160					12
	1954	612	3	422	311	111	14				167					6
United Kingdom	1950	81		36	—	36	11				22	17	5		1	11
	1951	66		22	—	22	14				10	8	2			20
	1952	80		28	—	28	8				44	38	6			
	1953	160		70	—	70	14				73	57	16			3
	1954	151		56	—	56	8				87	80	7			
Rest of Sterling Area	1950	329	2	237	214	23	1				89					
	1951	413		273	252	21	2				135					3
	1952	433	2	335	289	46	4				84					8
	1953	442	3	339	280	59	4				87					9
	1954	461	3	366	311	55	6				80					6
Nonsterling EPU area	1950	161	11	12			15			9	100	99	1		2	12
	1951	288	8	36			25			10	186	184	2		6	17
	1952	677	56	40			44			17	506	495	11		2	12
	1953	1,026	29	50			57			29	835	821	14		4	22
	1954	1,217	25	57			98			36	948	929	19		7	46
Cont. OEEC countries	1950	154	11	12			12			5	100	99	1		2	12
	1951	281	8	36			22			6	186	184	2		6	17
	1952	665	56	40			40			9	506	495	11		2	12
	1953	1,005	29	50			55			10	835	821	14		4	22
	1954	1,192	25	57			93			16	948	929	19		7	46
Cont. Overseas Territ.	1950	7					3			4						
	1951	7					3			4						
	1952	12					4			8						
	1953	21					2			19						
	1954	25					5			20						
Own Currency Area	1950							5	4	9						
	1951							6	4	10						
	1952							9	8	17						
	1953							10	19	29						
	1954							16	20	36						
United States	1950	240		29	23	6	85	84	1		43		4	39	33	50
	1951	281		39	23	16	105	105			48		8	40	40	49
	1952	350		57	23	34	104	104			64		20	44	51	74
	1953	349		51	25	26	102	102			63		17	46	46	87
	1954	303		45	22	23	86	86			61		17	44	46	65
Canada	1950	47		5	4	1	8				30	30			3	1
	1951	58		8	7	1	1				47	47			1	1
	1952	124		9	8	1	3				110	110			1	1
	1953	151		11	9	2	4				132	132			2	2
	1954	121		13	11	2	5				101	101			1	1
Internat. Organizations	1950	30		6	4	2	4	4			15	14	1		1	4
	1951	38		8	5	3	5	5			18	17	1		2	5
	1952	38		7	5	2	5	5			17	16	1		2	7
	1953	44		9	5	4	5	5			17	16	1		3	10
	1954	38		7	4	3	5	5			15	14	1		2	9
Latin America	1950	50	20	1	1		2	2			24	24				3
	1951	69	19	2	2		2	2			41	41			4	1
	1952	57	26	2	2		2	2			23	23			4	
	1953	72	29	3	3		2	2			35	35			3	
	1954	70	29	3	3		3	3			30	30			3	2
Other Countries	1950	340	9	51	51		4	4			271	269	2			5
	1951	815	12	53	53		3	3			742	740	2			5
	1952	1,059	14	38	38		6	6			994	992	2			7
	1953	1,048	21	53	52	1	7	7			955	953	2			12
	1954	832	21	41	40	1	4	14			747	745	2			9

TABLE B-20
Gross Government Transactions Between World Areas, Annually, 1950–54, as Reported by Area Debited (million U.S. dollars)

		All Areas	Unallocated	Sterling Area			Nonsterling EPU Area			Own Currency Area	U.S.	Canada	IO	Latin America	Other Countries
				All	U.K.	RSA	All	Cont. OEEC	Cont. OT's						
All areas	1950	1,814		487	367	120	166	153	13		920	32		118	91
	1951	2,691		592	440	152	170	162	8		1,629	44		154	102
	1952	3,577		703	484	219	192	181	11		2,363	73		121	125
	1953	4,306		717	484	233	250	237	13		2,944	130		143	122
	1954	4,374		737	504	233	284	267	17		2,979	112		134	128
Unallocated	1950	94		1		1	15	15						52	26
	1951	99		2		2	22	22						53	22
	1952	125		1		1	29	29						56	39
	1953	152		4		4	42	42						58	48
	1954	175		4		4	52	52						60	59
Sterling Area	1950	442		304	213	91	12	12			95	15		2	14
	1951	553		374	252	122	16	16			137	10		3	13
	1952	725		447	288	159	18	18			219	25		1	15
	1953	900		467	280	187	24	24			326	65		3	15
	1954	1,008		485	311	174	27	27			448	32		2	14
United Kingdom	1950			68		68					46	14		2	14
	1951			101		101					78	9		3	13
	1952			113		113					134	23		1	14
	1953			128		128					222	63		3	13
	1954			119		119					341	30		2	10
Rest of Sterling Area	1950			236	213	23					49	1			
	1951			273	252	21					59	1			
	1952			334	288	46					85	2			1
	1953			339	280	59					104	2			2
	1954			366	311	55					107	2			4
Nonsterling EPU area	1950	397		55	42	13	34	32	2	19	249	3		5	32
	1951	570		65	59	6	38	36	2	17	404	3		5	38
	1952	1,069		105	84	21	58	55	3	82	821	18		3	42
	1953	1,420		105	95	10	73	72	1	13	1,149	31		7	22
	1954	1,583		109	90	19	79	76	3	41	1,294	39		5	16
Cont. OEEC countries	1950										236			5	32
	1951										357			5	38
	1952										720			3	42
	1953										1,045			7	22
	1954										1,203			5	16
Cont. Overseas Territ.	1950										13				
	1951										47				
	1952										101				
	1953										104				
	1954										91				
Own Currency Area	1950						19	8	11	19					
	1951						17	11	6	17					
	1952						22	14	8	22					
	1953						33	22	11	33					
	1954						41	28	13	41					
U.S., Canada, & IO	1950	229		43	33	10	45	45			62	11		53	15
	1951	308		51	34	17	51	51			80	19		85	22
	1952	372		48	25	23	38	38			192	21		54	19
	1953	449		58	33	25	36	35	1		233	25		71	26
	1954	447		54	36	18	49	48	1		234	31		60	19
United States	1950			19			44	44				11		53	15
	1951			24			50	50				19		85	22
	1952			19			36	36				21		54	18
	1953			18			28	27	1			25		66	26
	1954			17			47	46	1			31		60	18
Canada	1950			3			1	1			34				
	1951			7			1	1			48				
	1952			6			2	2			162				1
	1953			7			8	8			204			5	
	1954			8			2	2			206				1
Internat. Organization	1950			11							28				
	1951			3							32				
	1952			–							30				
	1953			8							29				
	1954			11							28				
Latin America	1950	88		3	3		5	5			75	1		4	
	1951	114		3	3		8	8			94	3		6	
	1952	114		3	3		5	5			100	1		5	
	1953	116		–	–		6	6			104	1		3	2
	1954	115		–	–		9	9			99	2		4	1
Other Countries	1950	564		81	76	5	36	36			439	2		2	4
	1951	1,047		97	92	5	18	18			914	9		2	7
	1952	1,172		99	84	15	22	22			1,031	8		2	10
	1953	1,269		83	76	7	36	36			1,132	8		1	9
	1954	1,046		85	67	18	27	27			904	8		3	19

TABLE B-21
Net Government Transactions Between World Areas, Annually, 1950–54
(as reported by area at left, million U.S. dollars)

		All Areas	Unallocated	Sterling Area			Nonsterling EPU Area			Own Currency Area	U.S., Canada, and IO				Latin America	Other Countries
				All	U.K.	RSA	All	Cont. OEEC	Cont. OT's		All	U.S.	Canada	IO		
All areas	1950	-536	-52	-65			-258				365				-45	-481
	1951	-663	-60	-112			-403				919				-61	-946
	1952	-759	-27	-209			-876				1,470				-54	-1,063
	1953	-1,014	-70	-314			-1,196				1,748				-58	-1,124
	1954	-1,181	-97	-420			-1,322				1,622				-56	-908
Unallocated	1950															
	1951															
	1952															
	1953															
	1954															
Sterling Area	1950	-77	1	-31	146	-177	-43				68				-2	-70
	1951	-113	-2	-79	151	-230	-49				94				-3	-74
	1952	-190	1	-84	176	-260	-93				80				-3	-91
	1953	-115	-1	-58	152	-210	-87				102				—	-71
	1954	-125	-1	-63	192	-255	-95				113				—	-79
United Kingdom	1950	-286		-177		-177	-31				-11	-2	2	-11	-2	-65
	1951	-374		-230		-230	-45				-24	-16	-5	-3	-3	-72
	1952	-404		-260		-260	-76				19	19			-3	-84
	1953	-324		-210		-210	-81				40	39	9	-8	—	-73
	1954	-353		-255		-255	-82				51	63	-1	-11		-67
Rest of Sterling Area	1950	209	1	146	146	—	-12				79					-5
	1951	261	-2	151	151	—	-4				118					-2
	1952	214	1	176	176	—	-17				61					-7
	1953	209	-1	152	152	—	-6				62					2
	1954	228	-1	192	192	—	-13				62					-12
Nonsterling EPU area	1950	-5	-4	—			-19			-10	55	55	—		-3	-24
	1951	118	-14	20			-13			-7	135	134	1		-2	-1
	1952	485	27	22			-14			-5	468	459	9		-3	-10
	1953	776	-13	26			-16			-4	799	793	6		-2	-14
	1954	933	-27	30			19			-5	899	882	17		-2	19
Cont. OEEC countries	1950	1	-4				-20			-3	55	55	—		-3	-24
	1951	119	-14	20			-14			-5	135	134	1		-2	-1
	1952	484	27	22			-15			-5	468	459	9		-3	-10
	1953	768	-13	26			-17			-12	800	794	6		-2	-14
	1954	925	-27	30			17			-12	900	883	17		-2	-14
Cont. Overseas Territ.	1950	-6					1			-7	—	—				19
	1951	-1					1			-2	—	—				
	1952	1					1			—	—	—				
	1953	8					1			8	-1	-1				
	1954	8					2			7	-1	-1				
Own Currency Area	1950						-10	-7	-3	-10						
	1951						-7	-2	-5	-7						
	1952						-5	—	-5	-5						
	1953						-4	8	-12	-4						
	1954						-5	7	-12	-5						
United States	1950	-680		-66	-23	-43	-164	-152	-12		-19		-30	11	-42	-389
	1951	-1,348		-98	-55	-43	-299	-252	-47		-32		-40	8	-54	-865
	1952	-2,013		-162	-111	-51	-717	-616	-101		-128		-142	14	-49	-957
	1953	-2,595		-275	-197	-78	-1,047	-943	-104		-170		-187	17	-58	-1,045
	1954	-2,676		-403	-319	-84	-1,208	-1,117	-91		-173		-189	16	-53	-839
Canada	1950	15		-10	-10	—	5				19	19			2	-1
	1951	14		-2	-2	—	-2				28	28			-2	-8
	1952	51		-16	-15	-1	-15				89	89			—	-7
	1953	21		-54	-54	—	-27				107	107			1	-6
	1954	9		-19	-19	—	-34				70	70			-1	-7
Internat. Organizations	1950	30		6	4	2	4	4			15	14	1		1	4
	1951	38		8	5	3	5	5			18	17	1		2	5
	1952	38		7	5	2	5	5			17	16	1		2	7
	1953	44		9	5	4	5	5			17	16	1		3	10
	1954	38		7	4	3	5	5			15	14	1		2	9
Latin America	1950	-68	-32	-1	-1		-3	-3			-29	-29	—		-1	-2
	1951	-85	-34	-1	-1		-3	-3			-44	-44	—		-2	-1
	1952	-64	-30	1	1		-1	-1			-31	-31			-1	-2
	1953	-71	-29	—	—		-5	-5			-36	-31	-5		—	-1
	1954	-64	-31	1	1		-2	-2			-30	-30	—		-1	-1
Other Countries	1950	249	-17	37	37	—	-28	-28			256	254	2		—	1
	1951	713	-10	40	40	—	-35	-35			720	718	2		—	-2
	1952	934	-25	23	24	-1	-36	-36			975	974	1		—	-3
	1953	926	-27	38	39	-1	-15	-15			929	927	2		-2	3
	1954	704	-38	27	30	-3	-2	-2			728	727	1		-1	-10

TABLE B-22

Gross Miscellaneous Services Transactions Between World Areas, Annually, 1950–54, as Reported by Area Credited (million U.S. dollars)

		All Areas	Unallocated	Sterling Area			Nonsterling EPU Area			Own Currency Area	U.S., Canada, and IO				Latin America	Other Countries
				All	U.K.	RSA	All	Cont. OEEC	Cont. OT's		All	U.S.	Canada	IO		
All areas	1950	2,741	266	877			576				628				171	223
	1951	3,245	320	1,043			614				784				221	263
	1952	3,349	346	1,036			746				747				219	255
	1953	3,630	314	1,080			916				804				236	280
	1954	4,309	504	1,198			1,148				943				222	294
Unallocated	1950															
	1951															
	1952															
	1953															
	1954															
Sterling Area	1950	884	40	459	198	261	96				219				35	35
	1951	975	4	481	175	306	139				242				49	60
	1952	994	77	439	190	249	156				239				29	54
	1953	1,028	27	467	179	288	176				267				35	56
	1954	1,299	230	492	175	317	189				302				33	53
United Kingdom	1950	575	40	204		204	87				186	163	23		35	23
	1951	622	—	194		194	133				206	174	32		48	41
	1952	664	74	180		180	148				199	178	21		27	36
	1953	718	25	236		236	164				218	197	21		35	40
	1954	1,005	225	277		277	175				255	229	26		33	40
Rest of Sterling Area	1950	309	—	255	198	57	9				33				—	12
	1951	353	4	287	175	112	6				36				1	19
	1952	330	3	259	190	69	8				40				2	18
	1953	310	2	231	179	52	12				49				—	16
	1954	294	5	215	175	40	14				47				—	13
Nonsterling EPU area	1950	909	140	161			306			53	115	112	3		23	111
	1951	1,122	233	245			297			55	130	126	4		36	126
	1952	1,292	196	305			390			55	196	192	4		31	119
	1953	1,409	198	298			503			56	181	177	4		40	133
	1954	1,726	175	338			720			54	267	262	5		42	130
Cont. OEEC countries	1950	891	140	160			305			38	114	111	3		23	111
	1951	1,101	233	243			296			38	129	125	4		36	126
	1952	1,269	196	302			390			37	194	190	4		31	119
	1953	1,385	198	298			502			34	180	176	4		40	133
	1954	1,710	175	337			719			40	267	262	5		42	130
Cont. Overseas Territ.	1950	18		1			1			15	1	1				
	1951	21		2			1			17	1	1				
	1952	23		3			—			18	2	2				
	1953	24		—			1			22	1	1				
	1954	16		1			1			14	—	—				
Own Currency Area	1950						53	38	15	53						
	1951						55	38	17	55						
	1952						55	37	18	55						
	1953						56	34	22	56						
	1954						54	40	14	54						
United States	1950	497		169	137	32	65	64	1		104		76	28	105	54
	1951	545		192	159	33	83	81	2		98		83	15	127	45
	1952	576		190	150	40	85	85	—		105		97	8	146	50
	1953	608		213	164	49	99	96	3		92		91	1	148	56
	1954	684		274	224	50	112	108	4		95		95		135	68
Canada	1950	125		33	31	2	2				86	86			2	2
	1951	134		32	30	2	3				93	93			3	3
	1952	111		29	25	4	4				71	71			4	3
	1953	119		32	27	5	4				76	76			4	3
	1954	127		29	24	5	4				87	87			4	3
Internat. Organizations	1950	5									5	5				
	1951	6									6	6				
	1952	6									6	6				
	1953	8									8	8				
	1954	7									7	7				
Latin America	1950	123	19	4	4		9	9			83	82	1		6	2
	1951	167	37	9	9		12	12			100	99	1		6	3
	1952	166	22	11	11		22	22			100	99	1		9	2
	1953	226	34	14	14		32	32			135	134	1		8	3
	1954	214	37	11	11		23	23			133	132	1		7	3
Other Countries	1950	198	67	51	33	18	45				16	16				19
	1951	296	46	84	62	22	25				115	115				26
	1952	204	51	62	40	22	34				30	30				27
	1953	232	55	56	32	24	46				45	45			1	29
	1954	252	62	54	31	23	46				52	52			1	37

Gross Miscellaneous Services Transactions Between World Areas, Annually,
1950–54, as Reported by Area Debited (million U.S. dollars)

		All Areas	Unallocated	Sterling Area			Nonsterling EPU Area			Own Currency Area	U.S.	Canada	IO	Latin America	Other Countries
				All	U.K.	RSA	All	Cont. OEEC	Cont. OT's						
All areas	1950	2,509		881	525	356	718	676	42		224	251	50	186	199
	1951	3,316		1,167	744	423	1,000	952	48		286	290	53	224	296
	1952	3,223		1,061	690	371	1,082	1,025	57		294	250	56	212	268
	1953	3,652		1,107	675	432	1,225	1,187	38		382	251	56	287	344
	1954	4,168		1,231	770	461	1,524	1,482	42		420	271	54	285	383
Unallocated	1950	174		—	—		98	92	6					22	54
	1951	365		99	97	2	169	164	5					35	62
	1952	247		2	—	2	152	143	9					36	57
	1953	245		1	—	1	134	134	—					37	73
	1954	296		4	—	4	193	193	—					31	68
Sterling Area	1950	805		459	198	261	96	90	6		166	25		35	24
	1951	926		481	175	306	139	131	8		178	34		48	46
	1952	870		439	190	249	156	149	7		182	24		27	42
	1953	962		467	179	288	176	175	1		206	28		35	50
	1954	1,033		492	175	317	189	188	1		233	32		33	54
United Kingdom	1950			204	—	204					163	23		35	23
	1951			194	—	194					174	32		48	41
	1952			180	—	180					178	21		27	36
	1953			236	—	236					197	21		35	40
	1954			277	—	277					229	26		33	40
Rest of Sterling Area	1950			255	198	57					3	2			1
	1951			287	175	112					4	2			5
	1952			259	190	69					4	3			6
	1953			231	179	52					9	7			10
	1954			215	175	40					4	6			14
Nonsterling EPU area	1950	591		161	122	39	285	282	3	46	27	—	5	14	53
	1951	843		245	212	33	412	408	4	49	36	1	7	21	72
	1952	949		305	274	31	463	458	5	52	39	5	6	18	61
	1953	1,073		298	259	39	538	537	1	55	43	6	6	26	101
	1954	1,292		338	305	33	723	722	1	51	44	7	6	33	90
Cont. OEEC countries	1950										26		5	14	53
	1951										35		7	21	72
	1952										39		6	18	60
	1953										43		6	26	101
	1954										43		6	33	90
Cont. Overseas Territ.	1950										1				—
	1951										1				—
	1952										—				1
	1953										—				—
	1954										1				—
Own Currency Area	1950						46	19	27	46					
	1951						49	19	30	49					
	1952						52	17	35	52					
	1953						55	20	35	55					
	1954						51	12	39	51					
U.S., Canada, & IO	1950	733		205	168	37	95	95			10	226	43	106	48
	1951	883		243	189	54	130	129	1		19	254	44	107	86
	1952	827		233	175	58	124	123	1		19	216	48	117	70
	1953	910		254	191	63	147	146	1		9	213	48	168	71
	1954	1,071		312	248	64	203	202	1		10	227	46	169	104
United States	1950				137		94	94				226	43	106	48
	1951				159		128	127	1			254	44	107	86
	1952				150		120	119	1			216	48	117	70
	1953				164		145	144	1			213	48	167	71
	1954				224		199	198	1			227	46	169	102
Canada	1950				31		1	1			10			—	
	1951				30		2	2			19			—	
	1952				25		4	4			19			—	
	1953				27		2	2			9			1	
	1954				24		4	4			10			—	2
Internat. Organizations	1950														
	1951														
	1952														
	1953														
	1954														
Latin America	1950	74		4	4	—	45	45			17	—	1	7	—
	1951	116		9	9	—	46	46			49	1	1	9	1
	1952	150		11	11	—	70	70			48	5	1	13	2
	1953	208		14	14	—	59	59			110	4	1	19	1
	1954	224		11	11	—	63	63			124	5	1	16	4
Other Countries	1950	132		52	33	19	53	53			4		1	2	20
	1951	183		90	62	28	55	55			4		1	4	29
	1952	180		71	40	31	65	65			6		1	1	36
	1953	254		73	32	41	116	116			14		1	2	48
	1954	252		74	31	43	102	102			9		1	3	63

TABLE B-24
Net Miscellaneous Services Transactions Between World Areas, Annually, 1950–54
(as reported by area at left, million U.S. dollars)

		All Areas	Unallocated	Sterling Area			Nonsterling EPU Area			Own Currency Area	U.S., Canada, and IO				Latin America	Other Countries
				All	U.K.	RSA	All	Cont. OEEC	Cont. OT's		All	U.S.	Canada	IO		
All areas	1950	232	92	72			-15				-105				97	91
	1951	-71	-45	117			-229				-99				105	80
	1952	126	99	166			-203				-80				69	75
	1953	-22	69	118			-157				-106				28	26
	1954	141	208	165			-144				-128				-2	42
Unallocated	1950															
	1951															
	1952															
	1953															
	1954															
Sterling Area	1950	3	40	—	-6	6	-65				14				31	-17
	1951	-192	-95	—	-19	19	-106				-1				40	-30
	1952	-67	75	—	10	-10	-149				6				18	-17
	1953	-79	26	—	-57	57	-122				13				21	-17
	1954	68	226	—	-102	102	-149				-10				22	-21
United Kingdom	1950	50	40	6		6	-35				18	26	-8		31	-10
	1951	-122	-97	19		19	-79				17	15	2		39	-21
	1952	-26	74	-10		-10	-126				24	28	-4		16	-4
	1953	43	25	57		57	-95				27	33	-6		21	8
	1954	235	225	102		102	-130				7	5	2		22	9
Rest of Sterling Area	1950	-47	—	-6	-6	—	-30				-4				—	-7
	1951	-70	2	-19	-19	—	-27				-18				1	-9
	1952	-41	1	10	10	—	-23				-18				2	-13
	1953	-122	1	-57	-57	—	-27				-14				—	-25
	1954	-167	1	-102	-102	—	-19				-17				—	-30
Nonsterling EPU area	1950	191	42	65			21			7	20	18	2		-22	58
	1951	122	64	106	·		-115			6	—	-2	2		-10	71
	1952	210	44	149			-73			3	72	72	—		-39	54
	1953	184	64	122			-35			1	34	32	2		-19	17
	1954	202	-18	149	·		-3			3	64	63	1		-21	28
Cont. OEEC countries	1950	215	48	70			23			19	19	17	2		-22	58
	1951	149	69	112			-112			19	—	-2	2		-10	71
	1952	244	53	153			-68			20	71	71	—		-39	54
	1953	198	64	123			-35			14	34	32	2		-19	17
	1954	228	-18	149			-3			28	65	64	1		-21	28
Cont. Overseas Territ.	1950	-24	-6	-5			-2			-12	1	1				
	1951	-27	-5	-6			-3			-13	—	—				
	1952	-34	-9	-4			-5			-17	1	1				
	1953	-14	—	-1			—			-13	—	—				
	1954	-26	—	—			—			-25	-1	-1				
Own Currency Area	1950						7	-12	19	7						
	1951						6	-13	19	6						
	1952						3	-17	20	3						
	1953						1	-13	14	1						
	1954						3	-25	28	3						
United States	1950	273		3	-26	29	38	38	—		94		66	28	88	50
	1951	259		14	-15	29	47	46	1		79		64	15	78	41
	1952	282		8	-28	36	46	46	—		86		78	8	98	44
	1953	226		7	-33	40	56	53	3		83		82	1	38	42
	1954	264		41	-5	46	68	65	3		85		85	—	11	59
Canada	1950	-126		8	8	—	2				-140	-140			2	2
	1951	-156		-2	-2	—	2				-161	-161			2	3
	1952	-139		5	4	1	-1				-145	-145			-1	3
	1953	-132		4	6	-2	-2				-137	-137			—	3
	1954	-144		-3	-2	-1	-3				-140	-140			-1	3
Internat. Organizations	1950	-45					-5	-5			-38	-38			-1	-1
	1951	-47					-7	-7			-38	-38			-1	-1
	1952	-50					-6	-6			-42	-42			-1	-1
	1953	-48					-6	-6			-40	-40			-1	-1
	1954	-47					-6	-6			-39	-39			-1	-1
Latin America	1950	-63	-3	-31	-31		-5	-5			-23	-24	1		-1	—
	1951	-57	2	-39	-39		-9	-9			-7	-8	1		-3	-1
	1952	-46	-14	-16	-16		4	4			-17	-18	1		-4	1
	1953	-61	-3	-21	-21		6	6			-33	-33	—		-11	1
	1954	-71	6	-22	-22		-10	-10			-36	-37	1		-9	—
Other Countries	1950	-1	13	27	10	17	-8				-32	-32	—		—	-1
	1951	—	-16	38	21	17	-47				29	29	—		-1	-3
	1952	-64	-6	20	4	16	-27				-40	-40	—		-2	-9
	1953	-112	-18	6	-8	14	-55				-26	-26	—		—	-19
	1954	-131	-6	—	-9	9	-44				-52	-50	-2		-3	-26

TABLE B-25
Net Transfer Transactions Between World Areas, Annually, 1950–54
(as reported by area at left, million U.S. dollars)

Area	Year	All Areas	Unallocated	Sterling Area: All	U.K.	RSA	Nonsterling EPU Area: All	Cont. OEEC	Cont. OT's	EPU	Own Currency Area	U.S.	Canada	IO	Latin America	Other Countries
All areas	1950	-261	30	-539	-444	-95	-2,450	-2,462	17	-5		3,647	-6	-113	-10	-820
	1951	-218	34	-273	-136	-137	-2,122	-2,013	4	-113		3,141	-9	-61	-33	-895
	1952	-299	13	-481	-290	-191	-1,076	-1,082	-5	11		2,035	14	-59	-48	-697
	1953	-373	21	-482	-190	-292	-882	-886	4	—		1,882	79	-98	-35	-858
	1954	-450	42	-297	-80	-217	-936	-943	7	—		1,700	24	-54	-53	-876
Unallocated	1950															
	1951															
	1952															
	1953															
	1954															
Sterling Area	1950	406	—	-12	37	-49	-272	-125	—	-147		(710)	(3)	(-14)	—	-9
	1951	202	-2	3	71	-68	-18	-19		1		(243)	(-)	(-19)	—	-5
	1952	394	-2	-10	100	-110	-19	-19	—	—		(431)	(9)	(-5)	-3	-7
	1953	396	-2	-15	77	-92	-27	-27	—	—		(442)	(23)	(-17)	-3	-5
	1954	174	1	-6	89	-95	-27	-27	—	—		(212)	(8)	(-5)	—	-9
United Kingdom	1950	323	—	-49		-49	-272	(-122)	(-)	(-150)		666	3	-22	—	-3
	1951	65	—	-70		-70	-11	(-11)	(-)	(-)		177	—	-28	—	-3
	1952	220	—	-109		-109	-11	(-11)	(-)	(-)		372	-6	-17	-3	-6
	1953	157	—	-87		-87	-5	(-5)	(-)	(-)		283	5	-31	-3	-5
	1954	-17	—	-98		-98	-8	(-8)	(-)	(-)		117	—	-20	—	-8
Rest of Sterling Area	1950	83	—	37	37	—	—	(-3)	(-)	(3)		(-44)	(-)	(8)	—	-8
	1951	137	-2	73	71	2	-7	(-8)	(-)	(1)		(66)	(-)	(9)	—	-2
	1952	174	-2	99	100	-1	-8	(-8)	(-)			(59)	(15)	(12)	—	-1
	1953	239	-2	72	77	-5	-22	(-22)	(-)			(159)	(18)	(14)	—	-1
	1954	191	1	92	89	3	-19	(-19)	(-)			(95)	(8)	(15)	—	-1
Nonsterling EPU area	1950	2,398	2	203	(198)	(5)	93	(-51)	(2)	(142)	3	(2,067)	(1)	(-6)	42	-7
	1951	2,180	3	19	(9)	(10)	32	(-51)	(1)	(82)	—	(2,125)	(1)	—	28	-28
	1952	1,106	-2	26	(10)	(16)	51	(-40)	(-)	(11)	-8	(1,013)	—	—	23	3
	1953	870	-3	34	(13)	(21)	29	(23)	(6)	(-)	-4	(829)	(1)	—	18	-34
	1954	783	3	17	(4)	(13)	-41	(-47)	(6)	(-)	-7	(877)	(-2)	—	18	-82
Cont. OEEC countries	1950	2,408	2	56	(48)	(8)	237	(93)	(2)	(142)	18	2,065	1	-6	42	-7
	1951	2,073	3	20	(9)	(11)	115	(32)	(1)	(82)	7	1,927	1	—	28	-28
	1952	1,124	-2	26	(10)	(16)	62	(51)	(-)	(11)	-1	1,013	—	—	23	3
	1953	886	-3	36	(14)	(22)	35	(29)	(6)	(-)	3	830	1	—	18	-34
	1954	800	3	19	(5)	(14)	-35	(-41)	(6)	(-)	3	876	-2	—	18	-82
Cont. Overseas Territ.	1950	-15	—	—	—	—	-2	(-2)	(-)		-15	2	—	—	—	—
	1951	-6	—	—	—	—	-1	(-1)	(-)		-7	2	—	—	—	—
	1952	-7	—	—	—	—	—	—	—		-7	—	—	—	—	—
	1953	-16	—	-2	(-1)	(-1)	-6	(-6)	(-)		-7	-1	—	—	—	—
	1954	-17	—	-2	(-1)	(-1)	-6	(-6)	(-)		-10	1	—	—	—	—
EPU	1950	5		147	150	-3	-142	-142								
	1951	113		-1		-1	-82	-82				196				
	1952	-11					-11	-11								
	1953															
	1954															
Own Currency Area	1950						3	-15	18		3					
	1951						—	-7	7		—					
	1952						-8	-7	-1		-8					
	1953						-4	-7	3		-4					
	1954						-7	-10	3		-7					
United States	1950	-3,923		-734	-695	-39	-2,289	-2,286	-3				-10	-95	-52	-743
	1951	-3,412		-321	-251	-70	-2,196	-1,996	-4	-196			-10	-45	-62	-778
	1952	-2,402		-505	-437	-68	-1,130	-1,126	-4				-5	-60	-73	-629
	1953	-2,312		-501	-316	-185	-946	-941	-5				-2	-93	-55	-715
	1954	-2,134		-298	-192	-106	-970	-968	-2				2	-62	-73	-733
Canada	1950	-31		-5	-3	-2	5	5	—			-14		—	-1	-16
	1951	-22		1	—	1	16	16	—			-20		—	-1	-18
	1952	-48		-8	6	-14	14	14	—			-43		—	—	-11
	1953	-49		-15	1	-16	17	17	—			-38		—	1	-14
	1954	-41		-6	—	-6	14	14	—			-37		—	1	-13
Internat. Organizations	1950	—	-87	14	22	-8	-2	-2				91	—	—	—	-16
	1951	—	-47	19	28	-9	—	—				44	—	—	—	-16
	1952	—	-32	5	17	-12	—	—				60	—	—	—	-26
	1953	—	-22	17	31	-14	—	—				94	—	—	—	-89
	1954	—	-27	5	20	-15	—	—				61	—	—	—	-39
Latin America	1950	-9	-8	-5	-5	—	-2	-2				8	—	—	—	-2
	1951	-4	-8	-7	-5	—	-1	-1	—			13	—	—	—	-1
	1952	-9	-7	-6	-6	—	—	—	—			3	—	—	2	-1
	1953	-26	-9	-6	-6	—	-9	-9	—			-1	—	—	2	-3
	1954	-18	-13	-7	-7	—	-7	-7	—			9	—	—	1	-1
Other Countries	1950	898	123	—	2	-2	14	14				785	—	2	1	-27
	1951	838	88	13	12	1	45	45				736	—	3	2	-49
	1952	660	63	17	20	-3	16	16	—			571	10	6	3	-26
	1953	748	57	4	10	-6	58	58	—			556	57	12	2	2
	1954	786	78	-2	6	-8	102	102	—			578	16	13	—	1

Net Capital Transactions Between World Areas, Annually, 1950–54
(as reported by area at left, million U.S. dollars)

	Year	All Area	Unallocated	Sterling Area All	U.K.	RSA	Nonsterling EPU Area All	Cont. OEEC	Cont. OT's	EPU	Own Currency Area	U.S.	Canada	IO	Latin America	Other Countries
All areas	1950	306	124	-40	-410	370	233	168	60	5		117	-255	-32	72	87
	1951	1,067	1,083	-892	-395	-497	1,197	1,106	44	47		1,160	-490	-79	-826	-86
	1952	778	841	612	1,696	-1,084	592	729	-33	-104		607	-490	-130	-938	-578
	1953	869	400	407	384	23	1,296	1,407	-116	5		146	-844	93	-151	-478
	1954	270	286	106	595	-489	1,280	1,432	-122	-30		26	-624	-24	-455	-325
Unallocated	1950															
	1951															
	1952															
	1953															
	1954															
Sterling Area	1950	-27	147	-135	-687	552	-273	(-48)	(-)	(-225)		(426)	(-13)	(13)	-4	-188
	1951	1,316	385	-57	251	-308	853	(164)	(-)	(689)		(144)	(23)	(5)	90	-127
	1952	5	210	118	787	-669	-23	(-173)	(-)	(150)		(100)	(17)	(105)	-193	-329
	1953	559	164	202	-36	238	40	(-98)	(-)	(-58)		(359)	(-132)	(-68)	137	-143
	1954	474	38	290	472	-182	87	(-302)	(-)	(-215)		(119)	(-83)	(-53)	27	49
United Kingdom	1950	340	-70	552	—	552	-305	(-80)	(-)	(-225)		367	-13	—	-3	-188
	1951	697	280	-308	—	-308	826	(137)	(-)	(689)		-33	28	-42	89	-143
	1952	-1,299	48	-669	—	-669	-62	(-210)	(-)	(148)		-80	-10	-6	-187	-333
	1953	402	103	238	—	238	45	(-104)	(-)	(-59)		338	-159	-151	131	-143
	1954	-100	20	-182	—	-182	89	(307)	(-)	(-218)		124	-98	-112	28	31
Rest of Sterling Area	1950	-367	217	-687	-687	—	32	(32)	(-)	(-)		(59)	(-)	(13)	-1	—
	1951	619	105	251	251	—	27	(27)	(-)	(-)		(177)	(-5)	(47)	1	16
	1952	1,304	162	787	787	—	39	(37)	(-)	(2)		(180)	(27)	(111)	-6	4
	1953	157	61	-36	-36	—	-5	(-6)	(-)	(1)		(21)	(27)	(83)	6	—
	1954	574	18	472	472	—	-2	(-5)	(-)	(3)		(-5)	(15)	(59)	-1	18
Nonsterling EPU area	1950	55	-65	419	(451)	(-32)	16	(-117)	(-)	(133)	-8	-256	-18	-42	15	-6
	1951	-487	131	-676	(-649)	(-27)	96	(581)	(-)	(-485)	-2	87	-6	-42	-98	23
	1952	-649	67	127	(-166)	(-39)	-86	(+252)	(-)	(-338)	-8	-376	-7	-48	-149	-169
	1953	-1,191	1	52	(-47)	(5)	-71	(-22)	(-)	(-49)	-2	-1,223	-15	-15	73	9
	1954	-1,010	195	26	(-24)	(2)	106	(-108)	(-)	(214)	-5	-1,290	-20	-89	38	29
Cont. OEEC countries	1950	104	-82	194	(-226)	(-32)	138	(5)	(-)	(133)	36	-133	-18	-42	15	-4
	1951	-389	136	16	(-43)	(-27)	-382	(103)	(-)	(-485)	44	-80	-6	-42	-98	23
	1952	-780	73	276	(-313)	(-37)	-424	(-86)	(-)	(-338)	-65	-253	-7	-62	-149	-169
	1953	-1,233	1	-10	(-16)	(6)	-132	(-83)	(-)	(-49)	-29	-1,098	-15	-33	74	9
	1954	-1,086	195	-190	(-195)	(5)	310	(96)	(-)	(214)	6	-1,359	-20	-97	40	29
Cont. Overseas Territ	1950	-44	17	—	—	—	11	(11)	(-)	(-)	-44	-26	—		—	-2
	1951	-51	-5	-3	(-3)	(-)	-7	(-7)	(-)	(-)	-46	10	—		—	—
	1952	27	-6	1	(1)	—	—	—	—	—	57	-39	—	14	—	—
	1953	47	—	4	(4)	—	12	(12)	—	—	27	-13	—	18	-1	—
	1954	46	—	1	(1)	—	10	(10)			-11	40	—	8	-2	—
EPU	1950	-5		225	225	—	-133	-133				-97	—	—	—	—
	1951	-47		-689	-689	—	485	485				157	—	—	—	—
	1952	104		-150	-148	-2	338	338				-84	—	—	—	—
	1953	-5		58	59	-1	49	49				-112				
	1954	30		215	218	-3	-214	-214				29				
Own Currency Area	1950						-8	-44	36		-8					
	1951						-2	-46	44		-2					
	1952						-8	57	-65		-8					
	1953						-2	27	-29		-2					
	1954						-5	-11	6		-5					
United States	1950	149	—	-347	-204	-143	379	258	24	(97)		—	-236	-27	64	316
	1951	-1,272	—	-7	125	-132	14	171	—	(-157)		—	-522	-87	-891	21
	1952	-760		-67	181	-248	441	311	46	(84)		—	-250	-149	-586	-149
	1953	-117		-159	-45	-114	1,219	1,155	-48	(112)			-707	19	-234	-255
	1954	-575		-286	-70	-216	1,049	1,131	-53	-29			-520	38	-420	-436
Canada	1950	420	16	13	13	—	27	27	—	—		342	—	-5	27	—
	1951	834	—	-23	-28	5	37	37	—	—		832	—	-4	-8	—
	1952	1		-17	10	-27	46	46	—	—		8	—	-12	-20	-4
	1953	799		132	159	-27	93	93	—	—		596	—	-20	-2	—
	1954	679		83	98	-15	62	62	—	—		539	—	-14	9	—
Internat. Organizations	1950	32	—	-13	—	-13	56	(56)	(-)	(-)		15	12	—	-38	—
	1951	14	—	-6	41	-47	34	34		(-)		43	15	—	-59	-13
	1952	137		-82	29	-111	74	88	—	—		118	20	—	-29	36
	1953	-26	—	116	199	-83	44	62	-1	—		-8	8	—	-83	-103
	1954	3	—	115	174	-59	128	136	-8	—		-111	6	—	-112	-23
Latin America	1950	123	56	-21	-24	3	63	63	—	—		4	—	31	—	-10
	1951	1,019	570	-53	-55	2	218	218	—	—		178	—	52	-12	66
	1952	1,541	471	194	191	3	86	86	—	—		692	-5	17	58	28
	1953	278	193	-42	-47	5	-53	-53	—	—		249	3	73	-91	-54
	1954	598	-5	60	52	8	19	19	—	—		443	-8	82	21	-14
Other Countries	1950	-446	-30	44	41	3	-27	-27	—	—		-414	0	-2	8	-25
	1951	-357	-3	-70	-80	10	-53	-53	—	—		-124	0	-3	-48	-56
	1952	503	93	339	332	7	-26	-47		—		65	-3	-43	19	9
	1953	587	42	106	107	-1	26	47	-21	—		173	-1	104	49	68
	1954	101	58	-182	-155	-27	-166	-99	-67			326	1	12	-18	70

TABLE B-27
Net Gold Transactions Between World Areas, Annually, 1950–54
(as reported by area at left, million U.S. dollars)

		All Areas	Unal-located	Sterling Area All	Sterling Area U.K.	Sterling Area RSA	Nonsterling EPU Area All	Nonsterling EPU Area Cont. OEEC	Nonsterling EPU Area OT's	Nonsterling EPU Area EPU	Own Currency Area	U.S.	Canada	IO	Latin America	Other Countries
All areas	1950	132	216	964	1,277	-313	302	231	6	65		-1,731	99	34	155	93
	1951	489	681	-568	-285	-283	-7	-45	8	30		79	2	1	104	197
	1952	397	937	-500	-289	-211	-310	-164	2	-148		288	-9	100	-91	-18
	1953	397	549	530	748	-218	454	350	10	94		-1,195		36	127	-104
	1954	293	360	52	439	-387	322	302		20		-332		-9	-69	-31
Unallocated	1950															
	1951															
	1952															
	1953															
	1954															
Sterling Area	1950	-1,133	-110	-27	253	-280						-1,014		5	-6	19
	1951	1,178	591	12	229	-217	29	29				511		1	-7	41
	1952	1,211	705	4	203	-199	35	35				446		2	-7	26
	1953	-296	184	18	236	-218	34	34				-482		2	-7	-45
	1954	256	298	4	391	-387	19	19				-50			-5	-10
United Kingdom	1950	-1,550	-246	-280		-280						-1,020			-6	2
	1951	700	404	-218		-218	27	27				464			-7	30
	1952	700	408	-199		-199	32	32				440			-7	26
	1953	-800	-70	-218		-218	20	20				-480			-7	-45
	1954	-250	184	-386		-386	17	17				-50			-5	-10
Rest of Sterling Area	1950	417	136	253	253							6		5		17
	1951	478	187	230	229	1	2	2				47		1		11
	1952	511	297	203	203		3	3				6		2		
	1953	504	254	236	236		14	14				-2		2		
	1954	506	114	390	391	-1	2	2								
Nonsterling EPU area	1950	-172	197				-40	-40			11	-367		29	-1	-1
	1951	-250	1	-27	-27		-81	-81			9	-152				
	1952	-566	-77	-32	-32		-296	-148		-148	9	-174		33		-29
	1953	-610	113	-20	-20		-43	-43			2	-576		5		-91
	1954	-566	-82	-17	-17		-71	-71			-1	-377		-9		-9
Cont. OEEC countries	1950	-76	231				-40	-40				-294		29	-1	-1
	1951	-237	-15	-27	-27		-81	-81				-114				
	1952	-400	96	-32	-32		-296	-148		-148		-172		33		-29
	1953	-610	11	-20	-20		-43	-43				-472		5		-91
	1954	-562	-99	-17	-17		-71	-71				-357		-9		-9
Cont. Overseas Territ.	1950	3									11	-8				
	1951	1									9	-8				
	1952	8	1								9	-2				
	1953	-8									2	-10				
	1954	-1									-1					
EPU	1950	-99	-34									-65				
	1951	-14	16									-30				
	1952	-174	-174													
	1953	8	102									-94				
	1954	-3	17									-20				
Own Currency Area	1950						11	11			11					
	1951						9	9			9					
	1952						9	9			9					
	1953						2	2			2					
	1954						-1	-1			-1					
United States	1950	1,738		1,008	1,020	-12	383	312	6	65			99		162	86
	1951	-69		-514	-464	-50	180	142	8	30			2		124	139
	1952	-382		-449	-440	-9	121	119	2				-9		-63	18
	1953	1,165		482	480	2	547	443	10	94					132	4
	1954	327		50	50		329	309		20					-62	10
Canada	1950	57	157									-100				
	1951	-117	-107									-10				
	1952	109	102									7				
	1953	46	46													
	1954	73	73													
Internat. Organizations	1950	-45		-5		-5	-39	-39								-1
	1951	-37		-1		-1	-18	-18							-16	-2
	1952	-161		-3	-1	-2	-69	-69							-26	-63
	1953	-11		-2		-2	-7	-7							-1	-1
	1954	-38					-19	-19							-2	-17
Latin America	1950	-164	-2	6	6							-168				
	1951	-9	93	7	7							-112			3	
	1952	152	72	7	7							65		2	6	
	1953	-46	44	7	7							-123		29	3	
	1954	119	19	5	5							95				
Other Countries	1950	-149	-26	-18	-2	-16	-13	-13				-82				-10
	1951	-207	103	-45	-30	-15	-126	-126				-158				19
	1952	34	135	-27	-26	-1	-110	-110				-56		63	-1	30
	1953	142	192	45	45		-79	-79				-8				29
	1954	132	52	10	10		65	65								5

TABLE B-28
Net Settlements Transactions Between World Areas, Annually, 1950–54
(as reported by area at left, million U.S. dollars)

		All Areas	Unallocated	Sterling Area All	U.K.	RSA	Nonsterling EPU All	Cont. OEEC	Cont. OT's	EPU	Own Currency Area	U.S.	Canada	IO	Latin America	Other Countries
All areas	1950	-382	-245	-136	386	-522	-660	-53	-542	-65		1	-190	84	283	481
	1951	-129	-1,706	-93	164	-257	-266	744	-1,046	36		664	-2	155	309	810
	1952	768	-1,720	-715	-608	-107	388	1,169	-1,022	241		1,189	42	113	542	929
	1953	-81	-841	-705	-538	-167	-944	-182	-663	-99		954	109	28	596	722
	1954	-205	-631	-1,008	-489	-519	-1,043	-489	-564	10		1,304	42	139	574	418
Unallocated	1950															
	1951															
	1952															
	1953															
	1954															
Sterling Area	1950	204	-72	367	1,632	-1,265	83	(-460)	(171)	(-372)		(-464)	(31)	(-6)	21	244
	1951	-387	-887	274	792	-518	-135	(348)	(207)	(-690)		(-467)	(169)	(16)	-2	645
	1952	-156	-987	-231	45	-276	413	(418)	(145)	(-150)		(-400)	(517)	(-92)	-49	673
	1953	-201	-367	-206	474	-680	-177	(-380)	(145)	(58)		(-186)	(422)	(108)	-86	291
	1954	-257	-528	-426	78	-504	-67	(-416)	(134)	(215)		(44)	(398)	(-79)	-106	349
United Kingdom	1950	71	262	-1,075		-1,075	786	(268)	(143)	(375)		-9	57	16	26	8
	1951	-279	-618	-421		-421	303	(826)	(166)	(-689)		-96	194	67	41	251
	1952	69	-561	-151		-151	682	(716)	(114)	(-148)		-633	403	23	-36	342
	1953	45	-78	-561		-561	285	(113)	(113)	(59)		-221	352	190	-54	132
	1954	-122	-439	-312		-312	442	(112)	(112)	(218)		-125	377	136	-81	-120
Rest of Sterling Area	1950	133	-334	1,442	1,632	-190	-703	(-728)	(28)	(-3)		(-455)	(-26)	(-22)	-5	236
	1951	-108	-269	695	792	-97	-438	(-478)	(41)	(-1)		(-371)	(-25)	(-51)	-43	394
	1952	-225	-426	-80	45	-125	-269	(-298)	(31)	(-2)		(233)	(114)	(-115)	-13	331
	1953	-246	-289	355	474	-119	-462	(-493)	(32)	(-1)		(35)	(70)	(-82)	-32	159
	1954	-135	-89	-114	78	-192	-509	(-528)	(22)	(-3)		(169)	(-21)	(-57)	-25	469
Nonsterling EPU area	1950	-194	-162	-467	(-1,025)	(558)	-162	(-131)	(244)	(-275)	81	-137	58	42	507	46
	1951	-100	-282	70	(-396)	(466)	74	(-508)	(179)	(403)	-33	-464	144	66	376	-51
	1952	735	-88	-277	(-626)	(349)	125	(-515)	(165)	(475)	71	214	249	38	455	-52
	1953	320	-221	57	(-390)	(447)	-205	(-456)	(202)	(475)	166	330	125	34	242	-208
	1954	289	-64	-58	(-569)	(511)	-407	(-508)	(315)	(-214)	139	453	71	122	303	-270
Cont. OEEC countries	1950	-844	-176	91	(-499)	(590)	-175	(-144)	(244)	(-275)	-471	-301	66	42	47	33
	1951	-948	-148	-426	(-930)	(504)	640	(58)	(179)	(403)	-859	-113	144	66	-165	-87
	1952	-498	-175	-302	(-672)	(370)	634	(-6)	(165)	(475)	-877	42	240	52	-4	-108
	1953	-469	-21	263	(-214)	(477)	81	(-170)	(202)	(49)	-671	132	130	52	-153	-282
	1954	-450	57	293	(-236)	(529)	-428	(-524)	(310)	(-214)	-664	565	94	130	-176	-321
Cont. Overseas Territ.	1950	551	-20	-186	(-151)	(-35)	-262	(-262)	—		552	2	-8	—	460	13
	1951	900	-118	-194	(-155)	(-39)	-163	(-163)	—		826	-28	—	—	541	36
	1952	1,152	-87	-125	(-102)	(-23)	-182	(-182)	—		948	88	9	-14	459	56
	1953	792	-98	-148	(-117)	(-31)	-237	(-237)	—		837	-8	-5	-18	395	74
	1954	766	-104	-136	(-115)	(-21)	-193	(-198)	(5)		803	-103	-23	-8	479	51
EPU	1950	99	34	-372	-375	3	275	275				162				
	1951	-52	-16	690	689	1	-403	-403				-323				
	1952	81	174	150	148	2	-327	-327				84				
	1953	-3	-102	-58	-59	1	-49	-49				206				
	1954	-27	-17	-215	-218	3	214	214				-9				
Own Currency Area	1950						81	(552)	(-471)		81					
	1951						-33	(826)	(-859)		-33					
	1952						71	(948)	(-877)		71					
	1953						166	(837)	(-671)		166					
	1954						139	(803)	(-664)		139					
United States	1950	-33		300	-212	512	214	374	2	(-162)			-255	67	-492	133
	1951	472		412	125	287	505	167	15	(323)			-273	109	-562	281
	1952	509		631	632	-1	3	18	69	(-84)			-768	183	-156	616
	1953	296		197	26	171	-250	-225	181	(-206)			-424	59	-23	737
	1954	178		303	283	20	-213	-448	226	(9)			-428	3	-30	543
Canada	1950	-1	-173	-18	-42	24	-126	-132	6			305		6	17	-12
	1951	-1	107	-167	-185	18	-249	-247	-2			305		5	50	-52
	1952	-2	-102	-497	-404	-93	-387	-375	-12			1,129		13	7	-165
	1953	2	-46	-353	-293	-60	-269	-271	2			719		21	86	-156
	1954	-3	-73	-366	-336	-30	-162	-176	14			597		14	85	-98
Internat. Organizations	1950	—	87	-5	-27	22	-38	-38	—			-80	-13		35	14
	1951	—	47	-23	-74	51	-40	-40	—			-63	-16		68	27
	1952	—	39	+65	-50	115	-28	-42	(14)			-147	-21		47	45
	1953	—	22	-152	-234	82	-61	-79	(18)			-53	-9		73	180
	1954	—	27	-140	-197	57	-133	-141	(8)			87	-6		99	66
Latin America	1950	-145	100	-9	-30	21	-695	-189	-506			441	-8	-28	107	-53
	1951	-19	-553	27	-42	69	-631	-44	-587			1,355	-70	-45	115	-217
	1952	-145	-405	93	74	19	-300	234	-534			707	-49	-11	18	-198
	1953	-182	-64	20	-16	36	-443	46	-489			469	-82	-91	127	-118
	1954	-341	120	-58	-8	-50	-436	141	-577			365	-79	-67	222	-187
Other Countries	1950	-213	-25	-304	90	-394	-17	-29	12			-64	-3	3	88	109
	1951	-94	-138	-686	-56	-630	243	242	1			-2	44	4	264	177
	1952	-173	-177	-499	-279	-220	491	483	8			-314	114	-18	220	10
	1953	-316	-165	-268	-105	-163	295	346	-51			-325	77	-103	177	—
	1954	-71	-113	-263	260	-523	236	256	-20			-242	86	-12	222	15

C

EFFECTS ON THE RECORD OF REDIRECTING PETROLEUM TRADE

One of our objectives has been to adjust the merchandise matrix (Appendix Tables B-4 and B-5) so as to include petroleum on a purchase-sales basis rather than a trade records (origin-destination or consignment) basis. This means taking petroleum entering international trade from sources outside the U.S., U.K., and Continental OEEC countries as sold first to residents of the U.S. and the U.K. and then resold to the countries of refining or final consumption. For this purpose, it is necessary to estimate (1) the proportion of oil supplied from each source by U.S., British, and other companies and (2) the proportion of oil supplied by U.S., British, and other companies to each market area.[1] The first set of proportions can be obtained from sources on the international oil industry, notably from a Federal Trade Commission staff study[2] and from publications of the Bureau of Mines;[3] the second set of proportions has been estimated by Cornelius Dwyer for the broad market areas in the two-valued matrix based on an expert knowledge of the marketing conditions in the industry.[4]

Given these proportions and the exports of oil-source countries to partner areas in each of the five years, the procedure for adjusting from a trade records to a purchase-sales basis is straightforward. Oil imports are deducted from the merchandise imports of the importing area, partner by partner, and counted instead as imports in appropriate proportions from the U.S. or the U.K. Oil exports are deducted from the merchandise exports of the exporting area, partner by partner, and counted instead as exports in appropriate proportions to the U.S. or the U.K. The U.S. and U.K. accounts are adjusted to include both imports of oil from the source countries and sales to the countries of refining or ultimate consumption. This last adjustment evidently raises the total of world trade, both debits and credits, since the U.S. and the U.K. are counted as middlemen between the sources and destinations.

Table C-1 shows for the five-year period (A) the f.o.b. value of oil entering into the eight-area matrix as carried in the merchandise credit entries of our oil-source accounts, (B) the distribution of oil sales by the source area to the U.S. and the U.K., (C) the redistribution of the oil by the U.S. and the U.K. to refining and market areas, and (D) the net change in the gross matrix of merchandise (and hence goods and services) transactions between world areas.

Free world oil sources outside the three economic centers supplied $22,060 million of oil in the five years to other countries. Part of this was supplied to the U.S. and the U.K., leaving $17,791 million to be redirected through the U.S. and the U.K. The total of world trade had to be raised by that latter amount (not quite 4 per cent of all goods and services or about 5 per cent of merchandise alone). The proportions of world trade contributed by the U.S. and the U.K. are somewhat increased and those contributed by other areas decreased under this new accounting. Slightly more than half (53.7 per cent) of the redirected oil is channeled through the U.S., and the balance[5] through the U.K. This increases U.S. goods and services credits and debits by 10.8 and 12.4 per cent, respectively, and U.K. credits and debits by 14.3 and 14.4 per cent. The total credits and debits of other areas remain unchanged after the adjustment.

However, the direction of the trade of certain areas—notably the Continental Overseas Territories—is changed markedly. Table C-2 shows the revision of the goods and services matrix in Table A-1, and Table C-3 compares the revised percentage distributions of purchases and sales computed from Table C-2 with the corresponding percentage distributions in Table A-3.

Looking first at the distribution of purchases of

---

[1] British companies include the Royal Dutch-Shell Group, whose transactions were in sterling according to an agreement between the treasuries of the U.K. and the Netherlands.

[2] *The International Petroleum Cartel,* Staff Report to the Federal Trade Commission, U.S. Senate, Washington, 1952.

[3] *International Petroleum Trade.*

[4] Emil Nelson assisted Dwyer in these calculations. See also C. J. Dwyer "The Oil Trade and the International Balance of Payments in 1951," unpublished NBER study.

[5] Including the French share of Iraq Petroleum Company oil.

TABLE C-1

Adjustments of Merchandise Matrix (Tables B-4 and B-5) to Channel Oil Purchases from Free World Sources Outside the United States, United Kingdom, and Continent Through the United States and United Kingdom, 1950–54 (million U.S. dollars, f.o.b.)

A. DEDUCT OIL FROM FREE WORLD SOURCES OUTSIDE U.S., U.K., AND CONTINENT

Exporter \ Importer	All Areas	United Kingdom	RSA	Cont. OEEC	Cont. OT's	United States	Canada	Latin America	Other	Unallocated
All sources	22,060	2,285	3,604	4,430	3,731	3,342	853	1,845	1,283	687
Rest of Sterling Area	5,888	1,380	1,150	2,276	79	307	46	113	408	129
Cont. Overseas Territ.	3,726	453	304	529	167	698	60	962	124	429
Latin America	7,838	184	287	416	3,398	2,052	632	704	123	42
Other Countries	4,608	268	1,863	1,209	87	285	115	66	628	87

B. ADD OIL SOLD TO U.S. AND U.K. OIL COMPANIES[a]

Exporter \ Importer	All Areas	United Kingdom	United States
All sources	22,060	9,419	12,641
Rest of Sterling Area	5,888	3,931	1,957
Cont. Overseas Territ.	3,726	1,602	2,124
Latin America	7,838	2,563	5,275
Other Countries	4,608	1,323	3,285

C. ADD OIL SOLD BY U.S. AND U.K. OIL COMPANIES[b]

Exporter \ Importer	All Areas	United Kingdom	RSA	Cont. OEEC	Cont. OT's	United States	Canada	Latin America	Other	Unallocated
U.S. & U.K. sales	17,791	1,107	3,604	4,430	3,731	251	853	1,845	1,283	687
United Kingdom	8,241		2,135	2,641	1,876	251	185	207	584	362
United States	9,550[c]	1,107[c]	1,469	1,789	1,855		668	1,638	699	325

D. NET CHANGE IN GROSS MERCHANDISE MATRIX

Exporter \ Importer	All Areas	United Kingdom	RSA	Cont. OEEC	Cont. OT's	United States	Canada	Latin America	Other	Unallocated
All sources	+17,791	8,241	0	0	0	9,550	0	0	0	0
United Kingdom	8,241	0	2,135	2,641	1,876	251	185	207	584	362
Rest of Sterling Area	0	2,551	-1,150	-2,276	-79	+1,650	-46	-113	-408	-129
Cont. Overseas Territ.	0	1,149	-304	-529	-167	1,426	-60	-962	-124	-429
United States	9,550	1,107	1,469	1,789	1,855	0	668	1,638	659	325
Latin America	0	2,379	-287	-416	-3,398	3,223	-632	-704	-123	-42
Other Countries	0	1,055	-1,863	-1,209	-87	3,000	-115	-66	-628	-87

E. NET CHANGE IN NET MERCHANDISE MATRIX[d]

Exporter \ Importer	All Areas	United Kingdom	RSA	Cont. OEEC	Cont. OT's	United States	Canada	Latin America	Other	Unallocated
United Kingdom	0	0	-416	2,641	727	-856	185	-2,172	-471	362
Rest of Sterling Area	0	416	0	-2,276	225	181	-46	174	1,455	-129
Cont. OEEC countries	0	-2,641	2,276	0	529	-1,789	-60	416	1,209	-429
Cont. Overseas Territ.	0	-727	-225	-529	0	-429	-60	2,436	-37	-429
United States	0	856	-181	1,789	429	0	668	-1,585	-2,301	325
Canada	0	-185	46	-60	60	-668	0	632	115	115
Latin America	0	2,172	-174	-416	-2,436	1,585	-632	0	-57	-42
Other Countries	0	471	-1,455	-1,209	37	2,301	-115	57	0	-87
Unallocated	0	-362	129	429	429	-325	-115	42	87	0

[a] Including French share of Iraq Petroleum Company oil counted as sold through the U.K.

[b] Excluding U.S. company sales to the U.S. and U.K. company sales through U.K., but including U.S. company sales through U.K. companies domiciled in London.

[c] Including $341 million sold from U.S. company supplies to U.K. companies.

[d] Account of area at left with area at top.

TABLE C-2

Two-Valued Matrix of Gross Goods and Services Transactions Between World Areas, Adjusted to Redirect Petroleum Transactions, 1950–54 (million U.S. dollars)

Line A: As reported by area at left
Line B: As reported by area at top

		All Areas	Unallocated	Sterling Area			Nonsterling EPU Area			Own Currency Area	U.S., Canada, and IO				Latin America	Other Countries
				All	U.K.	RSA	All	Cont. OEEC	Cont. OT's		All	U.S.	Canada	IO		
All areas	A	478,463	5,489	131,253	65,624	65,629	139,853	121,285	18,568		107,910	82,312	25,182	416	43,439	50,519
	B	481,831	—	131,975	65,339	66,636	138,788	119,474	19,314		113,946	86,220	27,376	350	46,746	50,376
Unallocated	A	5,963		281	135	146	1,918	1,837	81						1,817	1,947
	B															
Sterling Area	A	127,657	748	63,721	24,489	39,232	27,183	24,103	3,080		18,695	14,668	3,997	30	4,366	12,944
	B	127,195	233	63,888	24,570	39,318	26,841	23,780	3,061		19,669	15,487	4,179	3	4,625	11,939
United Kingdom	A	65,967	870	28,757		28,757	18,127	15,552	2,575		8,731	5,785	2,916	30	3,637	5,845
	B	67,124	362	29,532		29,532	17,940	15,374	2,566		9,514	6,435	3,076	3	3,782	5,994
Rest of Sterling Area	A	61,690	-122	34,964	24,489	10,475	9,056	8,551	505		9,964	8,883	1,081		729	7,099
	B	60,071	-129	34,356	24,570	9,786	8,901	8,406	495		10,155	9,052	1,103		843	5,945
Nonsterling EPU area	A	135,847	1,822	26,048	17,401	8,647	54,223	52,680	1,543	15,833	17,461	16,580	846	35	7,578	12,882
	B	135,221	-429	26,421	17,639	8,782	53,342	51,828	1,514	16,246	18,499	17,344	1,120	35	8,121	13,021
Cont. OEEC countries	A	120,661	1,750	23,149	14,923	8,226	52,212	50,586	1,626	9,506	14,128	13,276	817	35	7,465	12,451
	B	120,604		23,491	15,143	8,348	51,208	49,616	1,592	10,260	14,811	13,692	1,084	35	8,189	12,645
Cont. Overseas Territ.	A	15,186	72	2,899	2,478	421	2,011	2,094	-83	6,327	3,333	3,304	29		113	431
	B	14,617	-429	2,930	2,496	434	2,134	2,212	-78	5,986	3,688	3,652	36		-68	376
Own Currency Area	A						15,833	6,327	9,506	15,833						
	B						16,246	5,986	10,260	16,249						
U.S., Canada, and IO	A	123,930	325	22,332	11,615	10,717	24,367	20,668	3,699		35,374	15,382	19,651	341	26,535	14,997
	B	121,470	325	21,804	11,139	10,665	23,042	19,348	3,694		36,186	14,862	21,022	302	26,405	13,708
United States	A	98,777	325	16,967	7,695	9,272	22,172	18,561	3,611		19,986		19,646	340	25,337	13,990
	B	97,994	325	16,467	7,242	9,225	21,401	17,769	3,632		21,318		21,017	301	25,556	12,927
Canada	A	24,671		5,286	3,895	1,391	2,042	1,954	88		15,233	15,232		1	1,149	961
	B	22,936		5,250	3,864	1,386	1,488	1,426	62		14,663	14,662		1	800	735
Internat. Organiz.	A	482		79	25	54	153	153			155	150	5		49	46
	B	540		87	33	54	153	153			205	200	5		49	46
Latin America	A	44,033	1,111	6,411	5,856	555	7,460	7,271	189		22,926	22,455	466	5	3,636	2,489
	B	43,492	-42	6,161	5,725	436	6,616	6,608	8		24,543	23,770	768	5	3,997	2,217
Other Countries	A	46,996	1,483	12,741	6,263	6,478	10,787	10,236	551		13,454	13,227	222	5	1,324	7,207
	B	48,490	-87	13,420	6,131	7,289	10,783	10,087	696		15,049	14,757	287	5	1,781	7,544

TABLE C-3

Percentage Distribution of Unadjusted and Adjusted Goods and Services Transactions Between World Areas, 1950–54

PART I: PURCHASES

Line A: Unadjusted distribution, calculated from Table A-1, line B
Line B: Adjusted distribution, calculated from Table C-2, line B

		All Areas	Unallocated	Sterling Area			Nonsterling EPU Area			Own Currency Area	U.S., Canada, and IO				Latin America	Other Countries
				All	U.K.	RSA	All	Cont. OEEC	Cont. OT's		All	U.S.	Canada	IO		
All areas	A	100.00		100.01	100.00	100.00	100.01	100.00	99.98		100.00	99.99	100.00	100.01	100.00	99.99
	B	100.00		100.00	99.99	99.99	100.00	100.00	100.00		100.00	100.00	100.01	100.00	99.99	99.99
Unallocated	A	1.29		.23	.24	.22	1.38	1.54	.42							3.86
	B	1.24		.21	.21	.22	1.38	1.54	.42							3.86
Sterling Area	A	25.63		48.78	38.56	57.53	17.78	19.60	6.54		16.89	17.72	14.76	.86	9.69	23.35
	B	26.40		48.41	37.60	59.00	19.34	19.91	15.85		17.26	17.96	15.27	.86	9.89	23.70
United Kingdom	A	12.69		22.14		41.11	9.67	10.66	3.57		8.70	8.07	10.56	.86	7.65	10.74
	B	13.93		22.38		44.32	12.93	12.87	13.29		8.35	7.46	11.24	.86	8.09	11.90
Rest of Sterling Area	A	12.94		26.63	38.56	16.41	8.11	8.94	2.97		8.19	9.65	4.20		2.05	12.61
	B	12.47		26.03	37.60	14.68	6.41	7.04	2.56		8.91	10.50	4.03		1.80	11.80
Nonsterling EPU area	A	29.14		20.67	28.88	13.64	38.94	43.82	8.70		16.41	20.76	4.31		19.43	26.09
	B	28.06		20.02	26.99	13.18	38.43	43.38	7.84		16.23	20.12	4.09		17.37	25.85
Cont. OEEC countries	A	25.99		19.99	26.52	12.53	36.90	41.53	8.24		14.19	17.86	3.96		17.52	25.10
	B	25.03		17.80	23.17	12.53	36.90	41.53	8.24		13.00	15.88	3.96		17.52	25.10
Cont. Overseas Territ.	A	3.15		1.69	2.36	1.11	2.04	2.29	.46a		2.22	2.90	.35		1.91a	.99a
	B	3.03		2.22	3.82	.65	1.53	1.85	-.40a		3.23	4.24	.13		-.15	.75
Own Currency Area	A						11.71	5.01	53.12							
	B						11.71	5.01	53.12							
U.S., Canada, and IO	A	24.12		15.54	17.57	13.80	13.98	14.70	9.52		34.02	19.38	74.35	86.29	52.98	25.32
	B	25.21		16.52	17.05	16.00	16.60	16.19	19.13		31.76	17.24	76.79	86.28	56.48	27.21
United States	A	19.06		11.23	10.74	11.64	12.79	13.38	9.20		19.78		74.33	86.00	51.17	24.27
	B	20.34		12.48	11.08	13.84	15.42	14.87	18.81		18.71		77.78	86.00	54.66	25.66
Canada	A	4.94		4.24	6.77	2.08	1.07	1.19	.32		14.05	19.12		.29	1.71	1.46
	B	4.76		3.98	5.91	2.08	1.07	1.19	.32		12.87	17.00		.28	1.71	1.46
Internat. Organiz.	A	.12		.07	.06	.07	.11	.13			.20	.26	.02		.10	.09
	B	.11		.06	.06	.08	.11	.13			.18	.24	.01		.11	.09
Latin America	A	9.37		3.29	5.86	1.08	7.52	5.88	17.63		21.03	26.80	5.11	1.43		4.65
	B	9.03		4.67	8.76	.65	4.77	5.53	.04		21.54	27.57	2.81	1.43		4.40
Other Countries	A	10.45		11.50	8.89	13.73	8.70	9.45	4.05		11.65	15.33	1.47	1.43	3.95	16.22
	B	10.06		10.17	9.38	10.94	7.77	8.44	3.60		13.21	17.11	1.05	1.43	3.81	14.97

(continued)

TABLE C-3 (concluded)

PART II: SALES

Line A: Unadjusted distribution, calculated from Table A-1, line A
Line B: Adjusted distribution, calculated from Table C-2, line A

		All Areas	Unallocated	Sterling Area			Nonsterling EPU Area			Own Currency Area	U.S., Canada, and IO				Latin America	Other Countries
				All	U.K.	RSA	All	Cont. OEEC	Cont. OT's		All	U.S.	Canada	IO		
All areas	A	100.00	1.19	26.71	12.46	14.25	30.36	26.33	4.03		21.35	15.79	5.47	.09	9.43	10.97
	B	100.00	1.15	27.43	13.72	13.71	29.23	25.35	3.88		22.55	17.20	5.26	.09	9.08	10.56
Unallocated	A															
	B															
Sterling Area	A	100.00	.43	50.40	18.37	32.03	20.95	19.88	1.07		13.95	10.69	3.23	.03	3.58	10.69
	B	99.99	.59	49.91	19.18	30.73	21.29	18.88	2.41		14.64	11.49	3.13	.02	3.42	10.14
United Kingdom	A	100.01	.88	46.12		46.12	23.58	22.37	1.21		14.37	9.59	4.73	.05	5.95	9.11
	B	100.01	1.32	43.60		43.60	27.48	23.58	3.90		13.24	8.77	4.42	.05	5.51	8.86
Rest of Sterling Area	A	100.00	.01	54.41	35.56	18.85	18.50	17.55	.95		13.55	11.72	1.83		1.36	12.17
	B	100.00	-.20	56.68	39.70	16.98	14.68	13.86	.82		16.15	14.40	1.75		1.18	11.51
Nonsterling EPU area	A	100.00	1.66	18.55	11.96	6.59	40.43	39.17	1.26	11.65	11.85	11.15	.67	.03	6.29	9.57
	B	100.00	1.34	19.18	12.81	6.37	39.92	38.78	1.14	11.65	12.85	12.20	.62	.03	5.58	9.48
Cont. OEEC countries	A	100.00	1.45	19.18	12.37	6.81	43.27	41.92	1.35	7.88	11.71	11.00	.68	.03	6.19	10.32
	B	100.01	1.45	19.19	12.37	6.82	43.27	41.93	1.34	7.88	11.71	11.00	.68	.03	6.19	10.32
Cont. Overseas Territ.	A	100.00	3.30	13.53	8.75	4.78	17.83	17.27	.56	41.66	12.95	12.37	.58		7.08	3.65
	B	99.99	.47	19.09	16.32	2.77	13.24	13.79	-.55	41.66	21.95	21.76	.19		.74	2.84
Own Currency Area	A															
	B															
U.S., Canada, and IO	A	99.99		17.27	9.19	8.08	18.12	16.50	1.62		30.34	13.45	16.59	.30	21.76	12.50
	B	100.00	.26	18.02	9.37	8.65	19.66	16.68	2.98		28.55	12.41	15.86	.28	21.41	12.10
United States	A	100.00		16.13	7.38	8.75	20.76	18.80	1.96		21.65		21.27	.38	26.56	14.90
	B	99.99	.33	17.18	7.79	9.39	22.45	18.79	3.66		20.23		19.88	.34	25.64	14.16
Canada	A	100.00		21.43	15.79	5.64	8.28	7.92	.36		61.74	61.74		—	4.66	3.89
	B	100.00		21.43	15.79	5.64	8.28	7.92	.36		61.74	61.74		—	4.66	3.89
Internat. Organiz.	A	100.00		16.39	5.19	11.20	31.74	31.74			32.16	31.13	1.03		10.17	9.54
	B	100.00		16.39	5.19	11.20	31.74	31.74			32.16	31.13	1.03		10.17	9.54
Latin America	A	100.00	2.62	9.81	7.90	1.91	25.60	17.46	8.14		46.18	43.68	2.49	.01	9.86	5.93
	B	100.00	2.52	14.56	13.30	1.26	16.94	16.51	.43		52.07	51.00	1.06	.01	8.26	5.65
Other Countries	A	100.00	3.34	28.83	11.08	17.75	25.71	24.35	1.36		22.49	21.76	.72	.01	2.96	16.67
	B	100.01	3.16	27.11	13.33	13.78	22.95	21.78	1.17		28.63	28.15	.47	.01	2.82	15.34

a The amounts of oil reported sold to Continental Overseas Territories and Latin America exceeded by a small amount the amounts of imports attributed to Continental Overseas Territories.

goods and services (Table C-3, line A), we see that the proportions purchased from the U.S. and the U.K. by other areas increased, while the proportions purchased from the oil-source areas (Rest of the Sterling Area, Continental Overseas Territories, Latin America, and Other Countries) decreased.

However, the proportions purchased by the U.S. and the U.K. from the oil-source areas are increased in most cases. Surprisingly, the U.K.'s added oil purchases from the Rest of the Sterling Area were not as large a proportion of all its imports from that area as all its added oil imports were of total imports; consequently, the proportion of U.K. imports from the Rest of the Sterling Area falls with the adjustment. Imports of the Continental Overseas Territories, which are heavily affected by the Netherlands Antilles import of oil from Latin America for refining, are markedly altered in direction: much higher proportions are purchased from the U.S. and the U.K., much smaller from Latin America. There are twelve instances in Table C-3 in which imports of one of the eight areas from a partner area changed by as much as 2 per cent of its total imports; but most of these involved shifts of less than 4 per cent; the only changes in direction of more than 4 per cent were the three instances involving the redirec-

tion of Netherlands Antilles imports from Latin America to the U.S. and the U.K.

Looking next at the distribution of sales of goods and services (Table C-3, line B), we see that the proportions sold to the U.S. and the U.K. by other areas are increased by the adjustment, while the proportions sold to other areas are decreased. As oil exports bulk large among sales of the oil-source areas, the shifts in their export pattern are somewhat larger than the shifts noted above in import patterns. Seventeen instances occur in Table C-3, line B, in which exports to a partner area changed by as much as 2 per cent of a supplying area's total exports. None of these was as large as the shift involved in the redirection of the imports of Continental Overseas Territories, but eight were larger than 4 per cent and four were between 7 and 10 per cent. All of the eight largest shifts were in the export patterns of oil-source areas. The exports of the U.S. were changed only modestly and those of the U.K. more than 2 per cent in only two instances: to the Rest of the Sterling Area where the added oil sales were not in proportion to the increase in total U.K. exports and to the Continental Overseas Territories where the added oil sales were large relative to the other British exports to Overseas Territories.

D

DIVERGENCE IN THE TWO-VALUED RECORD OF GOODS AND SERVICES TRANSACTIONS

AGREEMENT ON SIZE OF GROSS TRADE

The annual matrixes of gross goods and services credits and debits between world areas given in Tables B-1 and B-2 provide sixty-three trade flows between world areas each year for which paired records can usefully be compared. This number includes intra-area trade flows but excludes goods and services transactions of International Organizations (which in many cases were derived from a single source).[1] Over the five years the sixty-three trade flows provide 315 cases of annual paired records of gross trade between world areas.

To study the agreement of paired records for the magnitude of gross trade in a given year, we have computed three measures: the difference between the paired records without regard to sign (the absolute difference), the mean of the two measures, and the difference expressed as a proportion of the mean (the difference relative to the mean). The 315 cases were distributed according to the absolute difference and the difference relative to the mean (Table D-1). Consideration of both these differences for each case provides a way of evaluating the extent of disagreement between paired records. In nearly a third of

[1] Each entry in Table B–1 is matched by an entry in Table B–2 for seven partner areas of the U.S., the U.K., and Canada; for eight partner areas of Latin America, the Rest of the Sterling Area, and Other Countries (including the area itself); and for nine partner areas of Continental OEEC countries and Continental Overseas Territories (including the area itself and Own Currency Area).

the cases the two records diverged by no more than 2.5 per cent of their mean. In about half the cases they diverged by no more than 5.0 per cent. In 70 per cent the divergence was no more than 10.0 per cent.

For more than 10 per cent of the trade flows, however, only the order of magnitude was indicated by the record (i.e., the records diverged between 25.1 and 50.0 per cent), and in four instances the magnitudes were somewhat in question (the divergence exceeded 50.0 per cent). These last four were all instances of trade between Continental Overseas Territories and Other Countries, in amounts never more than $200 million and sometimes as small as $38 million (on one record). The thirty-five cases diverging from 25.1 to 50.0 per cent included four of the remaining six instances of trade between Continental Overseas Territories and Other Countries. The rest also were mainly trade flows among peripheral areas. None of the trade flows between centers showed a divergence of more than 25.0 per cent, but trade between the Continent and Canada showed seven instances, and Overseas Territories with the United States showed one case, of such a large divergence. The incidence of uncertainty in the record mainly affects transactions between peripheral countries, as can be seen in the following distribution of the number of divergences of more than 25.0 per cent (exporting area at left and importing area at top):

	Canada	OT's	Other Countries	Latin America	RSA	Cont. OEEC	U.S.	Total Number
Canada		4	3	5		4		16
Overseas Territories	2		4(1)				1	7(1)
Other Countries	1	4(3)		4				9(3)
Latin America	1				2			3
Rest of Sterling Area				1				1
Continental OEEC countries	3							3
Total number	7	8(3)	7(1)	10	2	4	1	39(4)

(The figures in parentheses indicate the number of instances within the total given where the divergence exceeded 50.0 per cent.)

TABLE D-1
Analysis of Divergence in Annual Gross Trade Flows Between Areas

Distribution of 315 Cases by Amount of Difference Between
Paired Records of Gross Goods and Services Trade and by
Difference Relative to Mean of Paired Records

Difference Relative to Mean (per cent)	Total	Absolute Difference (million dollars)					
		0–10	11–50	51–100	101–200	201–500	501–1,000
0–2.5	102	58	36	5	2	1	
2.6–5.0	55	7	23	12	10	2	1
5.1–10.0	63	5	10	12	24	12	
10.1–25.0	56	2	14	11	12	17	
25.1–50.0	35	6	9	12	8		
50.1–100.0	4		1	3			
Total	315	78	93	55	56	32	1

In assessing the implications of these large divergences, we should recall that the accounts of transactions of Continental Overseas Territories fail to include any provision for services other than transportation and that the Overseas Territories and Canada tend to channel trade heavily through their associated economic center. Partner countries are likely to count Canadian goods shipped or consigned through the U.S. as coming from the U.S. and to count goods destined for Canada sent via the U.S. as exports to the U.S. Since Canada maintains a record of trade by partner of consignment and since it is greatly concerned with its recording detail, its account is likely to be the more reliable; indeed, in the case of the trade with Continental countries, Canada's account consistently shows a larger trade both ways. In contrast, greater reliance can be placed upon the partner area accounts of transactions with Continental Overseas Territories. These countries on the whole have relatively poor statistical services and their accounts of services are incomplete.[2]

Transactions with Canada and the Overseas Territories constitute all but eight of the thirty-nine cases of interarea trades diverging by more than 25 per cent. The eight remaining cases were all transactions of Latin America and arose mostly in the transportation account, with the entry from the Latin American record being much the larger of the two. This error doubtless reflects our inclusion of the PHL fleet account with Latin American countries as a reporting country. Partners may well have charged transactions with Liberian flag vessels to Other Countries or to owners or operators in the U.S., the U.K., or on the Continent.

AGREEMENT ON YEAR-TO-YEAR CHANGES IN GROSS TRADE

Over the five years the sixty-three trade flows provide 252 cases of year-to-year change in gross trade for which paired records can usefully be compared. One way to make the comparison would be to compute amounts of year-to-year change in both of the paired records and for such amounts, as before, the absolute divergence between them, their mean, and the difference relative to the mean. However, the distribution of cases would be widely dispersed because differences between amounts of change would tend to reflect the large differences in order of magnitude of the different interarea trading relations. Large transactions can be expected to change by large amounts and show large differences between paired records of amounts of change. Moreover, in considering the record of year-to-year change in trade between different areas, one is more concerned

[2] Overseas Territories are unlikely to know either the destination of the goods they ship or the origin of many of the goods they import since their trade is channeled heavily through their associated center. Their goods record, therefore, may more closely approximate the purchase-sales concept than do partner records.

Analysis of Divergence in Year-to-Year Changes in
Gross Trade Flows Between Areas

Distribution of 252 Cases by Amount of Difference Between
Paired Index Numbers of Change in Gross Goods and Services
Trade and by Difference Between Indexes Relative to Their
Mean

Difference Relative to Mean (per cent)	Absolute Difference Between Paired Index Numbers (percentage points)				
	Total	0-5.00	5.01-10.00	10.01-50.00	50.01 and over
0-2.5	102 (4)	102 (4)			
2.6-5.0	52 (3)	41 (3)	10	1	
5.1-10.0	51 (6)	7 (1)	35 (5)	9	
10.1-25.0	35 (6)		6	29 (6)	
25.1-50.0	11 (3)			9 (3)	2
50.1-100.0	1				1
Total	252 (22)	150 (8)	51 (5)	48 (9)	3

NOTE: The figures in parentheses indicate instances of year-
to-year change recorded in opposite directions.

with the proportions in which trade changes from year to year.

To discover whether paired records show a reasonable measure of agreement on the proportions by which interarea trades increased from year to year, we have expressed each of the records for the sixty-three trade flows as a paired series of four year-to-year link relatives (chained index numbers). For each of the 252 pairs of index numbers we have then computed the absolute difference between the indexes, the mean of the two indexes, and the difference between them relative to their mean. That is, we have followed the same type of analysis as before but applied it to year-to-year link relatives rather than amounts of year-to-year change. The 252 cases of paired index numbers of year-to-year change were distributed according to absolute difference and difference relative to the mean of the paired index numbers (Table D-2).

Where paired records of trade diverge the divergence tends to be maintained systematically from year

to year, thus not necessarily obscuring the measure of annual change. In more than 90 per cent of the cases both records showed a movement from one year to the next in the same direction. Most paired index numbers also differed absolutely by less than 5 percentage points (the first column in Table D-2) and for most the difference relative to the mean of the two index numbers was no more than 5 per cent of the mean (first two lines). Even in the twenty-two instances in which paired index numbers showed changes in opposite directions, there were only nine cases in which the absolute difference between the two was as much as 10.01 percentage points and in these nine cases the difference relative to the mean of the paired indexes was also more than 10.0 per cent.

All nine involved peripheral area trading relations, as the tabulation below shows (exporting area at left, importing area at top).

No transactions among centers and only two transactions between centers and peripheral areas had

	Canada	OT's	Other Countries	Latin America	Total Number
Canada			1953/52		1
Overseas Territories	1952/51, 1953/52		1952/51		3
Other Countries	1953/52	1952/53			2
Rest of Sterling Area				1954/53	1
Continental OEEC countries	1952/51			1952/51	2
Total number	4	1	2	2	9

	Canada	OT's	Other Countries	Latin America	RSA	Cont. OEEC	U.S.	U.K.	Total Number
Canada		2	2	2					6
Overseas Territories	1	1	2	2		1	1		8
Other Countries	3	2		1					6
Latin America	1				4				5
Rest of Sterling Area				1					1
Cont. OEEC countries	2			1					3
U.S.								1	1
U.K.			1				1		2
Total number	7	5	5	7	4	1	2	1	32

such divergent movements. Seven of the nine instances were transactions of Canada and the Overseas Territories. As noted above, there are reasons for preferring one of the paired records in these cases. In the other two cases, both involving Latin America as a partner, link relatives for the movement over the five years 1950–54 agreed closely, and it would appear that the year-to-year divergences may have reflected time lags in reporting.

Besides the nine cases that disagreed on direction, there were thirty-two more instances of paired indexes that differed by more than 10.00 percentage points (last two columns in Table D-2) and by more than 10 per cent of the mean of the paired indexes (last three lines before the total). These were trade flows between the partners listed above (exporting area at left, importing area at top).

Trade between the U.S. and the U.K. showed two instances of such large divergence and centers were also involved in four other cases, but the main difficulties of measuring year-to-year change concerned trade between peripheral countries. Moreover, all but six cases involved the trade of Canada or the Over-Seas Territories.

AGREEMENT ON CHANGES IN GROSS TRADE OVER THE FIVE YEARS

The technique followed in the previous section has been used to examine the divergence in paired records of growth in trade flows from 1950 to 1954. The sixty-three cases of paired index numbers of change over the five years were distributed according to absolute difference and difference relative to the mean of the paired index numbers (Table D-3).

Time lags in reporting may, in many instances, account for large differences in records of year-to-year movement so that link relatives for the movement from 1950 to 1954 may not diverge greatly.

Fourteen of the sixty-three cases showed a difference between index numbers for the change in trade over the five years of more than 10.00 percentage points (last two columns in Table D-3) and also a difference of more than 10.0 per cent of the mean of the two indexes (last four rows before the total). The distribution of these fourteen cases and the percentages of divergence relative to the mean of the paired link relatives are tabulated below (exporting area at left, importing area at top):

	Canada	OT's	Other Countries	Latin America	RSA	Cont. OEEC	U.S.	Total Number
Canada		28.57	29.70					2
Overseas Territories		21.28				21.92	28.89	3
Other Countries	(12.27)	119.64						2(1)
Latin America	27.03			13.01	(54.73)			3(1)
Rest of Sterling Area		10.05						1
Cont. OEEC countries	36.87						12.31	2
U.K.							20.38	1
Total number	3(1)	4	1	1	1(1)	1	3	14(2)

(The figures in parentheses indicate cases that diverged in direction.)

TABLE D-3

Analysis of Divergence in Changes in Gross Trade Flows
Between Areas from 1950 to 1954

Distribution of 63 Cases by Amount of Difference Between
Paired Index Numbers of Change in Gross Goods and Services
Trade and by Difference Between Paired Index Numbers Rela-
tive to Their Mean

Difference Relative to Mean (per cent)	Absolute Difference Between Paired Index Numbers (percentage points)				
	Total	0–5.00	5.01–10.00	10.01–50.00	50.01 and over
0–2.5	24	23	1		
2.6–5.0	11 (1)	3 (1)	8		
5.1–10.0	14	1	5	8	
10.1–25.0	6 (1)			5 (1)	1
25.1–50.0	5			3	2
50.1–100.0	2 (1)				2 (1)
Over 100.0	1				1
Total	63 (3)	27 (1)	14	16 (1)	6 (1)

NOTE: The figures in parentheses indicate instances of change
recorded in opposite directions.

Several relations not in the distributions previously discussed now appear: those among the Overseas Territories and among Latin American countries seem to be subject to cumulative error. A new entrant is Continental exports to the U.S. which, like U.K. exports to the U.S., seem to be subject to a systematic and cumulative difference in reporting. Paired index numbers for growth in trade between centers otherwise did not exhibit a divergence over the five years larger than 10.00 percentage points and also more than 10.0 per cent of the mean of the two indexes.

TABLE D-4

Analysis of Divergence in Annual Trade Balances Between Areas

Distribution of 145 Cases by Amount of Difference Between
Paired Records of Net Goods and Services and by Difference
Relative to Mean of Paired Records

Difference Relative to Mean (per cent)	Absolute Difference (million dollars)						
	Total	0–10	11–50	51–100	101–200	201–500	501–1,000
0–2.5	10	10					
2.6–5.0	9	7	2				
5.1–10.0	22	6	11	4	1		
10.1–25.0	33	6	14	6	6	1	
25.1–50.0	39	5	12	8	9	5	
50.1–100.0	13	1	4	3	4		1
Over 100.0	19 (10)	1	6 (3)	6 (5)	4 (2)	2	
Total	145 (10)	36	49 (3)	27 (5)	24 (2)	8	1

NOTE: The figures in parentheses indicate instances of balances recorded in opposite directions.

A number of relations previously noted as showing large year-to-year divergence do not appear above, and the occasional instance of large divergence appears to have been canceled out over time: notably exports of the Rest of the Sterling Area to Latin America and Continental exports to Latin America. Again, most of the cases of poor agreement involved Canada and the Overseas Territories. The only other trade flow between peripheral areas that showed a large divergence (more than 10.00 per-

centage points of absolute difference and also more than 10.0 per cent of the mean) was Latin American exports to the Rest of the Sterling Area, and in this case the two indexes differed in direction of movement by a large percentage. This difference apparently reflects our inclusion of PHL transactions with Latin American countries in the reporting area total and a different treatment by countries in the Rest of the Sterling Area.

AGREEMENT ON NET TRADE EACH YEAR

The annual matrix of net goods and services transactions between world areas given in Table B-3 provides twenty-nine interarea trade balances for which paired records can usefully be compared. This number excludes intra-area balances, which should be

Balance	Year
U.K.–U.S.	1954
U.K.–Other Countries	1952
RSA–Latin America	1954
Cont. OEEC–Latin America	1953

zero, as well as the balances of International Organizations previously excluded.[3] Over the five years the twenty-nine trading relations provide 145 cases of annual paired records of net trade between world areas. To study the agreement of paired records in these cases we have computed the same three measures used in studying the agreement on size of gross trade. The 145 cases were distributed according to the absolute difference in paired records of the amount of the balance and the difference relative to the mean (Table D-4).

Out of 145 annual interarea balances in the matrix, only ten instances had paired records that showed balances of opposite sign. Balances were small in such cases, and the mean of the paired records tended to be close to zero (in five cases the mean was less than $10 million and in no case was it more than $33 million). With such a small denominator the percentage difference relative to the mean tended to be very large. The ten cases (three of which were for the same paired records) included a

[3] In addition to the twenty-eight paired combinations between the eight areas, we include the balance between Continental OEEC countries and Overseas Territories within their Own Currency Area.

number of the relations which have consistently been found among those with a relatively large divergence in gross trade. The ten are listed below with an indication of the years showing paired records with balances of opposite sign.

Balance	Year
OT's–U.S.	1952
OT's–Other Countries	1950, 1951, 1952
Canada–Latin America	1952
Canada–Other	1950

The Overseas Territories feature prominently in this list and represent cases in which, as noted, one side has a superior record. Relations among peripheral areas are mainly involved. The only surprising relation in the group is the balance of the U.K. with Other Countries in 1952.

The largest divergences in absolute terms—the nine exceeding $200 million—were not in relations exhibiting large divergences in gross trade. They included a number of big trade flows. Five of the eight involved the U.S. as a partner (with Latin America in three years, Canada once, and Continental OEEC countries once); two involved the U.K. with the Rest of the Sterling Area. The only strictly interperipheral case was the Rest of the Sterling Area with Other Countries in 1951. In all nine cases the divergence was more than 10.0 per cent of the mean of the two records. In three the divergence exceeding 50.0 per cent of the mean of paired records of the balance: the U.S. balance with Latin America in 1952 (absolute divergence of $589 million and relative divergence of 50.2 per cent) and in 1954 (absolute divergence of $408 million and relative divergence of 106.2 per cent), and the Continental balance with the U.S. in 1954 ($251 million and 167.9 per cent). These three represent the worst cases of divergence.

There were a number of other instances of relatively large divergence—twenty-two cases—but in most of these the size of the balance was small. In seven the mean of the balances was not more than $50 million and in another five not more than $100 million.

Well over half of all 145 cases showed an absolute divergence of no more than $50 million and no more than 10.0 per cent relative to the mean.

Comparison of Table D-4 with Table D-1 shows that the extent of agreement on the direction and magnitude of interarea goods and services balances is not as good as it is for gross transactions. Nonetheless, for all but a small number (the exceptions being mainly small balances) the paired records agree on the order of magnitude of the balance (to within 50.0 per cent). Most of the divergences of between 10.1 and 50.0 per cent involved absolute divergences of not more than $100 million. If one can be content with measures of balances diverging by no more than either $100.0 million or 10.0 per cent, two-thirds of the balances qualify.

AGREEMENT ON YEAR-TO-YEAR CHANGES IN NET TRADE

Over the five years the twenty-nine net trading relations provide 116 cases of year-to-year change in balances for which paired records can usefully be compared. We have examined the extent of agreement in the amount of year-to-year change rather than change in index numbers of balances since the interest in balances lies with changes in magnitude rather than in proportional changes.

Table D-5 shows the distribution of the 116 cases. Seventeen of them had paired records showing year-to-year movements in opposite directions, but half of these were instances of insignificant movement—a mean change of no more than $10 million—and another five were instances of small movements (mean of the two records of change no more than $50 million). However, records of U.S. transactions with Canada and Latin America show large opposing movements from 1951 to 1952, and the amount of the difference was large relative to the amount of the movement. In both cases the paired measures of the change lie between $100 million and $150 million. While such movements seem large in relation to other interarea balances, they were relatively small compared with the size of the U.S. surpluses and with

TABLE D-5

Analysis of Divergence in Year-to-Year Changes in Trade Balances Between Areas

Distribution of 116 Cases by Amount of Difference Between
Paired Records of Change in Net Goods and Services Trade
and by Difference Relative to Mean of Paired Records of
Amount of Change

Difference Relative to Mean (per cent)	Total	Absolute Difference (million dollars)					
		0–10	11–50	51–100	101–200	201–500	501–1,000
0–2.5	6	6					
2.6–5.0	5	4	1				
5.1–10.0	6	4	2				
10.1–25.0	18	5	6	4	3		
25.1–50.0	31	4	10	7	8	2	
50.1–100.0	16	1	5	4	4	2	
Over 100.0	34 (17)	3 (1)	10 (6)	6 (2)	6 (3)	7 (5)	2
Total	116 (17)	27 (1)	34 (6)	21 (2)	21 (3)	11 (5)	2

NOTE: The figures in parentheses indicate instances of change recorded in opposite directions.

other year-to-year movements in them. In both cases the partner records show approximate stability in the balance from 1951 to 1952 while the U.S. account shows a change. Possibly time lags in reporting influence the pattern of year-to-year movement in these cases when the series is flattening out or changing direction.

This is undoubtedly a factor in other cases. Most of the instances of differing direction of movement in paired records occurred in 1951–52 or 1953–54 —periods of marked trade reversal. Altogether seven of the cases of differing direction of movement came in accounts with the Overseas Territories, and another seven came in accounts with Other Countries; five were in accounts with Latin America and three with Canada. None involved trade between centers, but centers were partners several times, the U.S. three times, the U.K. and the Continent four times

each. Net transactions of Other Countries with Canada, Latin America, and the Overseas Territories represented five cases and Canada's balance with Latin America was involved once. The poorest agreement on direction of movement in net trade thus characterized the record of balances of centers with the Overseas Territories and the balance of Other Countries with peripheral areas (both diverging in direction in five out of sixteen cases).

From Table D-5 we see that paired records usually agreed on the order of magnitude of the change in direction or differed by a small amount (most of the cases lie in the first two columns or the first four lines of the table), but in a fair number of cases the paired figures agreed only on direction—the divergence was more than 100.0 per cent of the mean and differed by more than $50 million (eleven cases).

AGREEMENT ON CHANGES IN NET TRADE OVER THE FIVE YEARS

The twenty-nine cases of change in balances from 1950 to 1954 were distributed as shown in Table D-6.

Paired records differing in direction (four cases) were all instances of divergence in movement exceeding $50 million and the mean of the two records of change was less than $50 million; hence the difference relative to the mean was greater than 100.0 per cent. It is instructive to consider these four cases in some detail for they indicate the limits of relia-

TABLE D-6
Analysis of Divergence in Changes in Trade Balances Between Areas from 1950 to 1954

Distribution of 29 Cases by Amount of Difference Between Paired Records of Change in Net Goods and Services Trade and by Difference Relative to Mean of Paired Records of Amount of Change

Difference Relative to Mean (per cent)	Total	Absolute Difference (million dollars)				
		0–10	11–50	51–100	101–200	201–500
0–2.5						
2.6–5.0	2	1	1			
5.1–10.0	3	1	2			
10.1–25.0	8	1	5	1		1
25.1–50.0	3		1		1	1
50.1–100.0	4	2		1		1
Over 100.0	9 (4)		1	2 (1)	4 (1)	2 (2)
Total	29 (4)	5	10	4 (1)	5 (1)	5 (2)

NOTE: The figures in parentheses indicate instances of change recorded in opposite directions.

bility of calculations of balances over a period of years. In the following table, line A gives the balance according to the reporting area, line B the same balance according to partner area, and line C is the difference—line A minus line B (all in million dollars):

		1950	1954	Change 1950–54
U.K. with RSA	A	852	978	126
	B	1235	1030	– 205
	C	– 383	– 52	331
U.K. with U.S.	A	– 4	– 66	– 62
	B	– 91	71	162
	C	87	– 137	– 224
RSA with Latin America	A	6	26	20
	B	24	– 42	– 66
	C	– 18	68	86
Continental OEEC with Cont. OT's	A	– 246	– 316	– 70
	B	– 253	– 194	59
	C	7	– 122	– 129

In two cases—the U.K. with the Rest of the Sterling Area and Continental OEEC countries with the Overseas Territories—the changes over the five-year period were small by either record relative to the level of the balance and to the initial and final divergences between the paired records. In the case of the balance of the U.K. with the Rest of the Sterling Area, the divergence in movement brought the two records closer together in 1954 than they had been in 1950. In the case of the balance of Continental OEEC countries with the Overseas Territories, a close agreement in 1950 was destroyed by the divergence in movement. Because of deficiencies in the record of transactions by the Overseas Territories we have a reason in this case to prefer the account of the Continental OEEC countries.

In the other two cases—the U.K. with the U.S. and the Rest of the Sterling Area with Latin America —the initial balance was close to zero and the movement recorded on either side was less than $100 million. Most of the divergence in the change in the balance between the U.K. and the U.S. is attributable to the greater rise in the U.S. account of government disbursements than in the U.K.'s account of such receipts. The divergence in the paired records of net trade between the Rest of the Sterling Area and Latin America, as was previously noted, arose in the account of transportation transactions and reflects the problem of accounting properly for PHL fleet transactions.

Paired records show movements in the interarea balances in the same direction in twenty-five out of twenty-nine cases, and in half of these twenty-five the records agreed to within 25.0 per cent of the mean of the paired figures on the amount of the change. Only eight cases (about one-third of the twenty-five) showed both a relative divergence larger than 25.0 per cent and an absolute divergence of more than $50 million. In a third of the cases, agreement was as close as 10.0 per cent or within $10 million.

E

VALUING IMPORTS F.O.B.

The best way to estimate the freight and insurance on imports valued c.i.f., as Herman Karreman has illustrated in his analysis of the French and British freight bills, is to identify the bulk items which account for most of the freight charges paid by an importing country and to apply to the quantities moved freight rates selected according to the sources of and the routes taken by the imports.[1] This approach, while best, is also costly since it requires the collection of freight rate data for different commodities moved in different ways on different routes, a compilation of tonnage of different commodities moving on different routes, and some consideration of method of packaging or handling. It was not possible with our resources to make such a recalculation.

We found it necessary to employ a short cut which could be applied to the value of trade of a given country with reporting areas as recorded in the *Directions of International Trade* (*DIT*). The most cursory study of the problem indicated that, while a rough factor like 10 per cent might serve for total freight payments by most countries, such a factor might be seriously in error if applied to the freight on imports from some areas where the trade was largely composed of bulky items like petroleum or wheat. We sought to develop "freight factors" to apply to c.i.f. values of imports for each country for different partner areas in each year. Carmellah Moneta's study of the German freight bill on seaborne imports in 1951 provided one basis for developing such factors.[2] She went through a detailed computation multiplying tonnages of German imports in

1951 (classified by SITC group and partner country) by their respective freight rates, summing for each SITC code, each partner country, and each partner area, and thus relating the resulting freight costs to the c.i.f. value of the imports. The derived freight factors varied widely, both with different commodity groups and with countries and areas of origin, reflecting the specialization in exporting which is an inherent feature of international trade. Moneta was able to explain much of the variation of freight factors (F_i) by deriving a "freight function": $F_i = aX_i^{-0.75}$, where X_i stands for unit value (dollars per metric ton) of commodity i and $2 \leqslant a \leqslant 6$ varies with region of origin. Since the exponent is smaller than zero, the size of the freight factor is reduced with increases in unit values. When unit values are very high, the freight factors are very small and the absolute variation introduced by the distance parameter is insignificant .

The study of the German freight bill also disclosed that the commodity groups associated with the major part of the freight outlays accounted for only a small fraction of the value of imports. Commodities like petroleum, coal, fertilizers, ores, timber, and cereals move in great quantity but their prices per unit of quantity are relatively low, and hence a selection of internationally traded commodities that may represent a high percentage of the total value of trade may provide only partial tonnage coverage. Therefore, we made sure to include not only the groups of commodities accounting for most of the value but also the ones responsible for most of the tonnages of imports of the countries under consideration.

Some countries supplied merchandise imports already valued f.o.b., but we had to adjust about thirty country accounts covering the five-year period 1950–54. Taking into account the results in the German case, we constructed a schedule of freight factors for each of these accounts on the basis of the direct

---

[1] Herman Karreman made such a computation in arriving at the total freight bill on British and French imports in the years 1950–53 (*Methods for Improving World Transportation Accounts, Applied to 1950–1953*, NBER Technical Paper 15, New York, 1961, pp. 68ff.).

[2] See Carmellah Moneta, "The Estimation of Transportation Costs in International Trade," *Journal of Political Economy*, February 1959.

freight rate information available.³ Since a very high degree of accuracy could not be attached to the results of a freight adjustment made using freight factors, we did not try to refine freight factors of less than 2.5 per cent nor to distinguish freight factors on different routes for highly valued commodities.

We established the country and commodity breakdown of imports. Starting with the breakdown of imports by ten partner regions as recorded in the *DIT,* we determined the commodity composition (in value terms) of the imports coming from each of these regions, using the trade statistics of the country or comparable data. We classified the imports by about twenty commodity groups, the classification and coverage varying with the nature of the available statistics. Once we completed the selection of imports, we applied to each entry its freight factor and summed the freight cost for each of the partner areas and for all areas, thus deriving the respective weighted freight factors. For trade with contiguous countries, we applied a zero freight factor, assuming that the point of exportation was the same as that of importation, unless we had reason to believe that the imports were transported by sea (e.g., from Argentina to Chile). We used substantially increased freight factors for imports of landlocked countries in order to allow for the additional and relatively high cost of overland transport.

Unidentified imports, which sometimes amounted to a significant portion of imports from certain partner regions, posed a problem. Judging by the type of the possible exports of the partner region, we assigned to these unidentified imports freight factors

³ For freight rate tables, the information came from the Bank Deutscher Länder and from "F.O.B. Value of Imports," Addendum 1, "Cost of Transport," U.N. Economic Commission for Europe, June 1953.

For tankers, we used the London Award rates (for a two-year time charter for a 12,000-ton tanker with a speed of 11 knots established twice a year by a panel of London brokers on behalf of the oil companies).

For tramps, we used monthly averages of daily quotations, for coal, wheat, etc., on the markets of London and New York.

For liners, we used the following information: (a) for U.S. exports to and imports from all other countries, the files of the Maritime Commission; (b) for Brazilian exports to Europe, the files of the European Shipping Conference; (c) for Spanish exports to and imports from all other countries, *Statistica du Fletes e Seguros,* Madrid; (d) for South African exports to Europe, U.S. Embassy files; (f) for Indonesian exports to Europe, the files of the European Shipping Conference; (g) for Australian exports to Europe, *Quarterly Summary of Australian Statistics,* Canberra.

ranging between 5 and 10 per cent, with the net effect of reducing sharp differences between regional freight factors.

Our freight factors were originally estimated on the basis of the 1951 data. Since freight factors are ratios of freight rates to unit values, we did not estimate new freight factors for 1950, 1952, and 1953, but instead studied movements over this period of freight rates, on the one hand, and of commodity prices, on the other. Taking 1951 as 100 and relating the freight rate index to the price index, we derived for each of the major groups of imports an index of the freight factor. Applying these index numbers to the respective freight factors, we introduced the effect of changes in freight rates and price relationships over time into our calculation. Thus, changes in regional freight factors over time could reflect both changes in freight rate and price relations and changes in the direction and composition of trade. But whereas there was not a significant or definite change in the composition of imports or in the direction of trade of the countries under study, there was a definite behavior pattern of freight factors: both commodity prices and freight rates increased sharply from 1950 to 1951 and then started to fall gradually during 1952 and 1953. Since the change of freight rates and prices of commodities carried by liners was approximately the same, freight factors for commodities carried by liners could remain at the 1951 level. The variation in tramp freight rates was, however, much sharper than that of commodity prices, making tramp freight factors for 1951 exceptionally high. Tanker freight rates and factors moved rather independently, since they continued to increase in 1952 and went down only in 1953. The over-all effect of these changes in freight rate levels was that freight outlays represented the highest percentage of c.i.f. value of imports in 1951, remained about the same level in 1952, and was considerably lower in 1950 and 1953.⁴

We came to adjust the 1954 accounts after the 1950–53 set had been completed. Prices and freight rates displayed relative stability in this year and seemed to remain at about the same level as in 1953, which would suggest that for 1954 we could use the same factors as for 1953. To verify the validity of

⁴ For a more detailed discussion of the behavior of freight factors over the 1950–53 period, see Karreman, *Transportation Accounts,* p. 19.

this suggestion and also to provide an independent check of our calculations for the previous years, we compared unit values derived from the importer's c.i.f. record as given in the *Commodity Trade Statistics* with the partner's unit values f.o.b. derived from the same publication for a selected group of commodities carried by tramps for the years 1951–54. We took the difference between c.i.f. and f.o.b. unit values to represent "derived" freight and insurance, and their ratios to c.i.f. value to represent "derived" freight factors. The derived freight factors showed a general downward movement during the period under discussion, but their absolute level was higher than that of the factors we had used. The same applied to the derived freight rates when compared with actual freight rates available to us. This discrepancy can be explained by time lags:

1. In a period of falling prices (such as the years after 1951) imports will reflect higher prices than those used in partners' records for the same period, because there is a lapse of at least a few weeks between the date the transaction is registered in the export record and the date it is entered in the importer's record.

2. Changes in freight rate quotations may affect c.i.f. prices of imports at a date later than the effective date of the change, since previous contracts may still be in effect.

While the first lag calls for a timing adjustment of the trade record *prior* to the c.i.f.–f.o.b. adjustment, we should have made an allowance for the second lag in our computation of freight factors. Unfortunately, we had no adequate information that would have helped us determine the length of this lag and therefore could not make an allowance for it.

The discrepancy between derived and actual freight rates made it difficult to establish the direction of movement of freight factors in 1954. We observed, however, that the change was modest and its direction was sometimes upward and at other times downward. We therefore relied on the information we have about the general stability of prices in this year and applied the 1953 factors to the 1954 imports.

The quality and coverage of the statistics we used to determine the country and commodity breakdown of imports were not uniform, and not all systems of classification lent themselves easily to our classification of twenty commodity sections by ten partner areas. Burma, Israel, and French Overseas Territories, for instance, did not provide sufficient partner and commodity detail; a multiple exchange rate system made the use of the statistics provided by Argentina and Taiwan difficult; in other cases the breakdown was too detailed, which induced us to look for supplementary sources containing summary tables.

In general, when direct data were insufficient or inappropriate we turned to partner data, and as a last resort we superimposed the regional breakdowns of imports given in the *DIT* on the commodity breakdown given in the U.N. *Yearbook of International Trade Statistics* and estimated the missing cross-classified entries.

For the OEEC countries (Austria, Sweden, Switzerland, Turkey, and Ireland) we used the Series IV of the *Foreign Trade Statistical Bulletins* published by the OEEC. This publication provides for each of the reporting countries a classification of trade both by two- and three-digit SITC codes and by partner country and region. Our sample for each of these countries covered, on the average, 80 per cent of imports by value and included the commodities that move in great quantity.

We used the *Statistical Abstracts for the Commonwealth and Sterling Area Countries* as the source for data on imports of India, Ceylon, and all British Overseas Territories. The breakdown of commodities by partner countries published therein did not exhaust the total for most of the commodities and therefore reduced our coverage to about 60 per cent of the value of imports.

The reports of the U.S. Department of Commerce (*World Trade Information Service*) supplied the necessary information on trade for most of the Central American countries, the Sudan, and Egypt. The samples for Colombia, Chile, Finland, Spain and its Overseas Territories, Yugoslavia, Indonesia, and Portuguese Overseas Territories were taken out directly from the trade statistics.

Table E-1 gives the resulting freight factors which we used for each country for each partner for each year. The regional distribution of freight factors followed a definite pattern. A large proportion of the imports of the industrial countries was composed of low-valued raw materials and fuels which required high freight factors and originated mainly in the underdeveloped areas. The latter, on the other hand, imported from the industrialized countries mainly relatively highly valued manufactures. Since our area breakdown reflects, to a large extent, a division between industrial and nonindustrial countries, the pattern of freight factors reflects the difference in pattern of trade: freight factors for imports of industrial countries were higher on the average than those for the underdeveloped countries and varied greatly with partner areas. Imports of underdeveloped countries required low freight factors and displayed a relative uniformity with respect to partner areas and small variation over the five years under study.

The freight costs deducted from merchandise c.i.f. to arrive at the f.o.b. value were transferred to the transportation account as debits and allocated to partner areas.[5] Freights paid to domestic carriers were excluded, however, and the transportation credit account was appropriately modified to eliminate the counter entry.

[5] See Karreman, *Transportation Accounts,* Appendix A–1.

TABLE E-1

Share of Freight and Insurance in C.I.F. Value of Merchandise in Imports for Twenty-Seven Countries, by Partner Area, Annually, 1950–54

(per cent)

1950

	Total	U.K.	Sterling OT's	Other Sterling Countries	Nonsterling EPU Area	OT's	U.S.	Canada	Latin America	Other Countries
Total	7.7	6.8	8.5	6.7	5.6	21.9	7.2	12.4	10.7	10.2
Sterling Area	7.5	6.6	8.2	6.3	6.9	17.1	8.2	12.6	14.5	7.4
Ireland	8	6	13	8	6	25	11	15	9	14
Overseas Territories[a]	7	6	8	6	7	18	8	10	17	6
India	8	8	8	6	8	10	9	14	10	10
Burma	7	6	7	7	8		7			9
Ceylon	9	10	9	8	8		6			10
Iraq	10	10	10	10	10		10			10
Nonsterling EPU area	7.4	5.9	10.0	8.0	5.0	24.7	10.2	15.6	11.4	12.3
Austria	7	5	3	8	2		13	20	13	9
Sweden	9	6	10	10	6	23	11	10	13	16
Switzerland	8	5	7	7	2	30	11	15	12	15
Turkey	7	5	16	5	5		10	20	5	9
French & Portuguese Overseas Territories	6	7	5	5	6		6	9	8	7
Latin America	7.6	9.9	10.0	9.8	5.8	5.8	5.1	5.4	8.6	19.5
Argentina	11	13	13	13	6	30	7	3	10	22
Chile	7	5		5	5		9	15	6	5
Colombia	5	5			6	10	5	10	6	8
Costa Rica	6				6		5			10
El Salvador	6				5		6		6	10
Haiti	7						5			10
Mexico	3	5			5		3	5		10
Uruguay	7	5	10	8	5	10	8	6	10	12
Other Countries	8.5	6.6	8.6	6.5	6.5	21.7	7.7	16.0	12.1	11.4
Finland	7	6	8	5	8	29	5		5	7
Spain & possessions	13	11	43		9	24	10	25	18	13
Yugoslavia	7	6	5	5	6		7		5	13
Egypt	8	6	8	8	6	11	7	13	14	11
Indonesia	6	5	7	5	6	8	6	9		6
Iran	6	7	5	6	5		6			8
Israel	10	5	8	5	5	10	10	13	3	20
Sudan	5	5	3	4	7		8		10	6

(continued)

TABLE E-1 (*continued*)
1951

	Total	U.K.	Sterling OT's	Other Sterling Countries	Nonsterling EPU Area	OT's	U.S.	Canada	Latin America	Other Countries
Total	9.0	6.7	9.8	7.3	6.7	29.5	11.2	14.0	12.1	10.7
Sterling Area	8.6	6.7	9.0	6.3	7.5	21.4	15.1	14.6	17.8	7.6
Ireland	10	7	13	9	7	34	19	22	9	16
Overseas Territories[a]	8	6	8	6	7	21	10	10	21	7
India	10	6	10	4	8	10	18	17	10	9
Burma	8	7	7	9	9		8			8
Ceylon	10	9	15	10	11		8			11
Iraq	10	10	10	10	10		10			10
Nonsterling EPU area	8.9	6.2	16.8	7.5	6.1	34.6	16.6	16.7	12.1	12.9
Austria	10	5		8	4		24	20	12	10
Sweden	11	6	21	9	6	38	17	15	14	15
Switzerland	9	6	8	6	3	33	17	19	10	15
Turkey	8	4	15	5	5		17		5	18
French & Portuguese Overseas Territories	7	9		7	7		10	10	11	9
Latin America	9.0	9.2	16.7	9.7	7.3	39.6	7.0	9.8	10.2	14.7
Argentina	13	13	20	10	8	44	15	6	11	19
Chile	9	6		5	5		11	20	4	5
Colombia	5	5			6	10	5	12	7	8
Costa Rica	7				6		6			10
El Salvador	7				5		7		6	10
Haiti	7						6			10
Mexico	4	5	10	10	6		3	5	10	10
Uruguay	8	5	10	8	5	10	8	10	15	13
Other Countries	10.1	6.5	6.0	9.8	7.6	24.7	10.6	11.5	14.2	14.4
Finland	10	6	8	8	9	27	19	10	8	13
Spain & possessions	18	14	13	10	12	30	16		22	22
Yugoslavia	9	5	5	19	8		10	16	7	13
Egypt	10	5	8	14	7	15	12	18	21	16
Indonesia	6	5	6	6	6	8	6	9	8	6
Iran	6	7	5	6	5		6		10	3
Israel	13	5	8	5	5	10	15	13	10	27
Sudan	6	6	4	5	9		7		10	7

(continued)

144

TABLE E-1 (continued)
1952

	Total	U.K.	Sterling OT's	Other Sterling Countries	Nonsterling EPU Area	OT's	U.S.	Canada	Latin America	Other Countries
Total	9.0	6.9	14.5	7.4	6.2	32.8	10.1	12.9	13.6	10.5
Sterling Area	9.2	7.0	12.7	6.9	6.5	25.2	12.8	12.6	23.5	8.8
Ireland	10	8	13	8	6	23	15	15	13	16
Overseas Territories[a]	9	6	13	7	6	26	11	10	27	6
India	11	8	15	5	8	23	14	16		11
Burma	8	6	8	9	8		9			8
Ceylon	9	9	10	9	9		11			9
Iraq	10	10	10	10	10		10			10
Nonsterling EPU area	8.5	6.8	22.5	9.2	5.6	40.6	14.8	15.7	14.1	11.4
Austria	8	5		9	2	14	22	25	12	12
Sweden	11	8	25	11	7	41	15	9	17	13
Switzerland	8	6	7	15	2	48	15	17	12	12
Turkey	7	3	21	3	5	20	19		3	15
French & Portuguese Overseas Territories	7	9		8	7		10	10	12	8
Latin America	9.3	8.8	45.6	5.3	6.2	46.3	6.5	9.8	12.3	10.0
Argentina	15	15	46	10	7	55	15	4	14	12
Chile	8	5		5	5		10	15	5	5
Colombia	5	4			5	10	5	9	5	6
Costa Rica	7				6		6			10
El Salvador	7				5		7		5	10
Haiti	7						5			10
Mexico	3	5			5		3	6		9
Uruguay	9	5	10	8	5		8	10	15	10
Other Countries	9.2	6.1	7.0	8.3	7.2	20.0	10.0	11.4	11.7	12.9
Finland	9	7	8	7	9	15	12	12	7	10
Spain & possessions	14	12	18	5	8	26	10		17	20
Yugoslavia	9	5	4	21	8		11	13	5	7
Egypt	10	5	8	10	6	39	15	13	18	11
Indonesia	6	5	7	6	5	8	6	8	8	5
Iran	5	7	5	6	5		6		8	3
Israel	14	5	8	5	5		10	13	10	38
Sudan	7	6	14	7	10	10	20		10	4

(continued)

TABLE E-1 (continued)
1953

	Total	U.K.	Sterling OT's	Other Sterling Countries	Nonsterling EPU Area	OT's	U.S.	Canada	Latin America	Other Countries
Total	7.6	6.6	10.8	7.1	5.6	23.0	8.1	11.1	10.4	9.1
Sterling Area	8.1	6.7	9.9	6.8	7.3	19.0	11.7	9.5	14.9	7.8
Ireland	9	8	8	7	6	26	14	13	10	10
Overseas Territories [a]	8	6	10	7	7	18	9	8	16	7
India	9	7	11	7	8	8	15	14		9
Burma	8	6	7	8	8		7			8
Ceylon	9	8	11	7	9		10	10		10
Iraq	10	10	10	10	10		10			10
Nonsterling EPU area	7.0	5.8	15.6	7.8	5.1	29.0	11.2	16.7	10.6	9.6
Austria	6	4	3	6	2	12	15	21	12	11
Sweden	9	6	19	10	6	29	12	8	11	12
Switzerland	6	6	7	7	2	33	11	17	11	9
Turkey	7	5	12	3	5		16	18	3	11
French & Portuguese Overseas Territories	7	7		5	6		7	8	10	7
Latin America	7.1	7.9	24.2	6.3	5.4	23.0	5.5	8.7	9.0	10.1
Argentina	12	13	25	8	6	30	13	5	10	11
Chile	8	5		5	5		10	15	5	5
Colombia	5	5			5	10	5	12	4	7
Costa Rica	6				6		5			10
El Salvador	7				5		7		5	10
Haiti	7						6			10
Mexico	3	4			5		3	6		10
Uruguay	7	5	10	8	5		8	10	10	10
Other Countries	8.3	6.6	5.2	7.9	6.3	21.3	8.6	10.0	11.5	10.8
Finland	6	6	8	6	6	18	4	6	5	7
Spain & possessions	12	10	13	5	8	25	9	9	15	18
Yugoslavia	8	5	4	24	6		10	13	6	5
Egypt	9	5	8	10	6	27	12	13	14	11
Indonesia	6	5	7	7	6	6	6			5
Iran	4	7			3		5			5
Israel	11	5	8	5	8	10	10	10	10	24
Sudan	6	6	3	5	8	20	8			3

(continued)

TABLE E-1 (concluded)
1954

	Total	U.K.	Sterling OT's	Other Sterling Countries	Nonsterling EPU Area	OT's	U.S.	Canada	Latin America	Other Countries
Total	7.4	6.8	10.8	7.5	5.5	20.3	7.9	8.8	10.2	9.1
Sterling Area	7.9	6.8	9.9	7.2	7.5	17.1	9.7	9.6	14.4	7.4
Ireland	9	8	12	7	6	26	11	17	11	11
Overseas Territories[a]	8	6	10	7	7	18	9	8	16	7
India	8	8	9	7	8	13	10	10	10	8
Burma	7	6	7	8	8		7			8
Ceylon	9	9	12	8	12		7	10		9
Iraq	10	10	10	10	10		10			10
Nonsterling EPU area	6.6	6.3	13.4	7.8	4.9	23.4	10.3	13.2	10.1	9.6
Austria	5	4	4	5	2	13	17	20	11	9
Sweden	8	6	17	8	6	25	11	10	10	13
Switzerland	5	5	7	7	2	21	10	16	12	9
Turkey	8	6	16	4	5	5	13	5	3	9
French & Portuguese Overseas Territories	6	7	5	5	6		7	8	10	7
Latin America	7.3	8.3	23.2	7.7	5.6	23.9	5.8	3.6	9.3	9.6
Argentina	11	13	25	8	6	30	13	5	10	11
Chile	8	5			5		13	10	6	5
Colombia	5	5			5	10	5	10	5	7
Costa Rica	7	6			6	10	6	10	10	10
El Salvador	6	10			5		7	10	5	10
Haiti	7	10	10		10		6	10	10	10
Mexico	4	5	5	5	5		3	7	5	10
Uruguay	9	5	10	8	5	15	10	10	15	10
Other Countries	8.5	6.4	6.6	8.2	6.3	18.8	9.7	10.0	10.0	11.2
Finland	7	7	6	5	6	13	5	10	4	8
Spain & possessions	13	10	13	5	8	25	13	10	15	18
Yugoslavia	8	5	5	21	5	15	13	13	5	8
Egypt	8	5	8	4	6	29	12	10	22	12
Indonesia	6	5	7	10	6	6	5	10		6
Iran	6	7		6	6		6			6
Israel	11	5	8	5	8	10	10	10	10	25
Sudan	6	5	4	4	10	5	8		10	5

[a] Excluding Northern Rhodesia.

F

ESTIMATING BUNKER SALES

The value of bunker sales by country shown in Table F-1 was estimated by applying prices to the quantity of sales to ships bunkers compiled by the U.N. Secretariat. Prices were obtained from Esso Export Company. For 1950 the quantity of bunker sales was obtained in the U.N. publication *World Energy Supplies in Selected Years, 1929–1950* (New York, 1952, pp. 81–83); for 1951, 1952, and 1954 N. B. Guyol of the U.N. Secretariat supplied his worksheet data; for 1953 figures were obtained from the U.N. *Monthly Bulletin of Statistics,* March 1955, pp. xiii–xv.

TABLE F-1
Estimated Value of Sales to Ships' Bunkers, 1950–54
(*thousand dollars*)

Sold by	1950	1951	1952	1953	1954
Total	1,067,887	1,297,583	1,485,201	1,305,150	1,317,611
Sterling Area	334,853	412,004	493,753	411,813	413,946
United Kingdom	93,632	125,513	149,496	139,461	138,044
Overseas Territories	168,284	189,009	265,745	210,385	208,852
Gold Coast	1,085	1,312	1,470	1,132	788
Kenya	5,538	6,186	6,946	4,960	5,068
Nigeria	490	615	882	1,387	240
Sierra Leone	33				20
So. Rhodesia	285		740	512	
Tanganyika	23		56	98	23
Uganda	246	286	296	256	360
Bahamas	156	183	252	220	206
Bermuda	2,352	2,871	4,386	4,005	4,654
Br. Guiana	81				4,196
Br. Honduras	31	216			
Trinidad & Tobago	18,903	29,300	33,768	28,188	20,572
Trucial Oman					
Aden	79,317	57,025	68,770	62,708	62,087
Bahrein	2,240	11,115	15,308	14,722	14,535
Kuwait	9,680	3,762	17,784	20,570	19,712
Hong Kong	5,300	6,206	5,700	5,486	8,604
Malaya	14,476	31,763	38,788	32,500	39,755
Sarawak	1,073	1,863	2,632	2,522	2,626
Fiji	492	582	600	696	897
Cyprus	200	238	492	535	700
Gibraltar	22,113	30,266	34,504	21,648	14,022
Malta	1,625	1,387	3,775	3,996	3,503
Mauritius		218	225		220
Virgin Is.		1,215	1,344		1,055
Falkland Is.	420	450	832	518	252
Jamaica	2,125	1,950	26,195	3,726	4,757
Other sterling countries	67,475	90,690	70,047	52,448	57,449
Union of S. Africa	14,952	21,556	13,825	8,235	14,337
Burma	288	308	360	350	325
Ceylon	11,640	15,250	14,404	11,408	9,703
India	11,788	12,002	5,600	6,192	7,608
Iraq	635	2,002	640		1,200
Pakistan	5,320	7,203	3,174	2,220	
Australia	16,296	29,376	28,665	22,380	22,769
New Zealand	6,556	2,993	3,379	1,663	1,507
Other sterling Europe	5,462	6,792	8,465	9,519	9,601
Iceland	2,108	2,146	2,926	4,059	3,991
Ireland	3,354	4,646	5,539	5,460	5,610
Nonsterling EPU countries	210,887	323,861	358,751	309,050	345,378
Cont. OEEC countries	81,424	187,241	213,363	182,718	197,068
Austria					
Belgium & Luxembourg	6,480	15,048	16,450	11,803	12,318
Denmark	3,800	4,500	9,200	5,900	6,726
France	19,131	48,386	59,211	46,295	43,924
Germany	2,436	25,996	31,080	26,340	33,801
Greece	5,900	4,300	3,800	5,400	5,263
Italy & Trieste	14,400	25,000	27,000	28,000	31,859
Netherlands	17,700	37,000	39,000	34,600	38,883
Norway	4,000	7,600	7,800	6,500	6,761
Portugal		9,432	8,732	8,736	9,152
Sweden	3,300	6,600	7,600	6,100	6,090
Switzerland	2,392	3,379	2,825	2,548	2,205
Turkey	1,885		665	496	86

(continued)

149

TABLE F-1 *(concluded)*

	1950	1951	1952	1953	1954
Overseas Territories	129,463	136,620	145,388	126,332	148,310
French	27,600	57,800	60,600	49,300	64,365
Algeria	11,300	19,000	18,000	13,000	13,194
Cameroons					
Fr. Eq. Africa					114
Fr. W. Africa	13,600	28,000	30,000	23,000	25,478
Madagascar	500				10,566
Morocco	1,500	3,400	3,100	3,700	4,093
Tunisia	500				492
Fr. Somaliland		6,500	9,000	9,000	10,098
Indochina	200	900	500	600	330
Other	101,863	78,820	84,788	77,032	83,945
Angola					46
Netherlands Antilles	94,163	69,620	76,588	66,132	67,375
Cape Verde	7,700	9,200	8,200	10,900	15,444
Belgian Congo					1,080
Canada	41,600	33,372	37,968	30,135	31,352
U.S. and possessions	267,280	283,332	318,179	287,182	242,017
U.S.	171,600	260,263	288,757	264,957	222,301
Hawaii	94,080	19,598	24,805	19,425	15,759
Puerto Rico	1,600	3,471	4,617	2,800	3,957
Latin America	83,748	96,531	94,800	91,875	86,480
Argentina	16,100	5,300	4,800	6,300	6,503
Bolivia	294	595	369	321	1,000
Brazil	14,310	22,035	13,266	21,518	17,502
Chile	1,060	1,400	2,200	2,000	2,096
Colombia	2,500	2,700	700	730	740
Costa Rica	53	32	330	116	108
Cuba	1,600	2,100	2,200	2,300	2,413
Dominican Rep.	53	64	66	87	108
Ecuador	180	430	475	399	320
El Salvador	60	96	66	58	
Guatemala	90	128	1,221	261	
Haiti	30	32	33		
Honduras	60	64	462	58	
Mexico	18,000	4,100	5,500	4,200	3,509
Canal Zone	18,000	21,000	24,000	21,000	16,485
Paraguay		25		20	21
Peru		2,250	2,573	1,755	1,140
Uruguay	4,800	6,100	6,350	5,300	5,842
Venezuela	6,452	27,920	29,463	25,452	28,693
Nicaragua	106	160	165		
Panama			561		
Other Europe	41,808	62,904	66,841	55,366	102,767
Finland	108	104	189	118	43,923
Yugoslavia			752	1,148	2,608
Spain	300	7,700	8,400	7,500	8,169
Canary Islands	38,900	41,100	43,000	38,200	37,891
Sp. N. Africa	2,500	14,000	14,500	8,400	10,176
Other Countries	87,711	85,579	114,909	119,729	95,671
Egypt	21,800	8,600	26,000	20,600	19,493
Iran	26,240				
Israel	2,000	1,800	800	3,900	2,820
Lebanon	260	12,000	14,000	11,000	10,517
Saudi Arabia	13,296	20,904	23,920	34,010	22,774
Syria	540		405	590	330
Sudan	1,400	2,100	2,100	1,800	1,324
Indonesia	9,600	12,800	18,300	23,800	19,346
Japan	8,800	22,400	22,800	17,000	10,328
Philippines	2,900	4,500	5,900	6,600	6,069
Thailand	210	475	684	429	584
S. Korea	665	—			
Liberia					66
Libya					2,020

GLOSSARY

BIS—Bank for International Settlements.

Continental-oriented countries—Continental OEEC countries, Continental Overseas Territories (except Netherlands Antilles), Iceland, Argentina, Paraguay, Uruguay, Other Europe, Soviet Bloc, Syria, Lebanon, and Egypt.

Cont. OEEC—countries that were members of the OEEC, except U.K., Ireland, and Iceland.

Cont. OT's (or OT's)—Continental Overseas Territories: Belgian, French, Dutch, and Portuguese Overseas Territories (excluding Indonesia, but including Netherlands Antilles and French Indochina) in the early 1950's.

Dollar Latin America—Bolivia, Colombia, Costa Rica, Cuba, Dominican Republic, Ecuador, El Salvador, Guatemala, Haiti, Honduras, Mexico, Nicaragua, Panama, and Venezuela.

EPU—European Payments Union, an international financial clearing union of the OEEC countries in the early 1950's.

GATT—General Agreement on Tariffs and Trade.

IBRD—International Bank for Reconstruction and Development.

IMF—International Monetary Fund.

IO—International Organizations located in the U.S.: IMF, IBRD, and U.N.

Nondollar Latin America—Argentina, Brazil, Chile, Paraguay, Peru, and Uruguay.

Nonsterling EPU area—Continental countries and their Overseas Territories in the early 1950's.

OEEC—Organization for European Economic Cooperation in the early 1950's: U.K., Ireland, Iceland, Belgium, France, West Germany, Italy, Luxembourg, the Netherlands, Norway, Sweden, Denmark, Austria, Switzerland, Trieste, Greece, Turkey, and Portugal.

OEH—Other Eastern Hemisphere: Eastern Hemisphere except Western Europe (i.e., Rest of Sterling Area, Overseas Territories, and Other Countries).

OT's—see Cont. OT's.

Other Countries—Other Europe, Soviet Bloc, and nonsterling countries in Middle East, Africa, and Far East.

Other Europe—Spain and possessions, Finland, and Yugoslavia.

OWH—Other Western Hemisphere: Western Hemisphere except U.S. (i.e., Canada, Latin America, and International Organizations).

Own Currency Area—partner area for transactions between Belgium, France, the Netherlands, and Portugal and their own Overseas Territories. (Note that transactions of Own Currency Areas with Own Currency Areas are not included in transactions of nonsterling EPU area in matrix tables.)

PHL—the fleet of merchant vessels registered in Panama, Honduras, and Liberia.

RSA—Rest of Sterling Area, i.e., Sterling Area (as defined by U.K. Exchange Control) except U.K. (including Ireland and Iceland).

Sterling-oriented countries—Rest of Sterling Area (excluding Iceland), Thailand, Indonesia, Iran, and Ethiopia.

U.S.-oriented countries—Canada, Latin America (except Argentina, Paraguay, and Uruguay), Netherlands Antilles, Japan, Philippines, Taiwan, South Korea, Israel, Saudi Arabia, and Liberia.

Western Europe—United Kingdom and Continental OEEC countries.

INDEX

Allen, R. G. D., 8n, 37n
Argentina, 17, 141
Australia:
  error in account of, 34
  gold production, 15n

Belgian Congo, 51n, 65
Belgium:
  boundaries for reporting transactions, 7
  error in account of, 33
  foreign investments of, 45
  investment income of, 43
  middleman trade by, 38
  multilateral settlements with EPU partners, 65
Bilateral payments balances:
  offset by multilateral settlements and error, 16
  of U.S. and U.K., 54–55, 57–59, 78–79
British Arabian Gulf Protectorates:
  deficiencies in account of, 32
  gold disappearance, 12n
British Colonies:
  account of, 58n, 68
  gold production, 15n
  services transactions, 45–46
  sterling balances accumulated by, 58
Bunkers, 9, 43, 143
  allocation of unallocated marine, 10
  mainly by American and British-Dutch Companies, 45
Burma, 141

Canada:
  agreement between its and partners' trade records, 36, 39, 42, 130–131, 133, 135–137
  allocation of unallocated gold sales, 12
  error in account of, 34
  foreign investments of, 45n
  gold production, 15n
  investment income of, 43
  middleman trade and, 38
  payments surpluses and multilateral settlements with U.S. and U.K., 58, 79
  reinvested earnings in accounts of and with, 15
Capital:
  agreement between paired records of, 49–51, 74
  liquid, 15, 49, 54–55
  magnitude of flow, 31–32
  official and private, long- and short-term, 15
  pattern of interarea flow, 51–52, 71, 74
  regional specialization in supplying, 44–45
  unreported:
    by oil-source countries, 26
    net capital flow and, 29–31
    reporting discrepancies and, 27, 34, 78

China:
  Communist, gold disappearance, 12n
  Taiwan, see Taiwan
Common Market, see European Common Market
Comparability of paired entries in a two-valued matrix of international transactions, 6, 12–13
    See also Agreement on or Comparability of paired records under listings for countries, areas, and types of transactions
Continental OEEC countries:
  agreement between paired records for transactions of capital flows with Overseas Territories and Other Countries, 51n
    goods and services transactions, 37–38, 42, 134–138
    merchandise transactions, 37n
    transportation transactions, 44
  allocation of unallocated transactions, 10–12
  direction of trade and payments altered by redirecting petroleum transactions, 40, 68
  elaboration of transactions with EPU partners, 14, 47n
  gold disappearance, 12n
  middleman trade and, 38
  payments surplus, 57
  ranking in world trade, 35–36
  transportation credits disproportionate relative to merchandise, 43
Continental Overseas Territories:
  agreement between paired records for transactions of capital flows with Continental OEEC countries, 51n
    goods and services transactions, 39, 130–131, 133–135, 137–138
  allocation of unallocated transactions, 11
  direction of trade altered by redirecting petroleum transactions, 37, 40, 126, 129
  elaboration of transactions with EPU partners, 14
  middleman trade and, 38
  ranking in world trade, 36
Country accounts:
  groupings of, 14, 17, 38, 53–54, 63, 70
  microfilm of, 5, 18n
  number of, 7
  over-all errors in, 16, 26, 32–34
Currency devaluation of 1949, 20
Cutler, Frederick, 41n

Direction of transactions:
  capital flows, 10
  freight, 10, 15
  goods and services, 36–37, 39–41
  investment income, 10
  merchandise, 9–10, 15–16
  tourist transactions, 10
Dollar area, 66
Dwyer, C., 16, 18, 126

Eastman, H. C., 26n
Economic interdependence:
    expressed by multilateral settlements, 64
    need for world-wide analysis, 1–3
    network of international transactions, 3
    postwar period, 79
    three-area model analyzing, 2n, 70n, 80n
    U.S. balance-of-payments deficit and, 79–83
Egypt, gold disappearance, 12n
Ekker, M. H., 61
Ely, J. Edward, 8n, 37n
European Common Market, multilateral settlements patterns
        of countries in, 64–65, 79
European Free Trade Area, multisettlements patterns of
        countries in, 65–66
European Payments Union:
    excluded from measurement of amount of multilateral
        settlements, 63n
    need for introducing account for, 9, 13
    pattern of payments surpluses between U.K., Continental
        OEEC countries, and Rest of Sterling Area and,
        58, 79

Financial transactions:
    agreement between paired records, 26–32, 49, 51, 55ff, 74
    defined, 49
    magnitudes of, 31–32, 78
    pattern of, between areas, 49, 71, 74
Finland, unilateral transfers to Soviet Bloc, 33–34
France:
    boundaries for reporting transactions of, 7
    deficiencies in accounting for transactions:
        of franc area, 33
        with Own Currency Area, 19, 24n, 32, 77
            See also French Overseas Territories
        travel credits, 26
    foreign investments of, 45
    gold disappearance, 12n
    investment income of, 43
    multilateral settlements with EPU partners, 65
    petroleum transactions adjustment, 9
    share of Iraq Petroleum Company, 126n
Freight rates and freight factors, 139–142
        See also Merchandise transactions, valuation of
French Overseas Territories:
    deficiencies in account of, 19, 32, 141
    multilateral settlements with EPU partners, 65
        See also Continental Overseas Territories; Own
            Currency Area; France, deficiencies
Frisch, Ragnar, xv, 61

Gardner, Walter R., 8n, 37n
Germany, West:
    boundary definition and East Germany, 7, 77
    error in account of, 33
    freight bill of, 139–140
    multilateral settlements with EPU partners, 65
    petroleum transactions adjustment, 9
Gold:
    allocation of unallocated transactions and matrix recon-
        ciliation, 12
    comparability of paired entries in matrix of, 15, 26–29,
        31, 75
    disappearance, 12n, 26, 28, 34, 78
    magnitude of international flow, 31–32
    monetary and nonmonetary, 15, 55

pattern of interarea flow, 52
production, 6n, 15n
    See also Reserve assets
Government transactions:
    agreement between paired records of, 22, 24–25, 45
    allocation of unallocated petroleum exports and, 11
    contribution of total world trade, 22
    deficiencies in accounting for, 19
    growth and variation in, 22
    included in miscellaneous services, 46
    regional specialization, 43
        See also Merchandise transactions
Greaves, Ida, 58n
Greece:
    petroleum transactions adjustment, 9
    transportation transactions adjustment, 9–10
Guyol, N. B., 143

Hansson, Karl-Eric, 61n
Hazelwood, A., 58n
Hickman, Bert G., 20n
Hicks, Earl, 17n
Hicks, Whitney, 80n
Hilgerdt, Folke, 14, 17n, 53, 60n, 61n
        See also League of Nations, Network of World Trade
Historical developments, 1950–54, 20
Hong Kong:
    excluded from published payments account of British
        Colonies, 68
    gold disappearance, 12n
    middleman trade, 38
Høst-Madsen, Poul, 15n, 55n

Imlah, Albert H., 1n
India:
    error in account of, 33–34
    gold disappearance, 12n
    government purchases of merchandise, 15
    petroleum transactions adjustment, 9
Indonesia, gold disappearance in, 12n
International Organizations:
    capital flow and, 52
    need for an account of, 9
    transactions usually reported only on one side, 38n, 130
International transactions:
    comparability of accounting with other countries sought,
        17
    currencies employed in making, 17
    definition of, 6
    time referent for, 16
    types distinguished, 15
    unit of account measuring, 17
    "vertical" and "horizontal" consistency in reporting of, 17
Investment income transactions:
    agreement between paired records of, 22, 26, 43–45
    contribution to total world trade, 22, 26, 45
    growth and variation in, 22
    petroleum industry, 18n, 44–45
    regional specialization in, 43, 45
        See also Reinvested earnings
Iran, 20, 44
Iraq, deficiencies in account of, 32–33
Iraq Petroleum Company, 126n
Israel, 141
Italy:
    error in account of, 33

foreign investments of, 45n
multilateral settlements with EPU partners, 65
travel credits omitted from account of, 26

Japan, foreign investments of, 45n
Joesten, Joachim, 12n

Karreman, Herman, 18, 25n, 43n, 139, 140n, 142n
Korea, South, unallocated transactions in accounts of, 11

Latin America:
    agreement between paired records of goods and services transactions of, 38, 42, 131, 134–136, 138
    allocation of unallocated transactions in account of, 11–12
    multilateral settlements and bilateral payments balances with U.S. and U.K., 59
    pattern of trade altered by redirecting petroleum transactions of, 40, 129, 133
    payments difficulties of, 79
    ranking in world trade, 39
League of Nations, *Network of World Trade,* xv, 2n, 14n, 53, 60–61, 68, 78
Lebanon:
    allocation of unallocated merchandise trade in account of, 10–11
    conversion from local units of account to dollars, 17
    gold disappearance, 12n
Leontief, Wassily W., xv
Lichtenberg, Robert, 18, 37n, 38
Liquid assets, *see* Reserve assets
London Award rates, 140n

Macao, gold disappearance, 12n
Marine insurance, 15, 26
Marshall, Alfred, 1
Matrix of international transactions:
    agreement of world totals, 5, 24, 26, 29, 31
    comparability of paired entries in, 6, 19, 35n, 77–78
    country coverage in, 18–19, 77
    deficiencies in, 18–19, 77
    described, 3, 5, 77
    dimensions of, 6, 35
    disturbances during 1950-54 affecting, 20
    limitations to measurement of, 78
    over-all net error in, 26, 78
    relationship to definition of international transaction, 6
    reporting country boundaries, 7
    similarity to other national accounts, xv
    spatial dimension, 35
    trial-run matrixes used to locate errors and omissions, 7–8, 77
    U.S. balance-of-payments deficit and, 79ff
    See also particular types of transactions
Merchandise transactions:
    adjustment to a transactions basis, 8n, 18, 126–129
    agreement between paired records of, 22, 25, 37
        magnitude of world trade and, 29
        time lag in reporting and, 24
        unilateral transfers and, 26, 28
    contribution to world trade, 22, 34, 126
    government transactions and, 15, 25
    growth and variation in, 22
    insurance on, 15
    petroleum transactions in, 9, 126–129
    regional pattern of, 46–48, 53–54
    smuggling, 34

special study of, 18
    trade in used articles, 16n
    valuation of, 8n, 10, 15, 18, 25, 139–142
Mexico:
    cotton exports adjusted as to direction, 9
    travel credits, 11–12
Michael, Walther, 15, 18, 32, 55n
Michaely, Michael, 60n
Middleman transactions:
    accounting for, 9–10, 37, 68
    concentrated by commodity, 38, 68
    freight, 10,
    in U.K. account, 46
    in world trade, 36–38, 40–41, 126
    pattern of multilateral settlements and, 68
    significance of, 67
Modigliani, Franco, 2n
Moneta, Carmellah, 18, 139
Montague, Samuel, and Company, 12n
Mozak, Jacob, 2n
Multilateralism:
    bilateralism and, 59–60
    economic efficiency (specialization) and, 59, 62
    in trade, 59–62, 78
    measurement of, 49, 61–62
Multilateral settlements and error:
    agreement between paired records of, 52, 54, 70, 75
    amount of, 62–64, 79
    balances to be settled and, 52n, 78
    bilateral payments balances of U.S. and U.K. and, 57–59, 81–83
    defined, 49
    European Common Market negotiations and, 64–66, 79
    grouping of countries and, 53–54, 63, 70
    meaning of, 16, 54, 59, 64–66, 78
    multilateralism and, 49, 59, 64
    offshore U.S. aid purchases and, 58–59, 64, 79
    over-all error in system of accounts, 26, 28
    regional pattern of, 52–54, 68, 74–76, 78
    statistical limitations to, 67–70
    statistically a residual entry, 16, 51n, 68, 78
    within currency areas, offsetting of, 66–67, 70, 79
Mundell, R. A., 1n

Neisser, Hans, 2n
Nelson, Emil, 126
Netherlands:
    boundaries for reporting transactions, 7
    foreign investments of, 45
    investment income of, 43
    middleman trade by, 38, 68
    multilateral settlements with EPU partners, 65
    reinvested oil company earnings omitted from account of, 11, 26
Netherlands Antilles:
    deficiencies in account of, 33
    government transactions in account of, 25
    multilateral settlements payments to Latin America, 59n
    oil imports, 47n, 129
    unallocated transactions in, 11, 25
New Zealand, petroleum transactions adjusted in account of, 9
Norway:
    petroleum transactions adjusted in account of, 9
    shipping transactions, 10

Oil-source countries:
  deficiencies in accounts of, 18–19, 26, 32–33
  investment income originating in, 43
  need for introducing accounts of, 9
  petroleum exports by, 126ff
  reinvested earnings in, 15, 18–19, 26, 32–33
Order of magnitude, agreement on, 39
Other Countries:
  agreement between paired records of goods and services transactions, 130–131, 135, 137
  allocation of unallocated transactions, 11–12
  direction of trade altered by redirecting petroleum transactions of, 40, 129
  multilateral settlements with U.S., U.K., and Continental OEEC countries, 58
  ranking in world trade, 36
Over-all error, *see* Multilateral settlements and error
Overseas Territories, *see* Continental Overseas Territories
Own Currency Area (of Continental European countries and their territories):
  accounting for transactions of, 7, 13, 21, 63n, 135n
  deficiencies in accounting for transactions within, 18–19, 77
  multilateral settlements within, 54

Petroleum transactions:
  accounting convention in merchandise matrix, 9–10, 37
  allocation of unallocated transactions, 10–11
  freight adjustment for, 139–140
  geographic structure (regional pattern) of trading and, 37–38, 40, 126
  investment income of U.S. and U.K. companies, 44–45
  marine bunkers, 9, 18, 143
  multilateral settlements pattern and, 67–68
  special study of, 18
  world totals for transactions of different types and, 18
Philippines, error in account of, 33
PHL fleet, account of:
  combined with Latin America in matrixes, 8n, 131, 138
  need for, shown by trial-run audit, 8
  tanker transactions in, 18
  transactions mainly by residents in U.S., U.K., and Continental OEEC countries, 43
Pizer, Samuel, 41n
Polak, J. J., 2n, 20n
Portugal:
  boundaries for reporting transactions, 7
  deficiencies respecting transactions with Own Currency Area, 19, 32, 77
Principal trading interest:
  foreign investment pattern and, 43
  grouping of countries by, 14
  middleman transactions and, 38, 41
  miscellaneous services and, 43
  pattern of multilateral settlements and, 54, 68, 70
  reserve accumulations and gold transactions and, 58–59, 78
  trade orientation and, 36–41, 47–48

Reinhardt, H. R., 12n
Reinvested earnings:
  agreement between paired records of investment income and, 25–26, 44
  included in investment income and capital, 15
  omitted from Netherlands account, 11, 25–26
  U.K. account and, 44
Reporting country, 7

Reserve assets, 6n, 27, 34, 49, 54–55, 59, 78–79
Rest of Sterling Area:
  agreement between paired records of goods and services transactions of, 135, 138
  direction of trade altered by redirecting petroleum transactions of, 37, 40, 129
  gold production of, 15n
  middleman trade and, 38
  payments balances and multilateral settlements with U.K. and Continental OEEC countries, 58, 79
  ranking in world trade, 36
  regional elaboration of transactions of, 14
Review Committee for Balance of Payments Statistics, xvii
Rhomberg, R. R., 2n
Royal Dutch Petroleum Company, 11
Royal Dutch-Shell Group, 9, 11, 126

Salant, Walter S., 2n, 55n, 70n, 80n
Saudi Arabia:
  deficiencies in account of, 32–33
  gold disappearance, 12n
  petroleum sales of, 67
Scandinavia, multilateral settlements with EPU partners, 65
Services transactions:
  agreement between paired records of, 22, 24, 29, 46
  contribution to total world trade, 22, 46, 78
  growth and variation in, 22
  miscellaneous (type), 22, 24, 78
    included with unilateral transfers, 19
    in U.K. account, 12, 46
  regional patterns of trade in, 42ff, 46–47
  unreported related to unreported capital and gold, 27
Singapore, 38
South Africa:
  boundaries for reporting transactions, 7
  gold production, 15n
Southwest Africa, 7
Soviet Bloc:
  boundaries for reporting transactions of, 7
  deficiencies in account of, 18, 33, 77
  freight on merchandise trade in, 34n
  gold, 12n, 15n
  multilateral settlements pattern in account of, 66, 79
  need for account of, shown by trial-run audit, 8
  unilateral transfers from Finland, 33–34
Spain, 19, 77
Sterling Area, 65–66
Switzerland:
  foreign investments of, 45
  gold disappearance, 12n
  investment income of, 43
  multilateral settlements with EPU partners, 65
Syria, conversion from local units to dollar equivalents, 17

Taiwan, 141
Tangier, gold disappearance, 12n
Taylor, Arthur H., 12
Thailand, gold disappearance, 12n
Trade in goods and services:
  agreement between paired records of, 22, 24, 26, 29, 35–36, 38–39, 41–42, 46n, 48, 130–138
  composition of, 22
  geographic structure of, 35–38, 126–129
  growth and variation in, 20, 22
  product content of, 42
  radial structure of, 36, 42, 46

ranking of areas in, 35–36
regional pattern of, 39ff, 46–47, 71
spatial dimension in matrix of, 35, 46
specialization of countries in, 35, 71
   See also Middleman transactions; Petroleum transactions

Transfers, *see* Unilateral transfers

Transportation transactions:
agreement between paired records of, 22, 24–26, 43–44
contribution to world trade, 22, 26
freight payments, direction of, 10
growth and variation in, 22
Panama Canal tolls, 44n
regional specialization in, 42–43
special study of, 18, 139–142
tanker transactions, 9, 18, 140
   See also Bunkers; Greece; PHL fleet; United Kingdom

Travel transactions:
agreement between paired records of, 22, 24, 26, 44
contribution to total world trade, 22
growth and variation in, 22
included in miscellaneous services, 44
regional specialization in, 43

Trial-run audit of matrixes, 7–9, 18, 77

Unilateral transfers:
agreement between paired records of, 15, 26, 28–29, 41, 49, 51, 74
included in miscellaneous services, 19, 74
magnitude of, 31
mainly U.S. and U.K. aid, 28
official distinguished from private, 15
regional pattern of, 51, 71

United Kingdom:
agreement between paired records of goods and services transactions of 42–45, 134–135, 137–138
boundaries for reporting transactions, 7
error in account of, 33–34
foreign investments of, 45
freight bill of, 139
government transactions in, 25, 45–46
investment income transactions in, 11, 26, 43–44
liquid liabilities of, 55–59
marine insurance transactions in, 26
middleman trade and, 38, 46, 68
miscellaneous transactions, 44n, 46

oil company transactions of, 9, 26, 40, 68, 126–129
payments balance and matrix of international transactions, 55–59
ranking in world trade, 1–2, 36–37
regional elaboration of transactions in, 14, 47n
tanker transactions in, 9, 11, 18
transactions with the U.S., 51, 57, 58n, 134
transportation credits disproportionate to merchandise, 43
unallocated transactions in, 11–12

United States:
agreement between paired records of goods and services transactions of, 39, 42, 45, 134–138
balance-of-payments deficit and matrix of international transactions, 55–59, 79ff
bilateral balances of, 55–59, 81–83
boundaries for reporting transactions, 7
error in account of, 33, 57
foreign investments of, 45n
government transactions, 11, 19, 25, 45–46
investment income of, 43, 45
liquid liabilities of, 55–59, 81ff
marine insurance omitted from transportation account of, 26
middleman trade and, 38, 68
military expenditures of, 22
multilateral settlements of, 81–83
offshore aid purchases by, 58–59, 64, 79
Panama Canal tolls in account of, 44n
petroleum transactions of, 40, 126–129
PHL fleet, transactions with, 8n
ranking in world trade, 1–2, 36–37
reinvested earnings in account of, 15, 25–26, 28n
transport earnings relative to other countries, 43
unilateral transfers in account of, 28–29, 51

Venezuela:
deficiencies in account of, 33
exports to Netherlands Antilles, 47n
government transactions, 25
multilateral settlements earnings from Overseas Territories, 59n
unallocated transactions in account of, 11

Western Europe:
reserve gains and multilateral settlements, 83
transactions of, 70, 81-83

Woolley, H. B., 6n, 15n, 16n, 36n, 37n